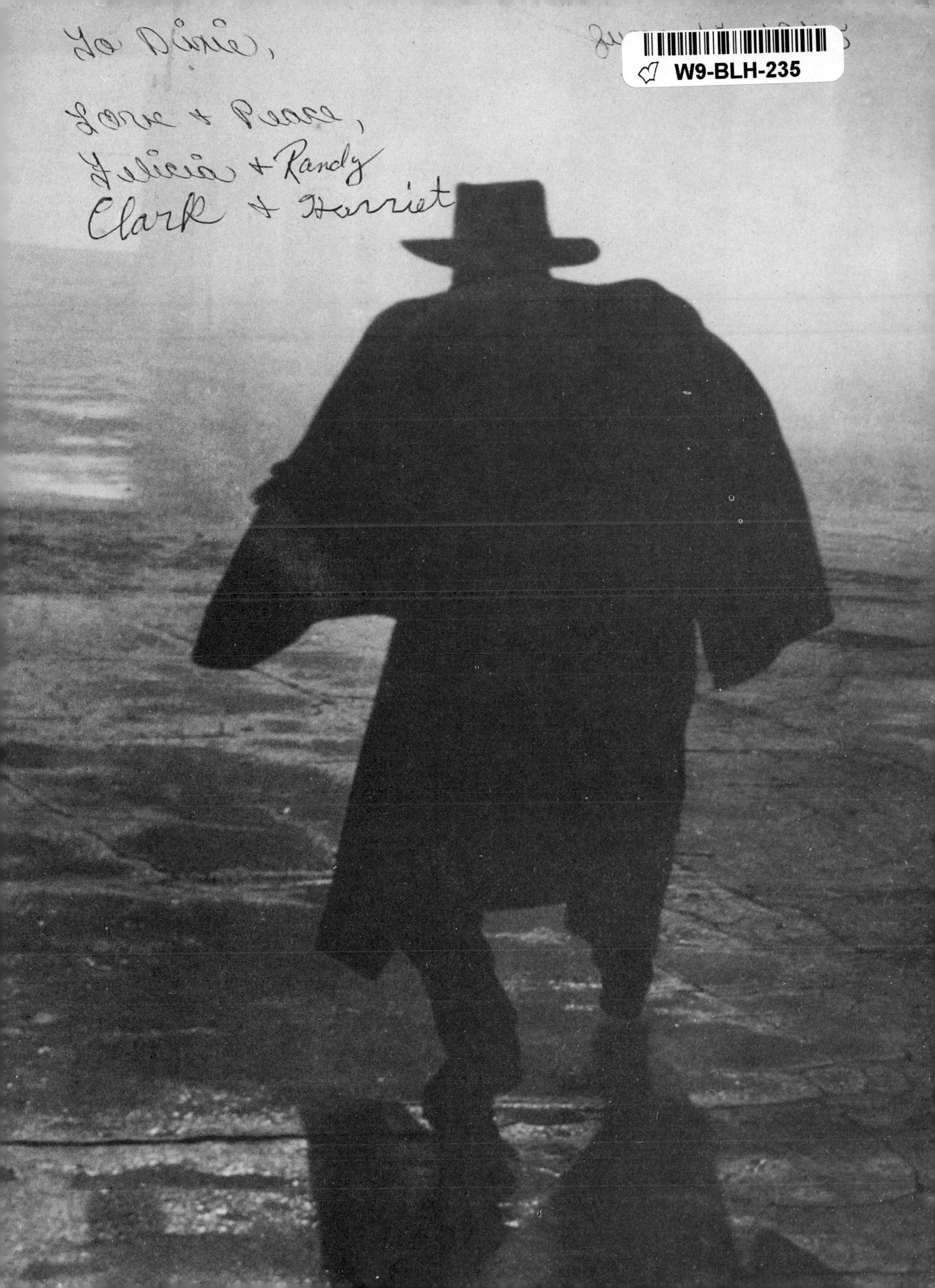
To Dixie,
Love + Peace,
Felicia + Randy
Clark + Harriet

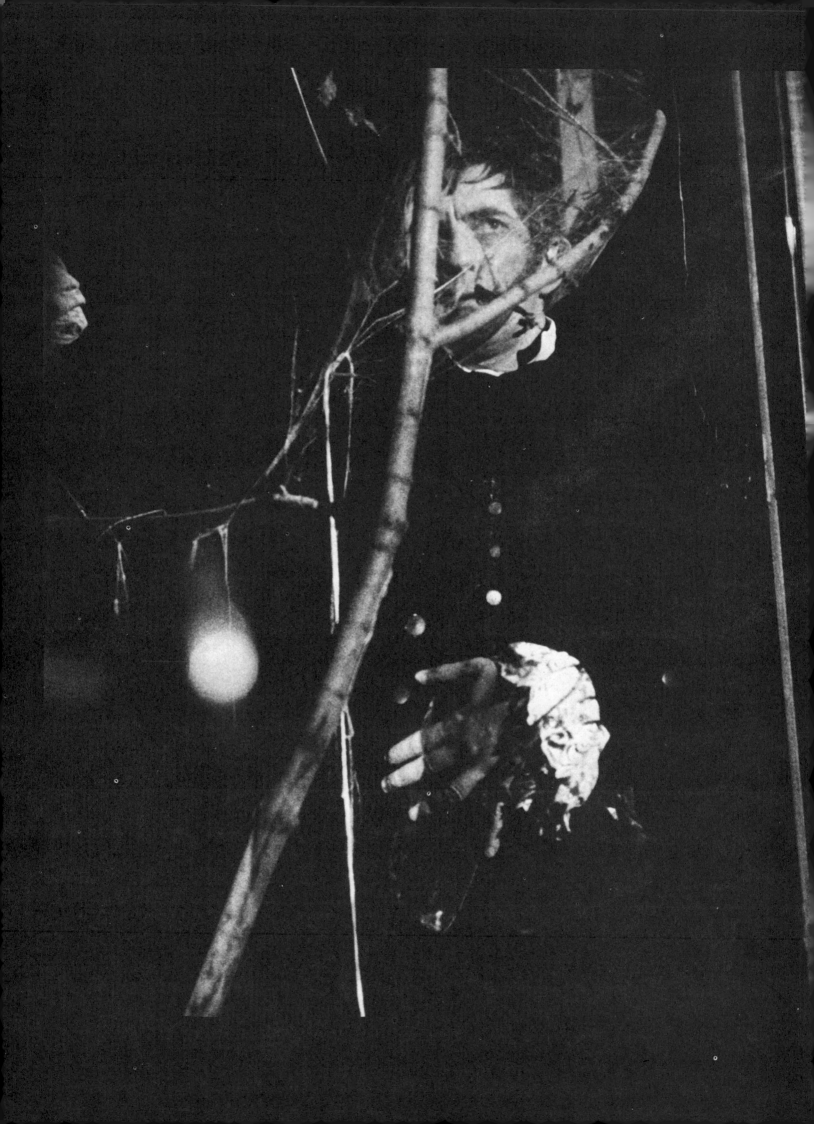

A Pictorial History of

HORROR MOVIES

And the Prophet said –
And lo, the Beast looked
Upon the face of Beauty.
And it stayed its hand
From killing. And from that
Day, it was as one dead.

Old Arabian Proverb
KING KONG (1933)

Front endpaper: *House of Wax* (Warner Bros 1953)
Half-title page: *House of Dark Shadows* (MGM 1970)
Title page: *The Ghost of Frankenstein* (Universal 1942)
Contents page: *Faust* (UFA 1926)
Quotations page: *Terror in the Midnight Sun* (Unger 1963)
Introduction page: *The Bat* (Liberty 1959)
                 Black Sabbath (Galatea 1963)
Back endpaper: *Dr Jekyll and Mr Hyde* (MGM 1941)

For Pandora Jane – one day.
Meanwhile in memory of
Bryan Berry
for whom *The Witching Hour*
sounded too soon.

A Pictorial History of

HORROR MOVIES

Denis Gifford

HAMLYN

LONDON NEW YORK SYDNEY TORONTO

CONTENTS

Published by
The Hamlyn Publishing Group Limited
London   New York   Sydney   Toronto
Hamlyn House, Feltham
Middlesex, England
© Copyright The Hamlyn
Publishing Group Limited 1973
Reprinted in 1973 (twice), 1974 (twice).
ISBN 0 600 36926 9

Publishing Group Limited 1973
Reprinted in 1973 (twice), 1974 (four times)
ISBN 0 600 36926 9
Printed in the U.S.A.

Text set in 12/14 point Century
Schoolbook Monophoto 227
Captions set in 9/10 point Century
Schoolbook Monophoto 227/477

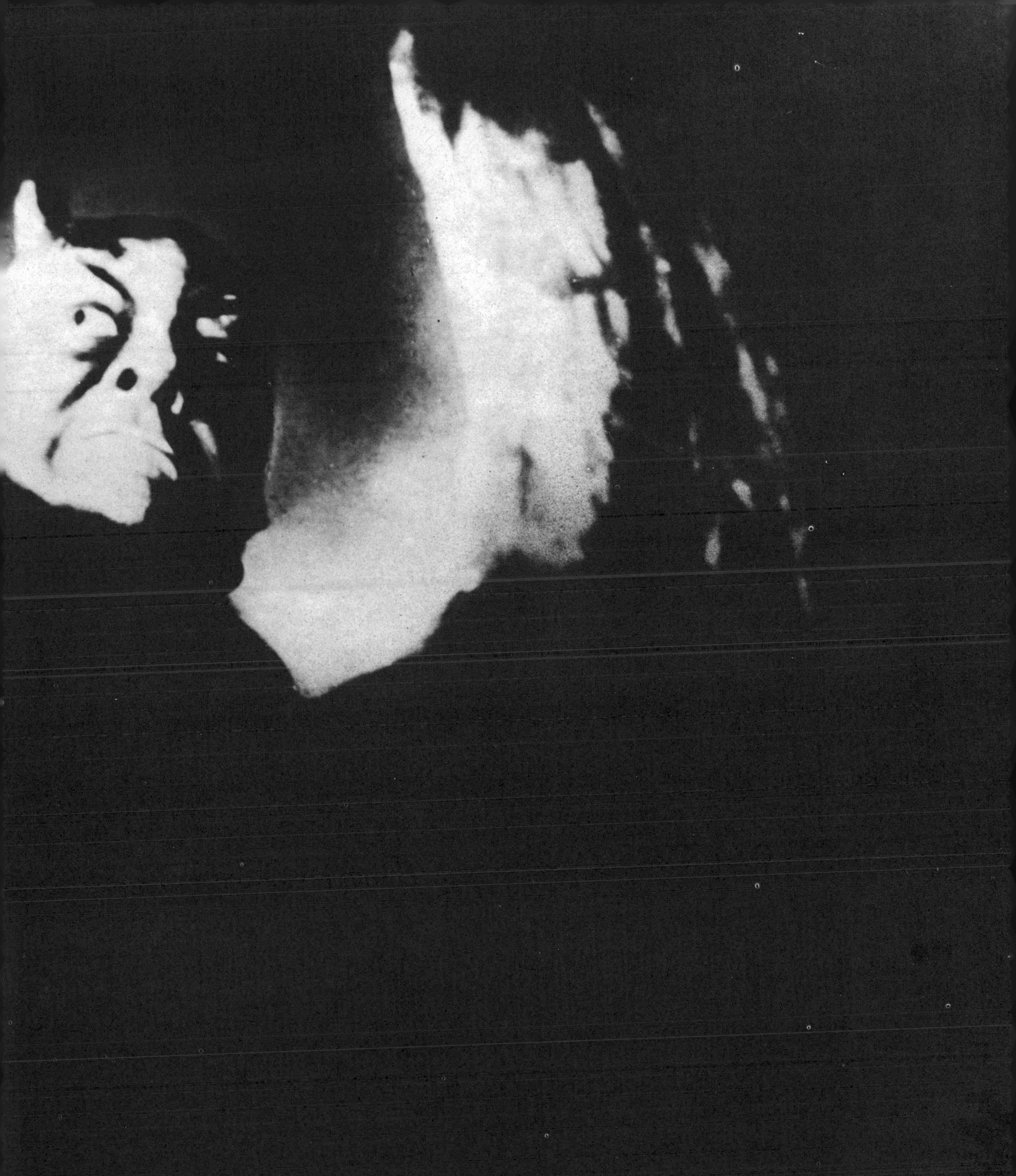

Also by Denis Gifford:
British Cinema
Movie Monsters
Science Fiction Film
Discovering Comics
Stap Me! The British Newspaper Strip
Six Comics of World War One
Test Your N.Q. (Nostalgia Quotient)
Fifty Years of Radio Comedy
The British Film Catalogue

I tell you, we haven't begun to discover
what science can do to the body and mind of man.
HENRY JEKYLL MD (John Barrymore) 1920

Think of it! The brain of a dead man, waiting to live again
in a body I made with my own hands!
HENRY FRANKENSTEIN (Colin Clive) 1931

Feast your eyes, gloat your soul, on my
accursed ugliness!
THE PHANTOM (Lon Chaney) 1925

This is the greatest moment of my life!
I have seen a living pterodactyl!
PROFESSOR CHALLENGER (Wallace Beery) 1925

I took a gorilla and, working with infinite care,
I made my first man!
DR MOREAU (Charles Laughton) 1932

Mad? I, who have solved the secret of life,
you call me mad?
DR OTTO VON NIEMANN (Lionel Atwill) 1933

It was Beauty killed the Beast!
CARL DENHAM (Robert Armstrong) 1933

I meddled in things that man must leave alone!
JACK GRIFFIN (Claude Rains) 1933

Alone you have created a man. Now together
we will create his mate!
DR PRETORIUS (Ernest Thesiger) 1935

The werewolf instinctively seeks to kill
the thing it loves best!
DR YOGAMI (Warner Oland) 1935

We belong dead!
THE FRANKENSTEIN MONSTER (Boris Karloff) 1935

To die! To be really dead!
That must be glorious!
COUNT DRACULA (Bela Lugosi) 1931

INTRODUCTION

WHEN IS A HORROR FILM NOT A HORROR FILM?

They were giants in the night: two tall men in two tall hats who swung out and away from each other and came at me, striding from the colossal window. And if I hadn't screamed and ducked under the seat they would have trampled me into the ice-cream wrappers. The site was the outsize Trocadero Cinema at the Elephant and Castle, London; the sight was no more than two top-hatted toffs, probably Jack Hulbert and Jack Buchanan, bidding themselves bye-bye; the night was the winter of 1930; the mite was yours truly the horror film fan; and the fright was simply dimensional – magnification plus depth. I in my three-year-old innocence was reacting classically to the concept of cinema, just as those first, older innocents had shrieked and shied from old Lumière's film of an oncoming engine, back in the beyond of 1895.

My early movie memories are all of horror: a long rifle nosing through the flap of a big top tent to pick off a man on a flying trapeze; two cowboys slugging away in the back of a jolting lorry as it racketed around a rocky mountain; a zoom into the open mouth of a cartoon character to see a similar face grimacing on its uvula. Horrid moments, yet not horror films.

I brushed the real thing but once in my bare-kneed days before the British Censor saved me with his 'H' for Horrific Certificate. Mum, daringly, considering all the embarrassing seat-banging she had been through, took me to see *The Invisible Man*. The experience was a treasured shudder for years, and now that I have my own print of it, I love the film all the more. For the curious thing about all the great horror films . . . *Frankenstein, Dracula, King Kong, The Old Dark House* . . . is that they are not only good for a first-time thrill, they can be seen again and again, savoured, rolled around the eyeballs. Unlike most movies they actually improve with the years, outmoded acting and production techniques adding a mouldering charm to the vintage. Where once *Dracula* was criticized for its contemporary setting, now it has developed a period crust of its own. Perhaps time will add its own patina to the Hammer horrors of today.

The Golden Age of the Horror Film passed me by as a direct experience, for once I was old enough to be allowed in by commissionaires with eagle-eyes for under-sixteens, the great days were over. I had to rely on that other curious British institution, the Sunday-For-One-Day-Only reissue bill. I sought out every side-street flea-pit for those treasured double-bills: *Buried Alive* and *The Monster Maker*, or *Devil Bat's Daughter* and *Mask of the Maniac*. I began to take notes, collect stills, collate press-books. Friends of a like mind joined me in winkling out films and facts. Bob Monkhouse, who became a star comedian, stirred my schoolboy zeal with tales of films seen surreptitiously in Worthing; Tony Hawes, who became a star writer, led me to tatty bug-hutches in wild Lee Green; Jennifer Jayne, who in time actually acted in horror films, came along for the fun; Bryan Berry, who became a great science-fiction novelist, helped me adapt remembered movies into playlets; Len Lurcuck, who became a TV director, supplied our sound effects; David Kodritsch, who draws maps for the War House, put on my imported Frankenstein Monster mask and stomped round the garden

to be photographed. I wrote the history of Horror Films twenty years ago, but nobody wanted to know (until Carlos Clarens finally came through with the right book at the right time). I created the first Horror Film magazine and called it 'H' – but nobody wanted to know (until Forrest J. Ackerman finally came through with the right mag at the right time). I even drew a horror comic, but nobody etc. etc. (until William Gaines finally etc. etc.). So you see, horror films and I are no strange bedfellows.

Yet ask me to define a horror film and I am stumped. Even the British Board of Film Censors, who actually officially christened the things with the creation of their 'H' Certificate, never got around to defining them. Witness the anomalies in their list which I append to this volume: *Boy Slaves*? *The United Nations War Crimes Film*? Egads! You'll find no mention of them in the text. Nor will you find movies with mere moments of horror, like *Psycho* or the descendants of *Les Diaboliques*. For me, an element of fantasy is essential to the true horror film: the impossible rather than the improbable. The vampire, the werewolf, the walking dead and the man-made monster – these are the heroes of horror films, not the Lodgers and the Rippers and the Hooded Terrors. But fear not, friends, for to trace the history of horror I have cast my web wide, digging deep in the cinematic sarcophagi to disinter long-dead ghosts of films and film-makers forgotten. Perhaps some are still forgotten, by myself: then I'm sorry.

And so I present to you this picture book; with the words of Professor Bruno Lampini, as portrayed by George Zucco in *House of Frankenstein*: 'I have here a collection of the world's most astounding horrors!'

HOW GRAND WAS MY GUIGNOL

In which Monsieur Méliès summons the Devil, Mr Smith photographs a ghost, Mr Porter takes a shot in the dark, and Quasimodo gets the hump.

The big, black bat flew into the castle room. It circled slowly, flapping monstrous wings. Suddenly – it changed into the Devil! It was the eve of Christmas 1896; the horror had begun.

Regular patrons of the little Théâtre Robert Houdin on the second floor of No. 8 Boulevard des Italiens, in Paris, were used to magic. For eight years now the prestidigitating proprietor had staged the most astonishing sequence of theatrical illusions ever seen: disappearances, decapitations, devilry undreamed by even the great Etienne Robertson, whose *Phantasmagoria* had brought horror to the magic lantern a hundred years before.

But now even Monsieur Méliès had excelled himself. Seizing upon the new scientific apparatus invented by the brothers Lumière – a machine to record movement by rapid photography they called *le cinématographe* – Méliès incorporated it into his act. Where once mere handfuls of Parisians had thrilled to the magician's trickery, now the world was his audience. Ordinary folk who had paid their pennies to gaze at 'Animated Photographs' of such mundane things as high tide at Brighton and rush hour at Piccadilly, gasped in fright as the bat flew and Satan laughed. In *The Devil's Castle* (1896) Mephistopheles made a magic pass.

'A large cauldron appears, out of which, in a great cloud of smoke, there emerges a beautiful lady. At another magic pass, a little old man comes out of the floor carrying a big book. Then the cauldron disappears. And so it goes. Cavaliers, ghosts, a skeleton and witches appear and disappear at a sign from the Evil One. Finally, one of the cavaliers produces a cross, and Mephistopheles throws up his hands and disappears in a cloud of smoke. From start to finish the action is rapid.'

It would have to be: the whole film ran for less than three minutes!

While the world wondered at the supernatural transformations unreeling so speedily before its boggling eyes, knowing Parisians nodded. They had spotted the twinkle in Satan's eye. For their mustachioed host at a hundred different magical spectaculars since 1888, and the moving picture Mephisto, were one and the same man.

Georges Méliès, former shoe manufacturer and cartoonist, had turned his hobby of spare-time conjuring into a career. It was to reproduce on film one of his favourite stage illusions, *The Vanishing Lady* (1896), that Méliès created the world's first cinematic device. As the magician, Méliès seated his charming victim in a chair and concealed her with his cloak. At this point he 'froze' his position. The cameraman stopped cranking, the lady left the set, and a stagehand slipped a skeleton into her seat. The cameraman continued the crank, Méliès whipped away the cape. When the printed film was projected without the stops and starts: hey presto! the lady vanished!

Audiences everywhere were astounded. They had seen a genuine physical disappearance, a macabre transformation from life to death, before their very eyes. In that split of a second they had seen even more: cinema taking its first step towards art.

Women had screamed the night cinema was born: a locomotive engine seemed to steam from the screen. Louis Lumière's innocent record of an everyday happening, *The Arrival of a Train at La Ciotat Station* (1895), had shock in its realistic approach. The shriek of surprise became a laugh of relief that was echoed around the world: six years later the memory was strong enough to be recalled by Robert Paul in *The Countryman and the Cinematograph* (1901). The scream of fear and the scream of laughter: an emotional combination that rings down the seventy-seven year history of the horror film.

Beautiful Beast: Jean Marais and Josette Day as Jean Cocteau's *Beauty and the Beast* (1945).

Cinema was but one year old when the Devil took over. A public already sated on Lumière's traffic scenes and burning weeds welcomed him with delighted fright. Merry Méliès gave them more of the same. *The Haunted Castle* and *The Laboratory of Mephistopheles* followed in early 1897, using the same sets, costumes and characters as *The Devil's Castle*. Méliès was a clever old devil.

In his country garden at Montreuil, Méliès built himself a movie studio. He designed it as a combination of standard photographer's studio and his own magic theatre. He filled his stage with concealed traps and hidden holes, movable panels and capstans, winches and pulleys: all the practicable impedimenta of the illusionist. He mounted his camera on a runway and in no time had created every trick in the movie book: stop-frame action, substitution, superimposition, animation, undercranking, split-screen, dissolves, fades both in and out, model work, miniature work, and the subtitle. Everything the horror film would ever need – including fantastic costume and grotesque makeup.

And in his first year of 1897 the world was startled to see Satan's head detach itself and float around a room (*The Laboratory of Mephistopheles*), a traveller flee in fright when his clothes came to life (*The Bewitched Inn*), a mesmerist put a girl in a trance and magically strip her naked (*The Hypnotist at Work*), a scientist use an X-Ray machine to extract the skeleton from a living body (*A Novice at X-Rays*), a boy chopped in half (*The Famous Box Trick*), a marble statue come to life (*Pygmalion and Galatea*), the moon zoom down from the sky to swallow a telescope (*The Astronomer's Dream*), and an old man sell his soul to Satan – twice (*Faust and Marguerite* and *The Damnation of Faust*)!

Meanwhile, across the English Channel, Mr Smith was photographing a ghost. This first cinematographical spectre stalked sunny Sussex in September 1898. It was summoned up by the ex-secretary of the Society for Psychical Research, George Albert Smith. Like Méliès, Smith had been both a conjurer and creator of conjurer's illusions. He had also been a hypnotist on the halls, and it was this mesmeric talent that had won him a place with the famous Society. He assisted in a series of spectacular spiritualistic seances that gained national notoriety. The year 1892 saw Smith's sudden disappearance from the Society staff; 1898 the appearance of a startling advertisement. 'The most marvellous films yet done! Protected under patent law!' They were made by George Albert Smith, initially known as G.A.S. Films.

'*Faust and Mephistopheles*. Faust discovered in his study. Mephistopheles appears in a cloud of smoke (fine effect), offers Faust renewal of youth if he will sign bond. As inducement, shows him charming 'vision' of Marguerite at spinning wheel in the garden. Faust hesitates no longer; signs bond; Mephistopheles triumphantly waves a drinking cup, causing it to emit a cloud of smoke, which falls around Faust as he changes to a handsome young man.'

The 'special photographic contrivance', by which Smith also produced a ghost in *The Corsican Brothers* (1898), was double-exposure, a simple method of 'spirit photography' born by accident in the early days of the camera. But that it was new to cinematography is proved by the granting to Smith of a British Patent. This 'Protection in Great Britain and Abroad' was much vaunted, but within weeks Méliès was advertising *The Cave of the Demons* (1898):

'Showing the interior of a cave, in which appear ghosts and skeletons busied in most mysterious proceedings. A young lady suddenly appears, who is immediately surrounded by the apparitions. The rocks and supports of the cavern are clearly seen through the transparencies of the ghosts' forms. A creepy and startling subject.'

Méliès subtitled his first essay into the spirit world '*scène fantastique avec spectres vivants et impalpables*'. Apparently Smith found Méliès equally untouchable, for no legal action was ever attempted. Indeed, the two film-makers shared the same distributor, Charles Urban. This American in London was the first to realize the box-office potential of the catchy title. In *Cléopâtre* (1899) Méliès made 'an old man of diabolical intent' hack a mummy to bits, then resurrected the living lady from a smoking brazier. Urban called it *Robbing Cleopatra's Tomb*. More catchpenny were the titles he gave to *Le Diable au Couvent* (1899) and *La Danse de Feu* (1899): cashing in on contemporary successes they came out as *The Sign of the Cross* and *Haggard's 'She'*.

Méliès, of course, played the Devil in the convent, leaping out of the holy font. He and 'a deformed imp of satanic type' turn themselves into a priest and a choirboy, changing back during the sermon: 'the nuns dispersing quickly in great

Monster Poster: Original advertisement for *Frankenstein* (Universal 1931).

16

fright'. In the end the ghost of St George appears, and 'overturns His Satanic Majesty, who descends below amid a cloud of smoke'. More serious in style than his earlier Mephistopheliana, Méliès issued an accompanying caution. 'There is not the least action in the film which would be obnoxious or shock the most sensitive audiences'. The first, but certainly not the last, movie producer to try to have it both ways.

Méliès' films link through to the modern horror movie in ways other than technique. *She*, Rider Haggard's 1887 novel, was no horror story, yet it has one classic horror scene: the lovely young Ayesha bathes in the flames of eternal life only to be overdone into incredible old age. It is a transformation scene of a type basic to the horror film, and in seventy-five feet of celluloid, 'coloured in a most surprising and artistic manner increasing the wonderful effects ten-fold', Méliès showed the core of a story which later film-makers would go to greater lengths to tell. A girl arises from a giant saucepan and executes a hasty skirt-dance before a pillar of fire shrivels her into 'a decrepit old hag'.

The outsize insect finds its harbinger in *A Midnight Episode* (1899). A sleeper, lit by the full moon, 'is suddenly awakened by a bug of gigantic proportions crawling over him. This he attacks and destroys, but before again retiring he notices three more climbing up the wall'. The hero shows all the resource of the modern monster exterminator. 'He lights the candle and applies the flame to each, causing them to explode with fine smoke effects.' A spectacular finale of which Inoshira Honda would be proud.

Méliès' influence was world-wide. In America Thomas Edison, having virtually invented the movies, left their production to his staff, Edwin S. Porter. A man with a mechanical turn of mind – he had been both plumber and projectionist – Porter was intrigued by Méliès' methods. Prints were imported and examined, frame by frame. In February 1900 Porter showed his first fantasy fashioned in the Méliès manner. His choice of subject was no more original than his achievement: *Faust and Marguerite* employed stop-motion photography to materialize Mephistopheles, who then used the same trick to summon up a skeleton. From this derivative beginning Porter would, in three years, reshape cinema.

Meanwhile, in London, another man of mystery was at work. Like Méliès, Walter R. Booth was a conjurer; unlike Méliès, national neglect has let the man himself sink into oblivion. Booth's earliest

Organ Gorgon: Vincent Price as *The Abominable Dr Phibes* (1971; *left*), a British-made American International Picture. The organ was designed by Brian Eatwell, the organs by Trevor Crole-Rees.

Bare Bones: George Méliès personally demonstrates that the hand – and the film – is quicker than the eye. Frames from *The Vanishing Lady* (1896; *below*) reduce a mademoiselle to her skeleton in three easy stages.

Skeleton Key: Dry bones have been walking around horror movies for more than seventy years. A lively skeleton was a bedtime surprise in Robert Paul's *Undressing Extraordinary* (1901; *far left*), a graveyard ghost in Pathé's *The Fairy of the Black Rocks* (1905; *below left*) and a shipboard shriek in Shochiku's *Living Skeleton* (1968; *left*). Edgar Allan Poe's 'Mask of the Red Death' hid Lon Chaney's living skull in *The Phantom of the Opera* (Universal 1925; *right*), while Nathaniel Hawthorne's 'Experiment of Dr Heidegger' bleached Mari Blanchard to her bones in *Twice Told Tales* (Admiral 1963; *below*).

film was probably *The Miser's Doom* (1899), made for Robert Paul. It used its spectre seriously: the spirit of a female victim returns to haunt a miser, who instantly dies of shock. Paul's studio at New Southgate was modelled on Méliès, down to the wheeled camera on rails. When trundled forwards during filming, it gave a gradual enlargement to the image, which was then double-exposed. It produced giants in *The Magic Sword* (1901) and *The Voyage of the 'Arctic'* (1903). This latter fantasy featured Cutcliffe-Hyne's popular magazine hero Captain Kettle, and his discovery of the North Pole. Méliès used his trucking device to create the inflating Satan of *The Gigantic Devil*, the *Amazing Colossal Man* of 1902.

Conversely, both men used the same contrivance to produce life in miniature. Booth's *The Cheese Mites* (1901), subtitled 'Lilliputians in a London Restaurant', showed six-inch sailors dancing the hornpipe on a diner's cheese! Méliès' *The Dancing Midget* came a year later and had more charm. Curious to consider that James Whale's miniaturized manikins in *The Bride of Frankenstein* (1935) included a ballerina.

Like Méliès, Booth treated fantasy lightly, but now and then horror broke through. *The Haunted Curiosity Shop* (1901) showed an antiquarian confronted by a living mummy. 'Before he can recover from the surprise this occasions, the wrappings fall away and the living Egyptian stands before him. Slowly the solid flesh melts away till only the bare skeleton remains.' Audiences of 1933 watching *The Mummy* were spared that additional touch of grue when the sight of a crumbling Karloff

Small World: Horror film makers have it both ways. You can shrink your star and enlarge the world, or enlarge your star and shrink the world. Either way the effect is much the same and the only thing guaranteed to expand is the box office. Henry B. Walthall and Rafaela Ottiana reduced Grace Ford to a *Devil Doll* (MGM 1936; *opposite*), Tod Browning's essay in electrical ecology. Atomic explosions expanded Dean Parkin in *War of the Colossal Beast* (American International 1958; *below*), Bert I. Gordon's essay in back-projection, and the Devil materialized in the form of a giant apeman in *Equinox* (Tonylyn 1969; *left*). Georges Méliès, of course, had done it all decades before in *The Gigantic Devil* (1902; *below left*).

taking 'a little walk' sent David Manners insane.

Méliès, too, looked to Egypt for inspiration, and brought a stone sphinx to life to wreak vengeance on the defiler of a temple tomb in *The Oracle of Delphi* (1903). Worse horror was to come. In *The Monster* (1903) an Egyptian Prince bribes a dervish to restore unto him his dead wife. 'Her skeleton begins to move about, and rises. The dervish covers it with a white cloth; a masque conceals its ghostly face.' It begins to dance, then starts to grow: 'its neck assuming enormous proportions, much to the horror of the Prince, who fails to see in this grotesque character the wife whom he seeks.' The twist in the tail is classic. The monster changes into the Princess and the Prince takes her into his arms. 'Removing the veil he finds he has embraced the skeleton.'

Cinema was giving a new, visual form to the traditional horror story at a time when, in print, imaginative literature was meeting an exciting new challenger. Science-fiction, as a label, was unknown. The trend-setting tales of Jules Verne were called 'Imaginary Voyages', while H.G.Wells' novels were publicised as 'Fantastic Romances'. Both authors met, uninvited, in Méliès' *A Trip to the Moon* (1902). Cinema's first sci-fi epic took the cannon-fired space-shell from Verne's 'From the Earth to the Moon' (1865) and the crustaceous Selenites from Wells' 'The First Men in the Moon' (1901). The explosive quality of the latter when struck by explorers' umbrellas was pure Méliès.

In 1903 Edwin S. Porter took a shot in the dark. Into *The Great Train Robbery* he cut a great closeup.

'*Scene 14:* A life-size picture of Barnes, the leader of the outlaw band, taking aim and firing point-blank at the audience. The resulting excitement is great.'

Indeed it was. For millions of moviegoers it was the first time they had been shot in the eyeballs. The secret of Scene 14 was its full-frontal relationship to the individual onlooker, a dimension of shock that flashed back to that first onrushing train. It went over the head of Méliès then, and now it did so again. For ten more years he marshalled his movies from stage left to stage right, dissolving from tableau to tableau. The head-on approach was not for him. *The Conquest of the Pole* might as well have been made in 1902, not 1912: Méliès as Engineer Mabouloff flying his Aerobus to battle the Giant of the Snows, an ogre articulated

to the eyeballs and operated by a score of stage-hands. This prehistoric King Kong was a swan song. The old alchemist's audience had grown beyond him; magic was no longer enough.

Georges Méliès, cinema's first producer, director, screen-writer and star, became cinema's first forgotten man. George Barnes had fired a pistol in the world's face and punctured the cardboard dream.

Cinema, born in a French salon, weaned in a London Polytechnic, misspent its youth in a fairground. It grew lustily, pulling in crowds bigger than its neighbour, that other sideshow where people paid to gape – the freak tent. Here nature's pathetic discards eked a living by sitting and being stared at. Naturally, the newest art, being of and by and for the people, absorbed a little of the freak show's aura.

The favourite French fable of Beauty and the Beast had reached its literary apotheosis in Victor Hugo's 'Notre Dame de Paris' (1831). The classic story of Quasimodo, the deaf, deformed, bell-ringing Hunchback of Notre Dame, and his hopeless love for a pretty Gypsy dancing girl, was an early epic. *Esmeralda* (1906) was directed by that rarity, a lady: Alice Guy. Henri Vorins and Denise Becker pantomimed the tale Goethe called 'the most detestable ever written' in ten terrible minutes. The plot was pirated around the world, in America by Vitagraph, *The Hunchback* (1909), and Selig, *Hugo the Hunchback* (1910), while the first production of that long-lived British emporium, Butcher's Films, was *The Love of a Hunchback* (1910). As with his transatlantic cousins, this humped hero followed in Quasimodo's pathetic footsteps by saving his unrequited beloved and dying with what passed for a brave smile on his face.

The following year the original hunchback became the first full-length monster in the movies. *Notre Dame de Paris* (1911) was filmed by Pathé in three parts. Quasimodo was played by Henri Krauss, Esmeralda by Stacia Napierkowska, a dancer who would become the first movie Queen of Atlantis.

For Quasimodo, there was only one transformation: from life to death. This is life's reality. Our escape clause is imagination, once into the fantasy of fable, now into the fantasy of film. When Beauty

Crustaceous Creatures: Spirit from *Night of the Demon* (Columbia 1957; *top left*) and Selenite from *A Trip to the Moon* (Méliès 1902; *centre left*).
Freak Show: *Horror of Malformed Men* (Toei 1969; *above right*), Victor Maddern in *Blood of the Vampire* (Eros 1958; *bottom left*) and Jane Adams in *House of Dracula* (Universal 1945; *below right*).

25

Ape Aped: *Balaoo the Demon Baboon* was made in France by Eclair in 1913, and in Hollywood by Twentieth Century-Fox in 1942. Fox called it *Dr Renault's Secret* and starred George Zucco as Dr Renault and J. Carrol Naish as his Secret (*opposite*).

Méliès' Monsters: Georges Méliès made monsters of many kinds, from bird-men of ancient Egypt (*below*) to an articulated Apocalyptic Horse (*The Merry Frolics of Satan* 1906; *bottom*).

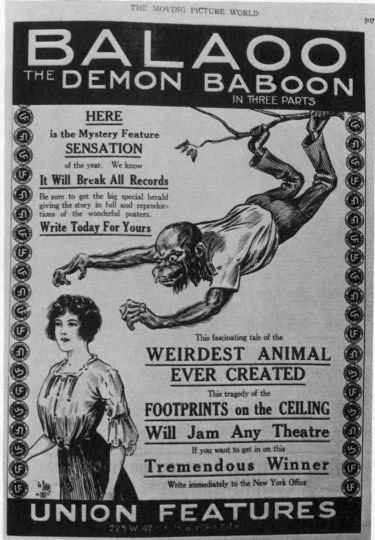

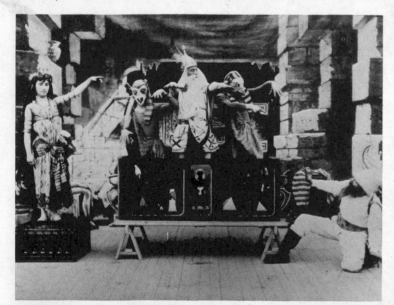

kisses the Beast, we can actually see him change into the handsome Prince. In the movies our dreams come true; but so do our nightmares.

The magical metamorphosis of *Beauty and the Beast* was first filmed by Pathé as early as 1899. But such was the overwhelming welter of pantomimic confusion in French films of the Méliès era that when the London firm of Clarendon produced their *Beauty and the Beast* (1905), they advertised it as 'A real fairy story told as it should be told – No French cooks, no ballet girls!' Three years later Pathé remade it, crediting Madame Le Prince de Beaumont as author of 'the interesting story of a beautiful girl who is loved by a hideous animal'.

The other great early inspiration for French producers was Darwin. *The Doctor's Experiment* (1908) was a monkey-gland injection that made unsuspecting patients act like apes, while *The Monkey Man* (1908) was a gruesome preview of transplants to come.

'While a surgeon is trepanning his patient, an accident happens to the grey matter and the surgeon has it replaced by the brain of a monkey. After this the man performs all sorts of eccentric actions. The surgeon, having become very much interested in this curious case, leads his patient through the streets to the great pleasure of all believers in the Darwin theory.'

Feature-length treatment of the topic came with *Balaoo* (1913), which American distributors subtitled *The Demon Baboon*. Victorin Jasset directed it from a newspaper serial by Gaston Leroux. Darwin disciple Dr Coriolis transforms an enormous baboon into a half-humanized monster. Having terrorized the locals Balaoo takes to the trees and turns up in Switzerland. Here he becomes the tool of a poacher called Hubert. Ordered to abduct the doctor's daughter, Balaoo builds a trap. Hubert falls in and breaks both his legs, while the wounded Balaoo explains all in mime, then expires. Lucien Bataille played Balaoo 'so like a baboon that we forgot he really wasn't one,' wrote H.C. Judson.

Night Fright: William Castle's 'Emergo' brought Leona Anderson screaming out at Carolyn Craig in *House on Haunted Hill* (Allied Artists 1958; *opposite above*), ten years ahead of the Japanese apparition in *The Snake Girl and the Silverhaired Witch* (Daiei 1968; *left*).

Kiss of Death: Virginia North as Vulnavia smiles in the face of death, Vincent Price as Dr Anton Phibes in *The Abominable Dr Phibes* (American International 1971; *opposite below*). Embracing fearlessly *below* are two of William Castle's *Thirteen Ghosts* (Columbia 1960).

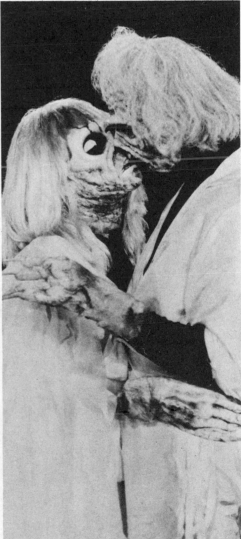

The Vengeance of Egypt (1912) was the first feature sold purely on the strength of its horror: 'A story in the Maupassant school, its object is horror, always a new horror.' This Gaumont film opened with no less a notable than Napoleon, digging up a mummy case. Lieutenant Girard steals the mummy's scarab ring and sends it to his sweetheart. When she puts it on she dreams of a mummy blinking its eyes and is promptly murdered by a burglar. An antiquary tries on the ring and dies of blotches on the arm. A toff buys it and gets shot; lovers find it and are killed in a plane crash. The uncanny catalogue only ends when an Egyptologist returns the ring to the mummy: its eyes glow again, presumably with satisfaction.

H.G.Wells' theory of evolution by vivisection, 'The Island of Dr Moreau' (1896), was thinly disguised by Eclipse as *The Island of Terror* (1913). Washed ashore somewhere in the Pacific is George Ramsey, a shipwrecked editor. His host, Dr Wagner, seems less hospitable when a stream of blood comes flowing under George's bedroom door. He discovers the doctor practising a grafting experiment upon a live black victim. The experiment fails and Wagner decides to try it on George. The editor escapes by raft, so Wagner, ever resourceful, substitutes his own assistant. In the struggle an oil lamp is overturned. Three victims push him into the flames and lock him in his blazing laboratory.

The terrible image of blood oozing under a locked door was repeated in *The Lunatics* (1913), Eclair's film of André de Lord's play, 'Le Système du Docteur Goudron et du Professeur Plume'. Henri Gouget and Monsieur Bahier played the mad characters based on Edgar Allan Poe's Dr Tarr and Professor Fether. Said trade critic George Blaisdell,

'It is a powerful story and a horrible one, yet fascinating in spite of its horror. Don't show it to your patrons without looking at it for yourself, for it is no food for infants or weaklings.' Said the advertising copywriter, 'Every scene a thrill – but the thrill of thrills, that terrifying thunderstorm with its awe-inspiring climax, stamps this feature as the greatest masterpiece of modern cinematography.' It was the first storm in horror movies; it would not be the last.

Brezard is dispatched to research an article on the Berneville Asylum, where Dr Maillard, the director, has developed a new way of treating psychopaths. Pretty Madame Brezard goes along for the ride. As they drive up to the old castle, a thunderstorm breaks. The inmates mutiny. Overpowering Dr Maillard, they hold him down as one lunatic raises a knife: 'to cure him quickly'. The Brezards' arrival interrupts the operation. Passing the knife to a colleague, the lunatic hurries into the director's office. 'His blanched face, glaring and staring eyes, and jerking motions cause the young couple great apprehension.' The 'director' describes his new cure for insanity. 'To their astonishment the chief step is cutting out an eye, and then, very carefully, the throat is to be sliced with a sharp knife!'

'Suddenly, a horrible and sickening rattle breaks up the interview. He rushes into the next room and returns a few minutes later, his hands covered with blood. For some little time strange beings have invaded the office. Their attitude is incomprehensible, their gestures wild. The sight of blood slowly oozing under the door awakens their murderous instincts, and they overpower Brezard. They prepare him for the operation. A wilder gust of wind blows the big window wide. The lunatics cower and this gives time for the keepers, now freed, to arrive with straightjackets and master the madmen.'

The *Grand Guignol* of Paris, that theatre of horrors which had replaced the guillotine as a public entertainment, had arrived in the cinema – belatedly but brilliantly. The new director – of the film, not the asylum – was a student of Rodin, an actor with Rejane, and the first great French filmmaker. Maurice Tourneur's brilliance with visuals was quickly lost to France. Eclair sent him to America to supervise their subsidiary studio. The horror film shifts with him.

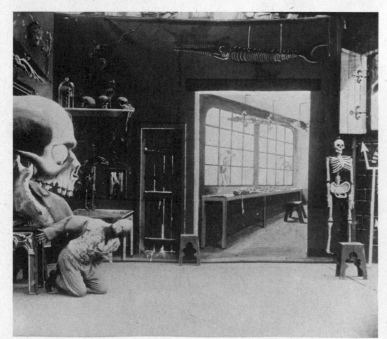

Heads of Horror: Georges Méliès menaced by a monster skull (*left*). Peter Cushing eyes the remains of the Marquis de Sade in *The Skull* (Amicus 1965; *opposite*).

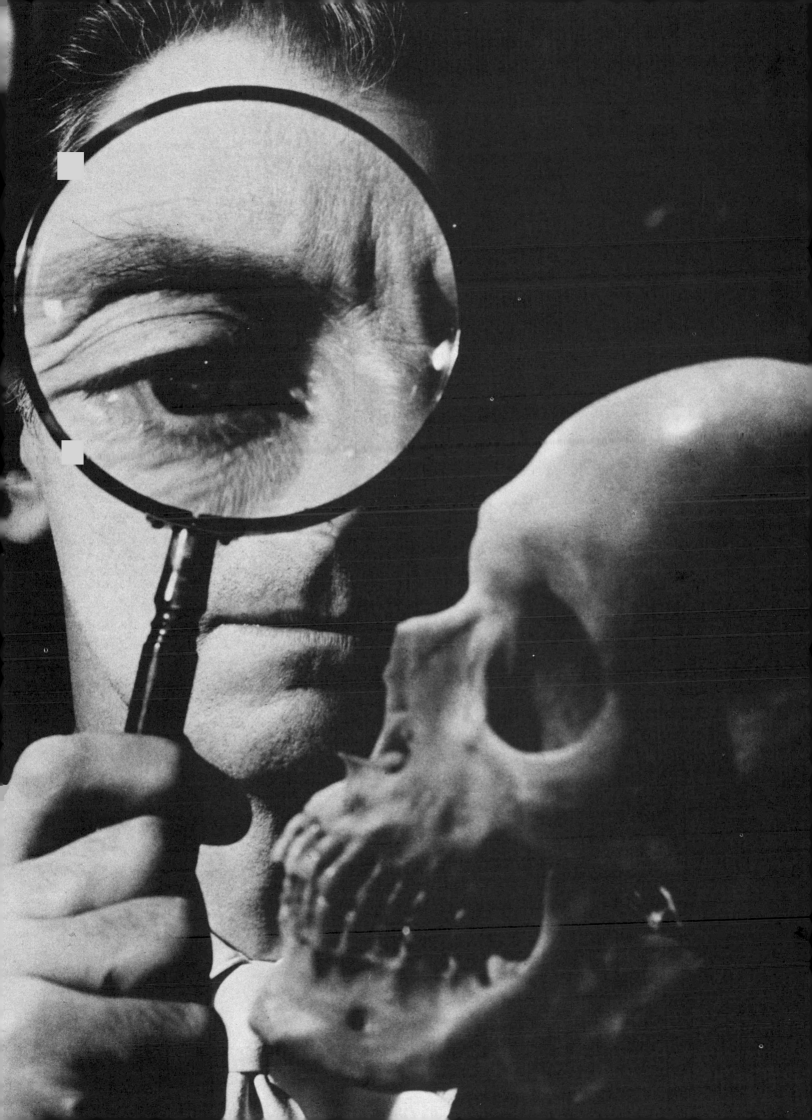

'DR. JEKYLL IS NOT HIMSELF'

In which James Cruze is Jekyll and Mr Hyde is somebody else,
Uncle Carl makes his first monster, John Barrymore loses his
Great Profile, and Mr Ogle's eyeballs leave Percy Darrell
Standing.

The transformation of man into monster, for long years a fairy tale, for longer a legend, finally achieved physical manifestation in 1887. American theatregoers could scarce believe it when handsome Richard Mansfield, thirty-year-old matinee idol, shrank into a hideous dwarf before their very eyes. As noble Henry Jekyll, M.D., he had drunk a drug that released the suppressed side of his personality as Edward Hyde. Robert Louis Stevenson wrote 'Dr Jekyll and Mr Hyde' in 1885; two years later Thomas Russell Sullivan dramatized it for the stage. It was the first science-fiction interpretation of the folk-tales of old, a modern rationalization of ancient superstition. For twenty years Mansfield toured in the title roles, mystifying millions with his on-stage change. A more concentrated, less literary, more sensational version was written by Luella Forepaugh and George F. Fish in 1897. This, too, had a long life and reached Chicago in 1908, a year after Mansfield's death. In the audience was Colonel William Selig, proprietor of the Polyscope Company. For the rest of the week the actors spent their daylight hours in Selig's studio, giving birth to the American horror film. *Dr Jekyll and Mr Hyde* (1908) condensed the play's four acts so tightly into one single spool of film that it even included the curtain! This rose to reveal Dr Jekyll and Alice, the Vicar's daughter, vowing their love in the vicarage garden.

'Then comes the transformation of the moral and physical character of Dr Jekyll from the admirable gentleman and scholar to the ferocious brute of a maniac known as Mr Hyde. He is irresistibly addicted to a drink of his own mixture. It sets him wild and his other self reigns supreme. He attacks his sweetheart. Her father approaches and interferes. With fiendish glee and demon strength, Hyde kills the Vicar, disappears, and the next moment is seen as Dr Jekyll.'

The transformation scene was, of course, the play's great gimmick. Selig filmed it directly,

recording the actor as he followed the formula of Forepaugh and Fish.

'Dr Jekyll writhes as though in physical pain; assumes crouching position; during this with one hand he pulls portion of the wig which is brought forward and falls in a tangled mass over his forehead and eyes.'

Despite super reviews ('the change is displayed with a dramatic ability almost beyond comprehension') the actor went unbilled. Anonymity was still accepted practice two years later, when Wrench released *The Duality of Man* (1910). In this variation Hyde indulges in high play in a pleasure garden, then makes off with the stakes.

'Detectives are hot on the trail when the criminal returns to his chambers and changes his identity. Hilda, the fiancée of the doctor, enters with her father, when again Hyde appears and murders him in the sight of the girl. The police enter, and the miscreant takes a fatal dose of poison.'

Nordisk's *Dr Jekyll and Mr Hyde* (1910) was the first version to name its star, Alwin Neuss. Director August Blom was called 'a sugar-coater of crime' for finding 'a very ingenious way of putting this drama before the young people and the various Boards of Censorship': 'The last scene shows Jekyll struggling with the nightmare in his chair, and, awakening in the presence of Maud, thanks God it was all a dream.' The reviewer added, 'We are inclined to think that Stevenson might just as well have done the same thing without hurting his story.' Already a new class of picturegoer – the middle class – was making its presence, and its predilections, felt.

All Change: Fredric March's not-so-easy switch from Jekyll to Hyde in *Dr Jekyll and Mr Hyde* (Paramount 1931).

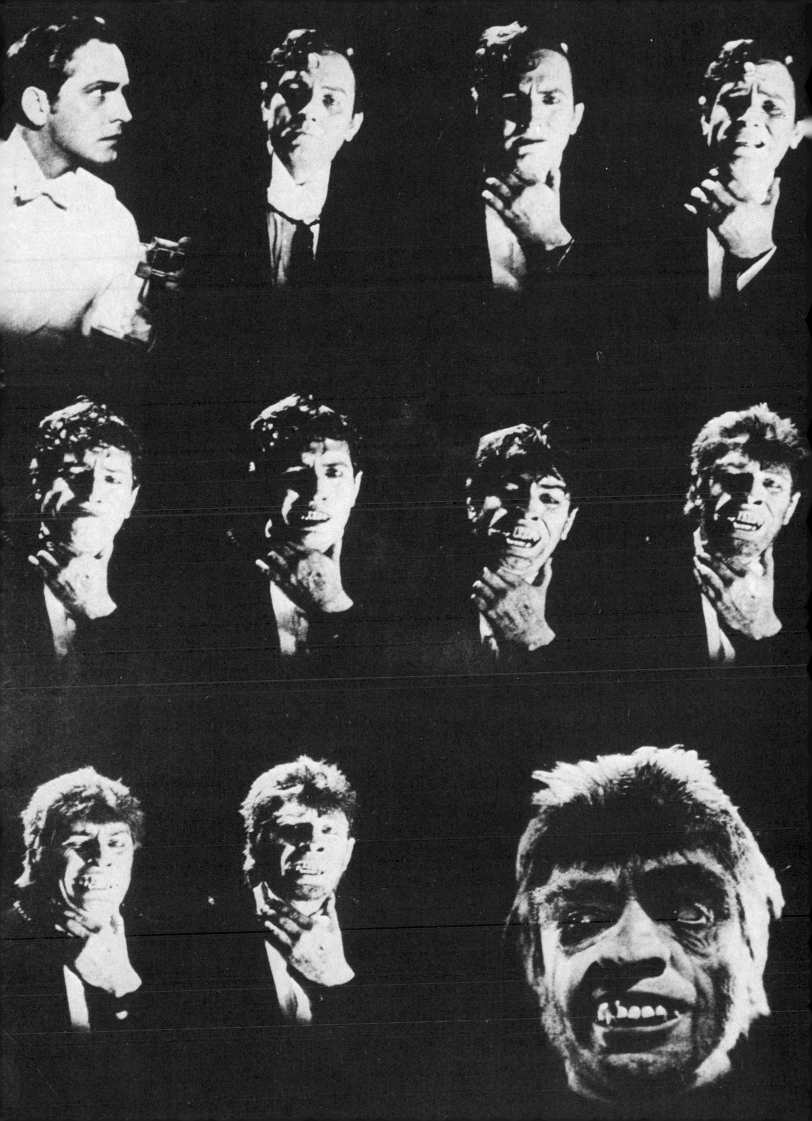

Vampire Vamps: Theda Bara, the first vampire star, gave the world a new verb but no nightmares. More supernatural (indeed more super) is today's vampire star Ingrid Pitt, who played the colourful Carmilla in Hammer's *The Vampire Lovers* (1970; *opposite*). Alice Eis repeated her stage success in Kalem's *The Vampire* (1913; *left*), luring her dancing-partner Bert French into the next trance. Everybody danced in Roman Polanski's *Dance of the Vampires* (Filmways 1967; *below*), which caught filmgoers on the hop. Made as *Your Teeth in My Neck*, it was released in America as *The Fearless Vampire Killers*.

No such cop-outs for Lucius Henderson, who directed the Thanhouser *Dr Jekyll and Mr Hyde* (1911). James Cruze played Jekyll, and his wife, Marguerite Snow, his village sweetheart. Whether Alice, Hilda, or Maud we know not; subtitles simply call her 'the Minister's daughter'.

We see genial, white-locked Dr Jekyll sampling his steaming potion in his laboratory. He chokes, and sinks into his chair, head slumped on chest. A quick frame-cut and Mr Hyde raises his black-curled head. Brows beetle over popping eyeballs and fangs poke out at the corners of his mouth. His tail-coat is pretty shabby, too. Crooking his fingers and clawing the air, he scuttles off to attack his fiancée and strangle her father. In the end he wrecks his lab and drinks poison as a burly bobby barges down the door. The most startling aspect of the whole production was not disclosed for more than fifty years. In 1963 the octogenarian actor Harry Benham revealed that he, and not James Cruze, had played Mr Hyde! Historic stuff; but there is more. The next version of the Stevenson story would be the first horror film produced by a studio that would corner the genre, letting loose upon the world more monsters than any other source in the history of the cinema.

Carl Laemmle, a spry little German with twinkling blue eyes, was born in Lauphein in 1867. He was forty before he had enough cash behind him to throw over book-keeping for buying cinemas in Chicago. An independent spirit, he bucked Edison's Patents Company and was forced into production to feed his own cinemas. There was demoniac humour in his choice of symbol: his Independent Motion Picture Company contracted neatly into Imp. He bedevilled the Trust so expertly that in 1912 he combined Imp and other independents into the Universal Film Manufacturing Company, and in 1915 opened Universal City, a great studio built on the 230-acre Taylor Ranch in Lankershim, Los Angeles.

Universal's big name was King Baggot: sometimes it was even bigger, as nobody, not even he, seemed quite sure whether to spell it with a second 't'. Lured by Laemmle in 1910 upon the sudden folding of a seemingly secure stage tour, Baggot's weekly one-reelers won him early international stardom. He was the first 'character star' in cinema: a wizard of the makeup box. In one memorable movie, *Shadows* (1914), he played every

Hyde's Hide: Christopher Lee in *I, Monster* (Amicus 1970).

character in the story, all ten of them. Meanwhile, as a warm-up, he concentrated on but two: *Dr Jekyll and Mr Hyde* (1913). With crêpe hair and greasepaint 'as the hideous Hyde he brings shudders aplenty'. More than ever before, there was help from the camera. 'We get the real dissolving view as the drug begins to manifest its influence, in the place of the crude facial manipulations employed on the stage.'

Simultaneously the American studios of Charles Urban's Kinemacolor Company released their version of *Dr Jekyll and Mr Hyde* (1913), the first horror film photographed in colour. The system required double-speed projectors fitted with revolving red-green filters; thus distribution of the film was such that even trade-paper reviewers were unable to catch it.

Trick photography had raised movie metamorphoses beyond the capabilities of theatrical mechanics, but the technique had changed little from Méliès' methods. A jump cut, or the slightly more sophisticated dissolve, was considered enough. Henry McRae, a Canadian director who would outlast even Laemmle in the service of Universal, was content with a quick dissolve to convert Watuma, a white-hating, half-caste Navajo, into a live wolf. *The Werewolf* (1913) was the first film to illustrate the legend of the lycanthrope and is still the only one to go to the American Indian original.

The first film truly to transform man into beast by blending several stages of makeup through a series of dissolves, was Thanhouser's *The Miser's Conversion* (1914). Sidney Bracy played the 75-year-old miser obsessed by Darwin's theory. He offers his daughter to the Maharajah of Lahaif in return for rejuvenation. Before an audience, seated in a chair wired to a pulsimeter, Bracy is dosed with elixir. 'The wrinkles leave his brow, his cheeks fill out, his hair changes colour, and he is transformed into a man of forty.' When the Maharajah isn't looking, Bracy grabs the bottle and swallows the lot. 'Immediately he is changed into an ape! It is the most lifelike ape that ever walked on to a studio stage, and you'll marvel, gasp, and exclaim at the transformation!'

John Barrymore, sweet prince of Broadway's royal family, was thirty-eight. As handsome Henry in Paramount's *Dr Jekyll and Mr Hyde* (1920) he looked eighteen years younger. Yet when he quaffed his concoction he crabbed and contorted into a grinning thing of ancient evil. He did it before your very eyes, following the famous feat of

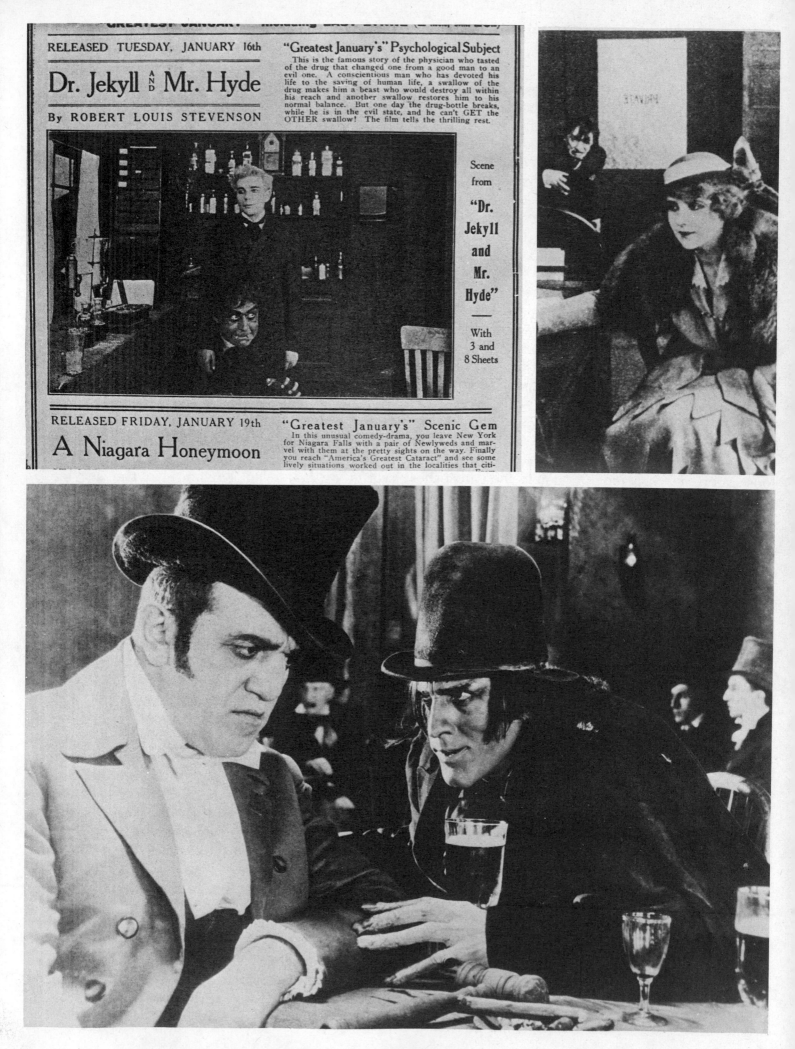

RELEASED TUESDAY, JANUARY 16th

Dr. Jekyll AND Mr. Hyde

By ROBERT LOUIS STEVENSON

"Greatest January's" Psychological Subject

This is the famous story of the physician who tasted of the drug that changed one from a good man to an evil one. A conscientious man who has devoted his life to the saving of human life, a swallow of the drug makes him a beast who would destroy all within his reach and another swallow restores him to his normal balance. But one day the drug-bottle breaks, while he is in the evil state, and he can't GET the OTHER swallow! The film tells the thrilling rest.

Scene
from

"Dr. Jekyll and Mr. Hyde"

—

With 3 and 8 Sheets

RELEASED FRIDAY, JANUARY 19th

A Niagara Honeymoon

"Greatest January's" Scenic Gem

In this unusual comedy-drama, you leave New York for Niagara Falls with a pair of Newlyweds and marvel with them at the pretty sights on the way. Finally you reach "America's Greatest Cataract" and see some lively situations worked out in the localities that citi-

Hyde and Shriek: Monster movies' most popular double act is *Dr Jekyll and Mr Hyde*. James Cruze and Harry Benham played the double-exposed duo in this publicity still from 1912 (Thanhouser: *opposite left*). 1920 saw a double-header: John Barrymore (seen with Louis Wolheim in the Paramount picture; *opposite below*) and Sheldon Lewis (seen with Pearl White in the 1915 Pathé serial *The Exploits of Elaine*; *opposite right*). Fredric March won an Oscar for Henry-and-Edward in Paramount's 1931 version (Holmes Herbert is at the revolver), while twenty years later Louis Hayward played the schizophrenic *Son of Dr Jekyll* (Columbia 1951; *left*) in makeup by Clay Campbell.

Richard Mansfield but under the cold-eyed closeup of the camera. Only then came the trickery: a shot of Jekyll's fingers dissolving into bony talons, then director John S. Robertson cut back to show Hyde's face in full, foul makeup. The concept of the character was horribly new: instead of hairy ape, this Hyde is a spider. Under his high hat his head comes to a point; when he walks he scuttles on crooked legs; his hands, so elongated he has trouble turning his key, are like outsize arachnids. And when Jekyll sleeps, 'in his hours off guard, outraged nature took her hideous revenge and out of the black abyss of torment sent upon him the creeping horror that was his other self'. A phantom spider of monstrous size crawls into his bedroom, up on to his covers, and melts into his body. Jekyll wakes as Hyde.

Clara Beranger's screenplay extended the original and doubled the 'romantic interest'. Martha Mansfield played Millicent, daughter of cynical Sir George Carewe and the chocolate-box innocent whom Jekyll loves. Sultry Nita Naldi was Miss Gina, 'the famous H'Italian dancer' with whom Hyde shacks up at No. 9 Barnesbury Road, Soho. The sapping of Gina's earthy health into shadow-eyed pallor between subtly slow fades adds an uncomfortable new dimension to man's baser nature. There is much of Wilde's Dorian in this beautiful Henry, and of W.T.Stead's London under his perverted Hyde.

This splendid film was a triumph for actor ('pure motion-picture pantomime on as high a level as has ever been attained by anyone') and director, a claim which can be indisputably proved: the Paramount picture had its own *doppelgänger*. Released simultaneously with Jesse L. Lasky's sumptuous super was a poverty-row piece of the same name. Thanks to a quirk of copyright an ex-exhibitor was able to rush through a carbon copy and found a fortune that would ultimately exceed even that of Lasky's. Louis B. Mayer set his *Dr Jekyll and Mr Hyde* (1920) in modern dress. This not only put the production apart from Paramount's just in case a suit should ensue, it also saved the cost of costumes. For his double star Mayer chose Sheldon Lewis, a name known mainly to serial fans. A shrewd move, for not only did Mayer gain a star of sorts, but Lewis brought along his 'Clutching Hand' kit at no extra charge. (He had played that monstrous menace in *The Exploits of Elaine*, 1915.)

The two films tell the story of Cinema 1920 – the one, beautifully tailored for the top box-office star of his time, told with all the expertise of the con-

temporary American movie; the other relying entirely on flatly filmed histrionics, hastily pasted together with high-flown, quasi-religious subtitles. The style of direction (which was anonymous), acting, and camera-trickery of the latter is exactly that of the James Cruze film of 1912: a one-reeler blown to five.

Lewis' Jekyll metamorphoses the easy way: a swig at a test-tube, a cut-away to a butler brushing his hat, and a cut-back to Hyde, crouching and clutching away. 'An Apostle of Hell!' shrieks a horrified subtitle. Proceeding to 'a squalid tenement district' Hyde indulges in 'crimes of his demon nature': he leaps out at a passing female and snatches her handbag. Hyde lurks in his laboratory as fiancée Bernice comes a-calling. 'Dr Jekyll is not himself,' warns the butler. Nabbed by Chief Barnes of the local precinct, Hyde is given the Third Degree. Strapped in the electric chair he dissolves to Jekyll dozing in his armchair. It was all a dream! 'I believe in God!' he cries, 'I have a soul – and I shall have *you*!' he adds, as Bernice bears him off to the opera.

Magic, myth, madness, metamorphosis. One more M came from Edison. He had made the movies; now he made a monster.

'Oh! No mortal could support the horror of that countenance!' The words of Victor Frankenstein, the Modern Prometheus of Mary Wollstonecraft Shelley's novel of 1816, must have found echo in many an exhibitor's exclamation as he opened his Edison envelope on the morning of 15 March 1910. For from the coloured cover of The Kinetogram, No. 4, Vol. 2, snarled 'Scene from *Frankenstein*, Film No. 6604': Charles Ogle.

'A giant in stature, Mr Ogle attracts instant attention whenever he appears on the screen, and from that moment never fails to hold it.' So wrote Edison's publicist, adding that Ogle in action 'has a power that is not easily forgotten'. Nor was his monstrous makeup. The theatrical tradition of the actor creating his own makeup had carried over into the movies, and Ogle's vision of the man-made monster came closer to Mrs Shelley's description than any other the screen has since seen. Only Ogle's eyeballs with their darkly distinctive pupils defied makeup and strayed from the watery original.

The film began in the Frankenstein home as the young student bade farewell to his father and sweetheart, then cut to his room at college where he sat 'absorbed in the mysteries of life and death'.

'He is convinced that he has found a way to create

Under the Hyde: Handsome Henry Jekyll was Spencer Tracy (seen with Ingrid Bergman, MGM 1941; *above*).

Oscar Hyde: Fredric March in *Dr Jekyll and Mr Hyde* (Paramount 1931, *opposite*).

the most perfect human being the world has ever seen. To Frankenstein's horror, instead of creating a marvel of physical beauty and grace, there is unfolded before his eyes an awful, ghastly, abhorrent monster.'

An aside by the synopsist now gives us a small hint of the cinematic quality of the creation scene. 'The formation of the hideous creature from the blazing chemicals of the huge cauldron in Frankenstein's laboratory is perhaps the most weird and fascinating scene ever shown in a moving picture.'

The horror piles up. Frankenstein rushes from the room, 'only to have the misshapen monster peer at him through the curtains of his bed. He falls fainting to the floor.' He returns home a broken man, but quickly recovers under the loving care of his sweetheart. This, moralizes the synopsist, 'brings out the fact that the creation of the monster was only possible because he had allowed his mind to be overcome by evil and unnatural thoughts.' Unable to live apart from his creator, the Monster returns on his wedding night and enters the bride's chamber. The film cuts to Frankenstein as he reacts to the sound of her scream. The girl rushes in and faints at his feet. The Monster is close behind; he overpowers Frankenstein and leaves. The final scene, claimed Edison, brought out the moral point 'that when love for his bride shall have attained full strength, it will have such an effect upon his mind that the monster cannot exist'.

Monster Rally: Charles Ogle was the first movie monster in *Frankenstein*, produced by Thomas Edison in 1910 (*left*). He created his own makeup, which was so effective it almost robbed him of his place in horror history. Boris Karloff did not make up his makeup for Universal's 1931 version (*below*). He supplied something else: artistry. The putty was applied by Jack P. Pierce. *Opposite page:* Hammer's remake *The Curse of Frankenstein* (1957; *above left*) teamed Peter Cushing and Christopher Lee as man and monster for the first time of many. Lee's makeup was by Phil Leakey, who did a slightly better job than the uncredited man at American International, where Gary Conway starred in *I Was a Teenage Frankenstein* (1957). Freddie Jones was Baron Cushing's creation in *Frankenstein Must Be Destroyed* (Hammer 1969; *bottom right*) wearing makeup by Eddie Knight. The Monster's striding power recalls the robots of *Metropolis* (UFA 1926; *centre right*) and *The Colossus of New York* (Paramount 1958; *top right*), played in female and male form by Brigitte Helm and Ed Wolff.

Carl Laemmle presents "Frankenstein" (The Man who made a Monster) A Universal production with COLIN CLIVE · MAE CLARKE · BORIS KARLOFF and JOHN BOLES

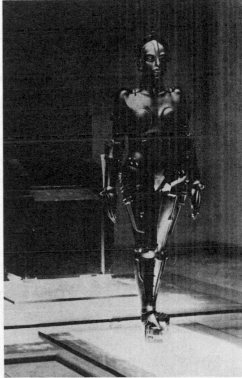

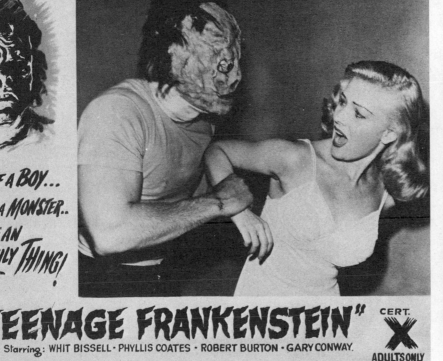

BODY OF A BOY...
MIND OF A MONSTER..
SOUL OF AN
UNEARTHLY THING!

"TEENAGE FRANKENSTEIN"

Starring: WHIT BISSELL · PHYLLIS COATES · ROBERT BURTON · GARY CONWAY.

CERT. X ADULTS ONLY

'The monster enters the room, stands before a large mirror, and holds out his arms entreatingly. Gradually the real monster fades away leaving only the real image in the mirror. A moment later Frankenstein himself enters. As he stands directly before the mirror we are amazed to see the image of the monster reflected instead of Frankenstein's own. Gradually, however, under the effects of love and his better nature, the monster's image fades and Frankenstein sees himself in his young manhood in the mirror. His bride joins him and the film ends with their embrace.'

Frankenstein ran to 975 feet in America, but only 967 feet in England. Was it the first horror film to be censored – or were the English simply better at counting?

Five years later the Ocean Film Corporation proudly announced their first five-reel feature, *Life Without Soul* (1915).

'The action is laid in the semi-tropics of Florida, the desert wastes of Arizona, the awe-inspiring mountainous regions of interior Georgia, the canyons of Colorado, the decks of a three-masted schooner, an ocean-going liner, and the parlors of refined New York.'

Exhibitors were surprised to discover that the film was actually *Frankenstein* again, as adapted by Jesse J. Goldburg, Vice-President and General Manager, and directed by Colonel Joseph W. Smiley, Preceptor of Directors. Percy Darrell Standing, an English actor, played 'the Creation':

'His embodiment of the man without a soul adequately conveys the author's intent. He is awe-inspiring, but never grotesque, and indicates the gradual unfolding of the creature's senses and understanding with convincing skill. At times, he actually awakens sympathy for the monster's condition, cut off as he is from all human companionship.'

Words which would be used of another English actor in a later version. But despite Standing's performance and the elaborately modernized script, the film failed, and it was taken over by the Raver Film Corporation. Mr Raver himself injected 'scientific scenes showing the blood coursing through the veins, the conjugation of cells, and the reproduction of life in the fish world'. Claimed he, 'In its new form, *Life Without Soul*, besides its entertaining value, also has an educational

worth.' Nobody went to his version, either.

'A sort of psychic Frankenstein' was the publicist's description of the Thought Monster, a creature conjured up by The Grand Master of the Black Order in the ultimate episode of *The Mysteries of Myra* (1916), a serial advertised as 'Fifteen Chapters of Science Versus the Supernatural'.

'This Monster is a huge and powerful creature. But his disposition is sort of like a child, in that he is easily distracted from his purpose. He starts to smash up things in the laboratory and to kill Myra. He sees his reflection in the mirror and forgets what he is after.'

Also cast in Frankenstein's monster mould was Q the Automaton, mechanical henchman of the villain in the Harry Houdini serial, *The Master Mystery* (1918).

'The creature is of immense size and fearsome aspect. It can batter down doors at a single strike, and barricades of furniture against them are of no avail against its immense strength. Its movements are ponderous and jerky, but always emphatic, and in spite of its grotesque appearance, the creature is never ridiculous.'

Purporting to be 'an automatic robot containing a human brain taken from a dying man and revivified by a mad genius', inside Q was actually actor Floyd Buckley. Meanwhile, in the European cradle of horrible legends, a human Frankenstein had unleashed a monster the like of which the world had scarcely dreamed.

Hyde and Find: *Abbott and Costello Meet Dr Jekyll and Mr Hyde* (Universal 1953; *above*); Peter Cushing catches Christopher Lee on the turn (Amicus 1970; *above right*); March sees his alter ego (Paramount 1931; *below right*).

THE CLAY MAN COMETH - AND COMETH BACK

In which the Student of Prague makes a Bargain with Satan, Herr Wegener makes a Golem, Dr Caligari makes a Cabinet, and Rotwang makes a Robot.

The German nightmare would begin, in reality, in the summer of 1914. As a foretaste, that favourite literary myth of the *doppelgänger* – a vision of oneself, the sight of which foretells death – had appeared on screen as early as 1909. *The Haunted Man* was produced by Düskes. 'Wherever he goes the same ghostly figure (apparent to none but himself) rises up with horrid imitations of his own actions.' Dogged by his remorseless spook, the haunted man flies to his lodgings where he is promptly doused by his landlady. A drier fate awaited Balduin, the doubled one of *A Bargain With Satan* (1913). This adaptation of Alfred de Musset's poem was publicized as 'a splendid modern allegory of the supernatural, crowded with meaning and mysticism. Better than Faust and Dr Jekyll and Mr Hyde put together!'

Balduin, penniless student of Prague, is visited by the shrivelled Dr Scapinelli, who offers him 100,000 gold pieces in return for permission to take whatever he wishes. Balduin takes the cash and Scapinelli takes Balduin's reflection, for Scapinelli is Satan and the reflection Balduin's soul. Now he is rich enough to woo a Countess. The lady, however, is engaged to Baron Waldis, who challenges his upstart rival to a duel. Balduin promises the Countess that he will not kill the Baron, then meets his victorious reflection, derisively wiping gory sword on cloak. The double pursues him; Balduin pulls a gun and fires. The double vanishes, and Balduin falls dead, blood gushing from his side.

A world success, there was praise for Danish director Stellan Rye, cameraman Guido Seeber ('As an example of ingenious double photography it will strike amazement into the uninitiated'), and the stage star from the Max Reinhardt theatre making a double debut in films. 'Perhaps the most remarkable feature of the film is the superb performance of Herr Paul Wegener. In his last fantastic flight from the spectre he conveys an expression of terror which is irresistibly communicated to the spectator.'

They made the film on location in Prague, where Wegener was much taken by the ancient Ghetto. One legend the old Jews told so intrigued him that he used it as the basis of his next picture. In *Der Golem* (1914) Wegener not only produced, co-wrote, and co-directed, he also played that stalking statue which his American distributors dubbed *The Monster of Fate*. Clad in clay-caked cloth, a thick wig on his head, the moon-faced Teuton stomped through the streets, smashing his way through glass doors and panicking the populace in his love-crazed pursuit of an antique dealer's daughter. The old man had bought the Golem from excavators who thought it was a statue. The dealer recognized it as the legendary clay-man created by a sixteenth-century Rabbi to protect his persecuted people from an evil Emperor. Brought back to life by a magic charm, the Golem reverts to stone when the girl snatches the charm from its chest. Falling from a tower it is broken on the cobblestones below.

The film itself met an equally shattering end. War was declared, preventing its export to England. It arrived in America somewhat belatedly and opened the week the US declared war. A key work in the monster genre, its influence was confined to its own country, where war had an unusual side-effect. German cinema, no longer dominated by America, grew fantastically. New studios were built to cope with the public's demand for escape and movies went back indoors, where it was safe from bombs. Under the bright lights native production bloomed. Cinema abandoned the reality of Lumière's open air and returned to first base: Méliès. To the artificially-created film was added the other Méliès line: fantasy.

Paul Wegener became the first film-maker since Méliès to specialize in the supernatural. From his

Pillar of Society: *The Golem* (Union 1920). Paul Wegener, monster and director.

"A BARGAIN WITH SATAN,

— OR —

The Student of Prague."

Now ready.   Length, approximately, 4,500 feet.

HERR PAUL WEGENER, in the Title Rôle.

The Sole Exclusive Rights for the United Kingdom of this Film are controlled by

The Walturdaw Co., Ltd.,

46 GERRARD STREET, SHAFTESBURY AVENUE, W.

Telephones: Regent 3310, 3311, 3312.   Telegrams: "Albertype, Telew, London" fantasies he evolved the first concept of pure cinema. *Kinetische Lyrik*. He proclaimed his 'New Aim of Cinema' at an Easter Conference in 1916. Unfortunately, his big words and bigger ideas were not borne out in his subsequent movies, as a critic complained of *Der Yoghi* (1916).

'The scenes in which the Yogi makes himself invisible and then torments the other are packed with tricks which we have known for a long time. We only find them now in advertising films, such as the firm of Pinschewer makes with great success.'

Had Wegener been less intellectual about his films, *Der Yoghi* might have been better received. It was the first serious film about invisibility, a power used by its Indian mystic to scare off a scientist. Wegener made the film itself a kind of personal *doppelgänger* by playing both ancient Yogi and youthful inventor.

Wegener doubled up again in *Der Golem und die Tänzerin* (1917: The Golem and the Dancer), by playing himself, the film star, going to the pictures to see himself as *Der Golem*. Then he puts on his old monster suit for a little farcical fun in a dancer's apartment. Scarcely in line with his famous precepts (the ads called it 'A Cheerful Caprice'), it still makes history as the first monster sequel.

Karl Freund had been photographing films of all sorts from as early as 1907, when he was seventeen. In 1920 he was assigned to Wegener's new version of *Der Golem*. To avoid confusion with his earlier work, the sequel was subtitled *Wie Er in die Welt Kam* (How He Came into the World). Dr Hans Poelzig of the Berlin Staatstheater constructed the crowded, crazy Ghetto of medieval Prague, for this time Wegener billed his film as 'Pictured from events in an old chronicle'. He had to: when last seen the Golem was broken in bits.

High Rabbi Loew sees in the stars that danger impends for the Jews of Prague. Instantly a flower-sniffing Junker arrives with a decree from Emperor Ludwig: leave before the end of the month. Loew consults his ancient archives.

'This figure called Golem was made long ago by a magician of Thessaly. If you place the magic word in the amulet on his breast he will live and breathe as long as he wears it. Astaroth guards the magic word which can endow even clay with life.'

Loew moulds a mighty giant of clay, then creates a magic circle of fire and summons forth the spirit. Astaroth, a floating head, speaks in smoke the word 'Aemaer'. Loew writes it down and puts it in the amulet: instantly the Golem's eyes light into life. His head turns, he sways, he lurches forward at Loew's command, then falls back stiffly, his eyes dimming as the Rabbi removes the charm. It is a superb sequence, one that would echo down the reels of time. The next scene is even better: fade in on the Golem in closeup, hacking away with his chopper. What bloody horror is he up to? Cutting back, Wegener shows the giant chopping firewood! More indignity: we next see the monster, bag on arm, doing the shopping!

'If you have brought the dead to life through magic, beware of that life. The lifeless clay will scorn its master and turn to destroy him.'

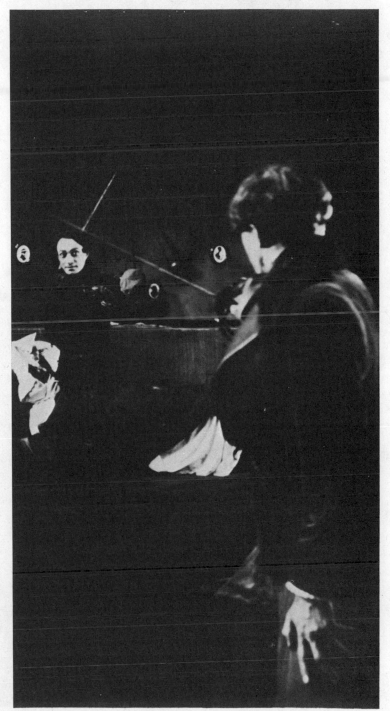

50

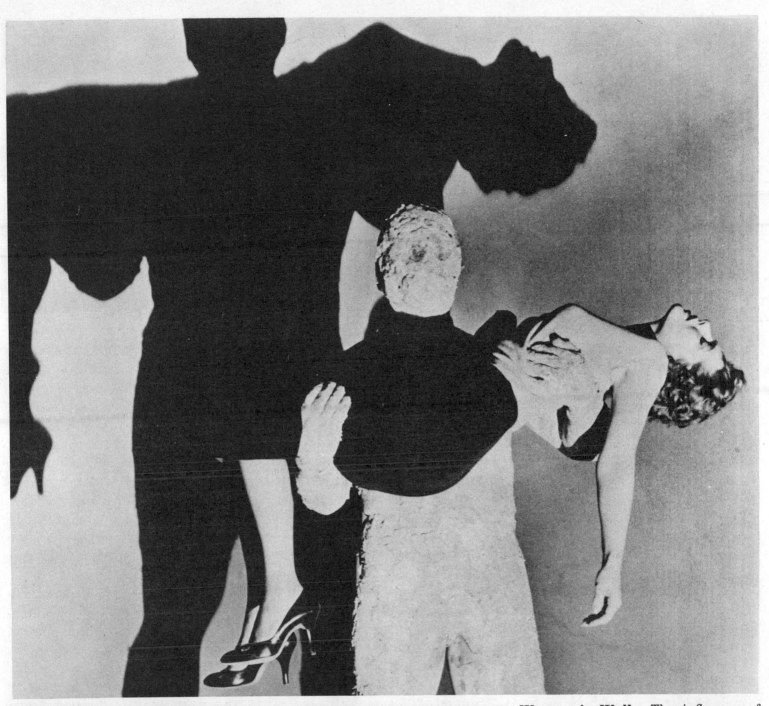

Wegener's Walk: The influence of Paul Wegener as a fantasy maker was felt throughout films. In Wegener's fatherland Emil Jannings played Ma the Mummy in Lubitsch's *The Eyes of the Mummy* (Union 1918; *opposite top left*) and was enough to make Pola Negri swoon on the stairs. Wegener played the Golem three times, best in 1920 (*opposite top right*). Ferdinand Hart brought the house down in Julien Duvivier's *The Legend of Prague* (AB 1936; *opposite below*) while Allan Sellers carried off Jill Haworth in the British *It* (Goldstar 1966; *left*). *Above:* an encrusted Etruscan (Bob Bryant), petrified at Pompeii, proves to Elaine Edwards his heart is not made of stone: *The Curse of the Faceless Man* (UA 1958).

Famulus, Loew's assistant, discovers the old man's daughter in bed with the Junker. The jealous youth orders the Golem to kill. All hell breaks loose. The clay man punches through the girl's door, throws her lover from a tower, grabs up a blazing log. Soon the whole cramped Ghetto is ablaze as the Golem drags the swooning girl away and drapes her over an accommodatingly-curved rock. He crashes open the great gates: children flee screaming. One little girl stands and smiles. She offers him her apple. The Golem picks her up. She plays with his amulet, takes out the charm: he stiffens, falls, a statue of stone.

Wegener's way with cinema attracted other intellectuals from the arts. A discharged lieutenant tried his hand at scenario writing whilst convalescing from war wounds. The result, *Hilde Warren und der Tod* (1917), inspired Fritz Lang to forsake his pre-war career as a painter and take up films. Director Joe May's wife Mia played Hilde Warren, and Lang himself played Tod (Death): a suitably supernatural beginning for a cinematic career that would stretch to the sixties.

The end of the war saw Lang a scenario editor, 1919 a director. Too busy to take on a horror story he had accepted from two young pacifist poets, Lang passed the script to Robert Wiene, but not before he had added two framing scenes. These, complained Hans Janowitz and Carl Meyer, took their tale of insanity out of reality and into explicable illusion. Nevertheless, *The Cabinet of Dr Caligari* (1919) is still not only a great horror film, it is a classic of cinema.

'Ladies and gentlemen. You are about to see what is without a doubt the strangest motion picture ever made. It may add to your appreciation if you know something of the aims of the producers. They believed that the screen could be made something more than a mere medium for the exact photographic reproduction of conventional stories. They considered that motion pictures could be made to reflect the newest and most interesting development in modern art, and that, in so doing, produce sensations and emotions in an audience that have hitherto been impossible. They have told a thrilling and fantastic story in somewhat the same manner in which an artist transfers his own emotions upon canvas – in vivid and unusual strokes of colour and composition. To do this they have made the backgrounds an important part of the story. In every scene there is a special setting made and painted by hand [designed by Hermann Warm, Walter Reimann and Walter Röhrig, painters from *Der Sturm* group in Berlin], which fits the mood of the action that is taking place. You will see Cesare, the sleep-walker, floating down the street that seems to have been ripped from some nightmare – a street of misshapen houses with brooding windows, streaked by dagger strokes of light and darkened by blots of shadow – and you will immediately feel the terror in the movements of that floating grotesque.'

This was how the British distributors introduced the film in 1922, by which time hostilities had cooled sufficiently for it to be billed, cautiously, as 'Europe's Greatest Contribution to the Motion Picture Art'. German publicists put it more simply: 'You Must Become Caligari!'

'In Holstenwall where I was born': Francis tells the tale in flashback, of a village fair and a hypnotist: 'Step up! Step up! See Cesare the Somnambulist! Cesare who has slept for twenty-five years and

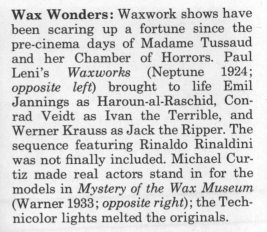

Wax Wonders: Waxwork shows have been scaring up a fortune since the pre-cinema days of Madame Tussaud and her Chamber of Horrors. Paul Leni's *Waxworks* (Neptune 1924; *opposite left*) brought to life Emil Jannings as Haroun-al-Raschid, Conrad Veidt as Ivan the Terrible, and Werner Krauss as Jack the Ripper. The sequence featuring Rinaldo Rinaldini was not finally included. Michael Curtiz made real actors stand in for the models in *Mystery of the Wax Museum* (Warner 1933; *opposite right*); the Technicolor lights melted the originals.

Doctor's Orders: The influence of *The Cabinet of Dr Caligari* (Decla 1919, *below left*) can be seen in Jean Hersholt's gloves in *The Cat Creeps* (Universal 1930; *left*) and the coffin in *Dance of the Vampires* (Filmways 1967; *below*).

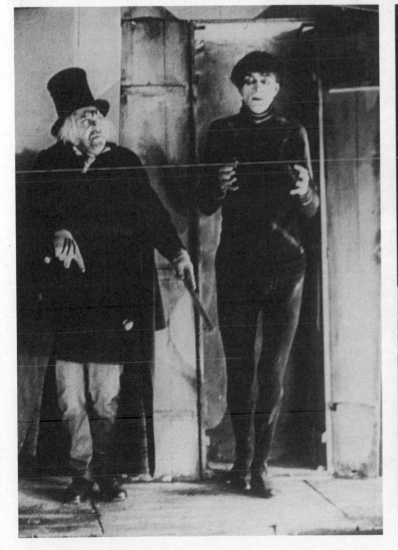

Shadow Shudder: The Germans were so fond of shadows that they made a film about them, *Warning Shadows* (Pan 1923), a year after Schreck's shadow crept in *Nosferatu* (*above*). The shadow of Vincent Price frightened Phyllis Kirk in *House of Wax* (Warner 1953; *opposite above*), a three-dimensional remake of *Mystery of the Wax Museum*. Shadows also struck home a point in Polanski's *Dance of the Vampires* (Filmways 1967; *opposite below*).

'I am Dracula. I bid you Welcome.': Max Schreck was Dracula but had to be called Graf Orlok to fool Bram Stoker's widow. F.W.Murnau's dodge failed, but his film did not. *Nosferatu* (Prana 1922; *above left*) remains a frightening thrill unequalled even by Tod Browning's *Dracula* (Universal 1931; *left*), with Bela Lugosi as the legal, lethal Count.

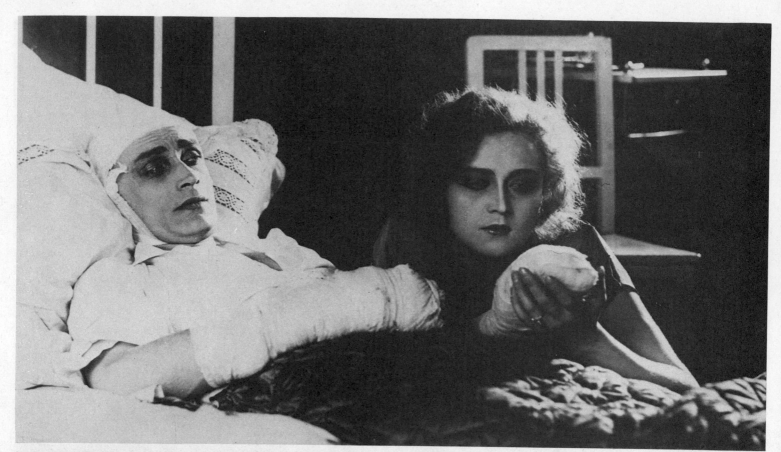

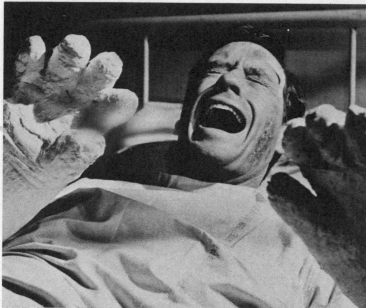

Veidt Fright: Conrad Veidt was the first great figure of fright in cinema. Following in the sturdier footsteps of Paul Wegener he created a unique creature in Cesare the skeletal Somnambulist, whose awakening was an eye-opener in *The Cabinet of Dr Caligari* (Decla 1919: *opposite right*). In *Waxworks* (Neptune 1924; *opposite left*) he was mad Ivan the Terrible, who went even madder trying to stop an hour-glass from emptying away his life. In Robert Wiene's *The Hands of Orlac* (Pan 1924; *top*) he was a concert pianist on to whose severed stumps were grafted the hands of a murderer. Peter Lorre played the part in Karl Freund's version, shown in America as *Mad Love* (MGM 1935; *right*) and Mel Ferrer did it again for Edmond T. Greville (Pendennis 1960; *above*).

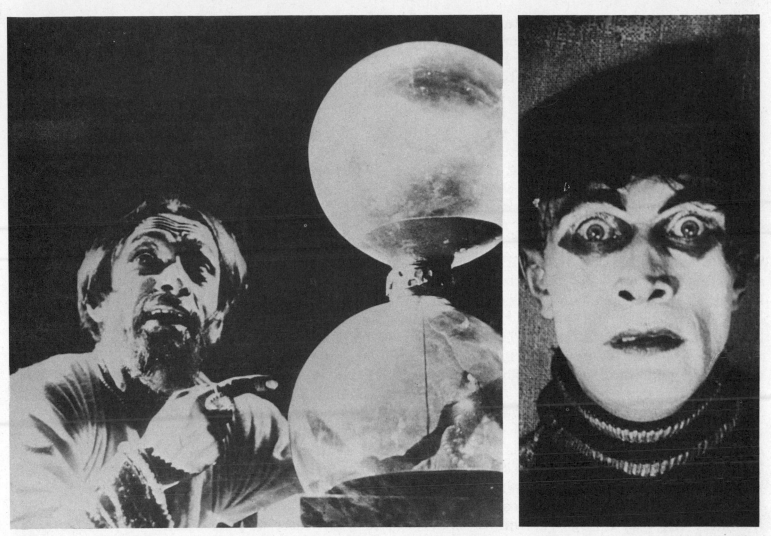

is about to awake!' At a command from Caligari (Werner Krauss in Mutt and Jeff gloves: three stripes on each to match his hair), Cesare (Conrad Veidt at his most skeletal in skin-tight leotards) opens his black-lidded eyes and cat-foots forth from his coffin. It is a moment of death into life that still chills. 'Cesare knows all secrets – ask him to look into your future!' Francis' frail friend asks, 'How long shall I live?' And Cesare answers, 'Until dawn!' The awful prediction comes true: Cesare murders him. Commanded to kill Jane Olsen (Lil Dagover, all mascara and white drapery) Cesare comes creeping through her window, knife at the ready. Her beauty gives him pause – she wakes – he snarls – she screams – they struggle – she swoons – he bears her off over the crooked roofs, a pack of outraged villagers at his heels. A classic sequence, classically constructed; as well made as any made today.

Francis exposes Dr Sonnow, head of the local lunatic asylum, as Caligari, insanely obsessed by exploits of an eleventh-century mountebank – but then Francis is exposed as a lunatic himself! This was the twist, added by Lang to 'explain' the unrealistic decor, that so upset Hans Janowitz. Even so the film was successful enough to create a whole

new school of cinema, Expressionism. Immediately Janowitz was given *Dr Jekyll and Mr Hyde* to adapt for the newest star of German horror, Conrad Veidt (another Reinhardt refugee). This film was another inexpensive piece. To avoid possible royalties it called its doubled hero Dr Warren and Mr O'Connor and itself *Der Januskopf* (1920). The fine physician who turned into a Whitechapel murderer under the influence of a statue of Janus, was photographed by Karl Freund and directed by F.W.Murnau.

Friedrich Wilhelm Murnau, whose real name was Plumpe, was yet another Reinhardt-trained man. His success at pirating Stevenson now led him to another late English novelist, and from Bram Stoker's 'Dracula' (1897) he evolved *Nosferatu* (1922). He subtitled it *Eine Symphonie des Grauens* (A Symphony of Shudders). He changed the characters' names: hero Harker became Hutter; his wife Nina, Ellen; Lucy Westenra became Annie Harding; Renfield, Knock; and Count Dracula, Graf Orlok. He changed London to Bremen and put the clock back to 1838. All this, and still the widow sued. Mrs Stoker won her case and all copies of the film were destroyed; or so the order went. In 1930 there turned up a talkie called *Die Zwölfte Stunde* (The Twelfth Hour), concerning a vampire called Fürst Wollkoff. He was Orlok-Dracula with a music-and-effects track added. Whatever man's law may decree, a vampire cannot die – as long as a film duper shall live. *Nosferatu* is the classic example of art saved from destruction by piracy.

Hutter arrives at a crumbling castle after a frightening ride in a high-speed coach drawn by shrouded horses. His hook-nosed host, skull-capped and skeletal, comes only by night. Creeping into his guest's room, Orlok is about to bite him when Ellen Hutter, in distant Bremen, wakes screaming from her sleep. This telepathic miracle interrupts the vampire, who packs his coffin and heads for the docks. Once aboard the *Empusa* the feast is on: soon only the mate and the captain are left alive. The mate chops open Orlok's crate – rats come swarming out. From his coffin Orlok swings upright, stare-eyed and smiling, as if on some horrid hinge. The mate plunges overboard and the captain ties himself to the wheel as the vampire creeps forth. The dead ship sails into harbour. Orlok scuttles away, his coffin tucked underneath his arm. Soon funerals fill the streets. Orlok stares in at Ellen's window. She welcomes him, embraces him, deceiving him to linger. Dawn warms the sky and as the sun strikes him, the vampire dissolves: a puff of smoke, and then that too is gone.

Thin Max Schreck played the bony blood-sucker in Spock-ears and eagle-claws. A skin wig made him look much older than his forty-three years. Schreck died in 1936, a veteran of more than fifty films: all but this forgotten. He was the first and foulest vampire in the movies.

Nosferatu used real settings, selected, framed, and lit with care. The interplay of light and shade replaced Caligari's black paint: in the horror film Expressionism had found its form. Unrealistic set design rolled on. Paul Leni, who had created great stage settings for Reinhardt, directed *Waxworks* (1924). An omnibus film following the Fritz Lang formula from *Destiny* (1921), it allowed Leni's designing mind to run wild. Opening in a crazy carnival, Wilhelm Dieterle (later William, the director) played a starving poet hired to create tales around the models in a waxworks show. In his fantasies Emil Jannings is Haroun-al-Raschid, bulbous lecher; Conrad Veidt is Ivan the Terrible, maniacal torturer; Werner Krauss is Jack the Ripper, relentless pursuer. Veidt's wrought performance as the insane Ivan is still one of the most compellingly disturbing in all cinema. He went on to play the obsessed amputee of *The Hands of Orlac* (1924), from a French science-fiction prediction of transplant surgery. Maurice Renard's popular novel was given much medieval trappery, as may have been expected from director Robert Wiene, who had helped create Caligarism five years before. Paul Orlac is a concert pianist whose hands are crushed in a crash. A surgeon sews on those of a murderer (Fritz Kortner), and sensitive Paul feels a subsequent urge. The consequent killings are, however, nothing more than a foul plot to drive the mended man mad. Strictly supernatural, however, was the remake of *The Student of Prague* (1926), in which Veidt sold his soul to Satan: Werner Krauss in top-hat, tail-coat and gamp.

Meanwhile, Fritz Lang had spent more than a year and most of UFA's money on *Metropolis* (1926), a symbolic prediction of the year 2000. Rudolph Klein-Rogge played Rotwang, a madly medieval scientist who single-handedly (literally: his right hand was a black-gloved claw) created a robotrix in the image of a 'girl of the people'. This *doppelgänger* was played both in flesh and steel sheathing by a student spotted in an amateur play. Brigitte Helm acquitted herself erotically enough to play later both Alraune, the man-created woman of *A Daughter of Destiny* (1928), and Antinea, queen of Atlantis; the former twice.

Metropolis, essentially a science-fiction spectacular, also sought to reform the boss-worker relationship: a fantasy on two levels. However, Lang put enough cracked magic into his laboratory sequences to spark off monsters unborn. The undoubted prototype for Frankenstein's, and every other mad movie doctor's lab, it added the new futurism to the old Expressionism. Alchemy both ancient and ultra-modern came together in the contrast of flashing light and frightening shadow. And as Lang looked into tomorrow and saw some of yesterday, Murnau looked back and found *Faust* (1926). From that old, much-filmed legend Murnau and Freund conjured cinema's definitive devil: Emil Jannings, horned and huge, flies through the night, enfolding a whole rolling town in the blackness of his cloak. This unequalled sequence, together with Lang's epic vision, makes 1926 the climax to an incredibly creative decade: a heritage of horror that was Germany's silent gift to the cinema.

Sleep Walkers: Conrad Veidt drags over Lil Dagover in *The Cabinet of Dr Caligari* (Decla 1919).

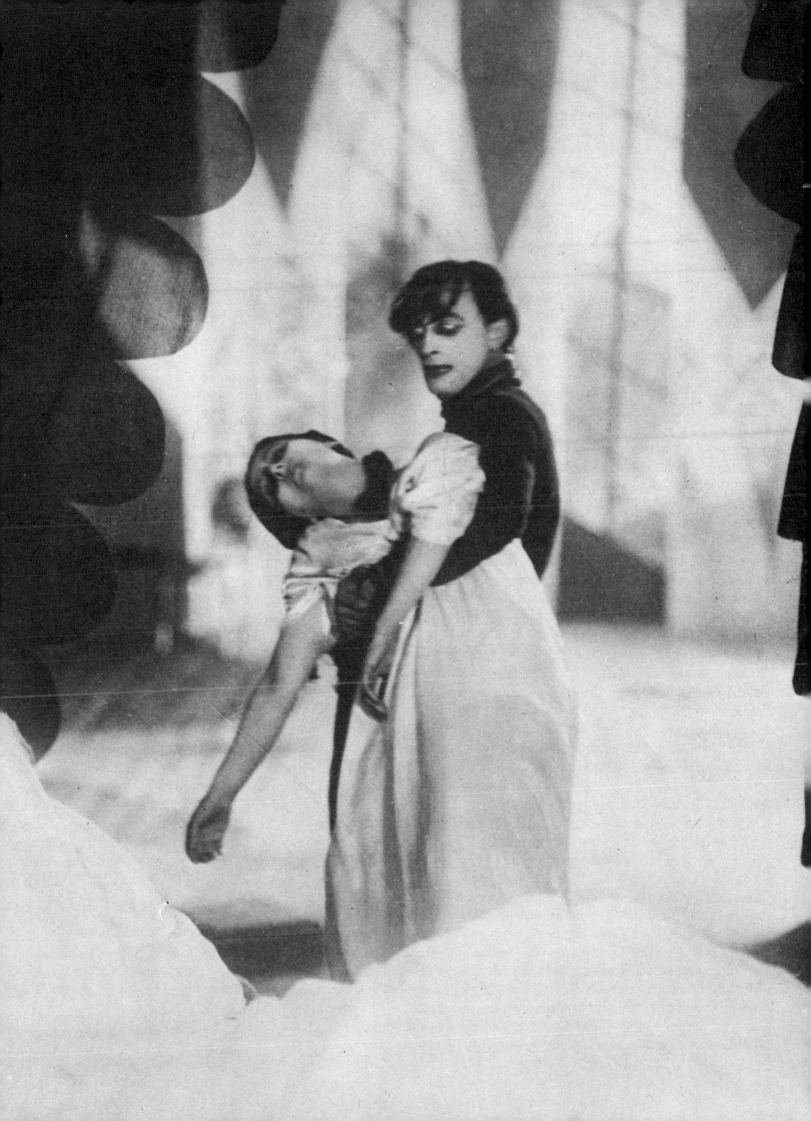

LON CHANEY WILL GET YOU IF YOU DON'T WATCH OUT!

In which the Miracle Man unwinds, the Hunchback unbends, the Phantom unmasks, and Professor Challenger is undone.

Dr Caligari arrived in America in 1921. Samuel Goldwyn, tycoon in bloom, imported the controversial Cabinet. It was the first film by the conquered to be seen by the conquerors; it was also the first horror film to be taken seriously by the intellectuals – although The New York Times mistakenly labelled it 'a Cubistic shocker'.

The horror of Caligari inspired Goldwyn to produce something similar, and from an old and whimsical thriller by Barry Pain, 'The Octave of Claudius', Wallace Worsley directed *A Blind Bargain* (1922). Trendy twenties trimmings in the shape of monkey-gland graftings 'to promote virility and longevity' were added to the 1897 original. The hero, topically promoted from wastrel to unemployed ex-serviceman, offered himself as a guinea-pig in return for an operation on his ailing mother. The experimentalist, benignly named Dr Lamb, kept a cripple: a dumb, half-animal hunchback, anthropoid end-product of some sinister surgery. Caged in the cellar are two further experiments. Luckily for our volunteer, the apeman lets them loose in time to save him from the knife: they break the doctor's back. An incredible piece by any standards, yet even more incredible: both surgeon and monster were played by the same actor – Lon Chaney.

Alonso Chaney was one of nature's April Fools. Born on 1 April 1883, his mother and father were both deaf mutes. So were his relations on his mother's side; indeed, his grandmother had helped found the Colorado State Institute for the Deaf and Dumb. This grounding in gesture, amplified by mimic descriptions of his daily doings to entertain his bedridden mother, gave the young Lon a unique technique for acting in the Silent film. Heartbreak and courage added to the man's character: divorce from an alcoholic wife gave him custody of their eight-year-old son, a child of destiny. By the time he played 'Frog', a fake cripple in *The Miracle Man* (1919), he had appeared in a hundred films. Yet so skilled was he with his make-up box that only a few knew the name of Lon Chaney when he was hailed as a star overnight.

'In the first place I planned to be a cripple, have a withered hand, a hump on my back, but when I discovered I had to unfold twice before the camera, these three infirmities were, of course, impossible. Finally, after several sleepless nights and a number of experiments, I decided on paralysis. I let my beard grow, and altogether I worked out a convincing makeup, horrible as it was.'

Chaney, unhooking his dislocated body and straightening out from a paralytic twist in one single, uninterrupted shot, remains a riveting sight unique in the movies. It gave rise to a national joke: 'Don't step on it – it may be Lon Chaney!'

Chaney's part was a turning point in more ways than one. He became the first film star to be boosted for each new appearance rather than for his own. He started a search for ever stranger, ever more difficult roles. A curious challenge, it drove the actor beyond the normal call of career. It was a personal quest into self-torture, and the public loved it. They revelled in each new monster, and revelled again in the revelation of how Chaney suffered pain for their pleasure. Fan magazines vied to publish the grisly details and grislier pictures. Was there a masochistic drive behind Chaney's agonizing contortions? And what was his world appeal at a time when genuine grotesques, the victims of war, begged at every street corner?

The Golem stomped onto the screens of America in 1923. Three years was a long time in movie evolution, yet such was Paul Wegener's mastery of the

Living Death: Lon Chaney as *The Phantom of the Opera* (Universal 1925).

medium that his film towered above current Hollywood products like the clay giant himself. Its style and spectacle inspired both pride and envy in German-born Carl Laemmle. His new production executive was a bright young man called Irving Thalberg; also on contract again was Lon Chaney, who had begun his career at Universal back in 1912. Wallace Worsley, who had worked with Chaney on his more startling creations, was brought in as director, and together, working on Laemmle's hunch, they fashioned a monster of a movie. Twelve reels long, it was shot on the biggest set yet built: a stone by stone replica of the Cathedral of Notre Dame de Paris.

The Hunchback of Notre Dame (1923) was impressive on all counts. 'Without a doubt the greatest individual studio setting yet created', was the mildest of tributes. Yet dwarfed as he was by artifice and architecture, it was Chaney who stole the scene every time: 'A veritable living gargoyle, he plays Quasimodo as a fearsome, frightful, crooked creature, one eye bulging but blind, knees that interfere, sharp, saw-edged, protruding teeth, high, swollen cheekbones, and a twisted nose, a monstrous joke of nature.'

Revealed to the fascinated world were the painful details of Chaney's makeup. First, a thirty-pound breastplate attached in front to shoulder-pads of the kind American footballers use. Next, a hump moulded from forty pounds of rubber was joined to the false front by a leather harness. Once in the rig, Chaney could no longer stand upright. Over the whole he wore a tight, pink, hairy skin, also made of rubber. On his head a matted wig; on his face lumps of putty; in his mouth fanged false teeth. It was a triumph of man over makeup; through all the gear came Chaney, not so much an actor, more a human being.

'The makeup is, I hope, merely a frame for the picture, and it is the picture with which I am concerned. It is not morbidity that made me turn

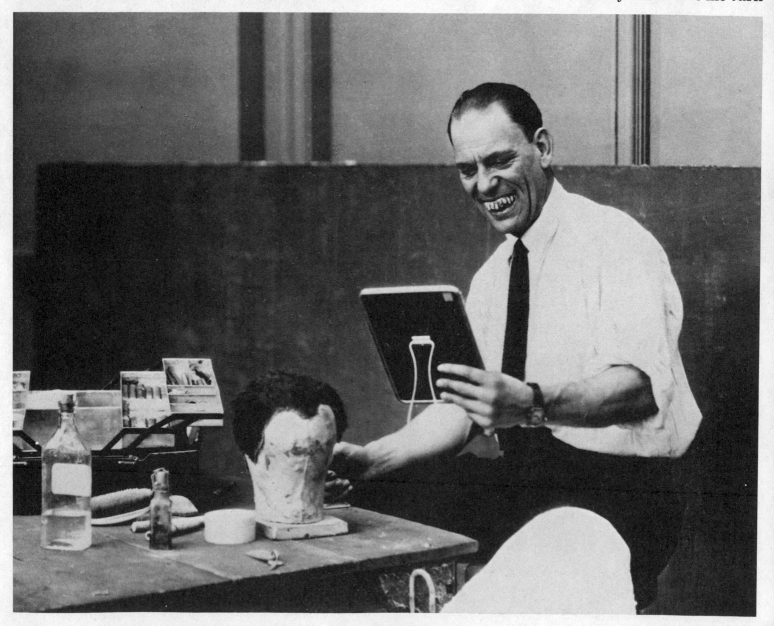

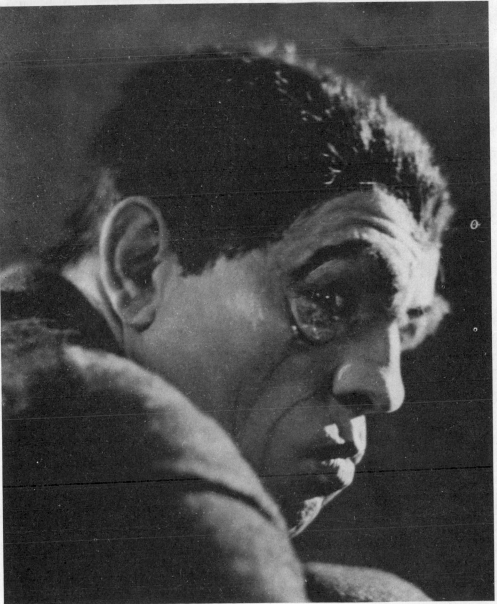

Makeup Man: Christopher Lee tries out his teeth, made by Harry and Peter Frampton for *I, Monster* (Amicus 1970; *left*). Lon Chaney for *A Blind Bargain* (Goldwyn 1922) supplied his own (*opposite*). In that film he also played the scientist who made the apeman (*below*). A creation of super-science on screen, he was created off-screen out of the paint and putty Chaney carried in his celebrated 'box of tricks'.

Chaney Reaction: Lon Chaney, the first American monster, influenced horror films far beyond his early death. As Quasimodo, Victor Hugo's *Hunchback of Notre Dame* (Universal 1923; *below*), his humanity surmounted his make-up in a way even James Cagney, a greater actor, could not achieve: *Man of a Thousand Faces* (Universal 1957; *opposite above*). Cagney, playing Chaney, was also unable to match the old master's *Phantom of the Opera* (Universal 1925; *bottom left and right*). Chaney was out-monstered by his own monster in *The Monster* (MGM 1925; *opposite below*). He played a ventriloquial jewel thief in Tod Browning's *The Unholy Three* (MGM 1925; *right centre*), for which he donned skirts. Chaney remade the film in 1930 (*right*), his first talkie – and his last.

UNIVERSAL MONTHLY

Vol. 1   No. 5.   May · 1924.

CARL LAEMMLE Presents

The

HUNCHBACK of NOTRE DAME

with

LON CHANEY

THE GREATEST SCREEN ATTRACTION OF THE AGE

Monkey Business: Bull Montana played a missing link in *The Lost World* (First National 1925; *right*). This ex-wrestler found help in the hirsute suit made by makeup man Cecil Holland. Jacques Lerner, a small French actor, came to Hollywood to star in *The Monkey Talks* (Fox 1927; *below*). His monkey suit was made by Jack P. Pierce. *The Gorilla* (First National 1927; *below right*) was actually Walter Pidgeon in disguise.

What the Dinosaur: Prehistoric monsters battle to the death in *The Lost World* (First National 1925; *opposite bottom right*) and live again to battle to the death in *One Million Years BC* (Hammer 1966; *opposite bottom left*). Willis O'Brien was the animator who inspired it all, and who worked on both *King Kong* (RKO 1933; *opposite top right*) and the 'live' remake of *The Lost World* (Twentieth Century-Fox 1960; *opposite top left*). His finned fauna lacked the charm of his animated animals and upset the Preventors of Cruelty.

to the type of role with which I have become identified. I hope that I shall never be accused of striving merely for horrible effects. I want to dig down into the mind and heart of the role. But as a man's face reveals much that is in his mind and heart, I attempt to show this by the makeup I use; and the makeup is merely the beginning.'

Irving Thalberg moved from Universal to MGM, lured by Louis B. Mayer. He signed Lon Chaney to a long-term contract which was still in force when the actor died. *The Monster* (1925) played its horrors for laughs, as suited the popular play by Crane Wilbur upon which it was based. Chaney was the mad Dr Ziska, mesmeric vivisectionist, who garnered fresh subjects for surgery by manipulating mirrors at motorists. He shot them through chutes, peeped through holes in walls, trapped Gertrude Olmstead in a descending couch, and generally sent himself up. For Chaney it was a welcome relief to return to comedy, a field he had

not played since his barnstorming days. For his next film he was reunited with a director who also had a comedy background. But Tod Browning would never return to the slapstick acting he had done with Fay Tincher in the Komic Komedies of 1914.

The partnership of Chaney and Browning had begun in 1921 with the Chinatown thriller *Outside the Law*. Tod Browning's schooldays were spent in the circus: he ran away from his old Kentucky home and toured as half of an act called 'The Lizard and the Coon'. Which half is not recorded. The double life of the carnival, the tears behind the tinsel, the con-men and the suckers, were his constant inspiration in his movie career. He drew upon his own experiences time and again, and always for the macabre behind the makeup. Then Browning's three years on the bottle broke the budding team. Thalberg ended studio prohibition with a movie reunion that grossed two million dollars – for MGM.

The Unholy Three (1925) were Echo (Chaney), a ventriloquist, Hercules, a strong man, and Tweedledee, a midget. Seeking to expand their extra-curricular activity of picking the pockets of circus customers, the incredible partnership sets up shop with Echo in charge as 'the Little Lady who Sells Parrots'. Their scheme is mind-blowing. Echo, beaded and bombazined, sells a talking parrot to a rich client. When the client complains that the bird no longer talks (it never did; Echo was ventriloquizing, of course), the Little Lady comes a-calling. She brings along her baby, who promptly clambers from his pram to stuff any spare jewellery down his diaper (the midget in disguise, you see). By way of a climax, Browning introduces a giant gorilla. 'Startling and original', exclaimed one reviewer.

Delighted with his *Hunchback* profits, Carl Laemmle determined to do the whole exercise again. He looked to France for another epic and found in Gaston Leroux's 1908 novel everything he could hope for: a magnificent set to build that would rival Notre Dame, and a horrible monster to create that would outdo Quasimodo. *The Phantom of the Opera* (1925) brought Lon Chaney hurrying back home to Universal.

'Sanctuary of song lovers. The Paris Opera House, rising nobly over medieval torture chambers, hidden dungeons long forgotten. One night each year all Paris mingled, forgetful of caste, at the merry, mad Bal Masqué de l'Opéra. In the midst of the revelry strode a spectral figure robed in red.'

This fearsome figure in crimson cloak and scarlet skull – Poe's 'Red Death' in two-tone Technicolor – is the Phantom. Erik, a born freak, lives only for music. Periodically he slinks from the shadows to whisper unseen tuition to Christine the chorus girl. When the directors of the Opera spoil her chance to deputize for a diva, the Phantom is angry. He sends a giant crystal chandelier crashing into the audience. In black cloak and white mask he emerges from a mirror to conduct Christine through cobwebby catacombs and across an underground lake to his lair. The Phantom sits at an organ and plays 'Don Juan Triumphant', his own composition (first heard four years later when David Broekman and Max Hayman added it to the film for a synchronized reissue). What follows is classic, of horror cinema and of cinema itself. Christine (Mary Philbin), unable to resist the fascination of fear, unmasks the Phantom.

Chaney's makeup had been kept secret by the studio during the shooting. When it was eventually revealed, quite late in the film, it was by as cunningly contrived a sequence of shots as was ever devised in the history of montage. Women screamed and strong men fainted. By careful placement of characters and camera, Rupert Julian doubles the shock. The first is for us: Christine is behind Chaney and cannot see his face. The second is for her when Chaney turns. Thus, through her shock, his face shocks us again.

'Feast your eyes, gloat your soul, on my accursed ugliness!' We can scarce do otherwise as Julian's camera cuts closeups, longshots, distorted shots, together into a film thrill unequalled until James Whale's revelation of his Frankenstein Monster. This was the original unmasking sequence in horror movies, and of a hundred seen since is still the best. It thrilled again when Universal spliced it into their 1951 mystery, *Hollywood Story*. Yet two full remakes and a third reconstruction for Chaney's biography, all in colour, have failed to catch that awful shock.

Chaney created a makeup intended to suggest a living skull. He designed a device that, inserted into his nose, tilted the tip and spread open his nostrils. Another device drew his mouth back at the corners, prongs attached to protruding false teeth. Inside his mouth, circles of celluloid accentuated his cheekbones, and on top of his head was a domed wig of skin, stranded with lank hair.

The film ended with a wild chase and an in-joke: pursued by a torch-bearing mob the Phantom drives his frantic coach past Notre Dame. Universal's most expensive production was banned in Britain, not because of its horrors, but from Parliamentary outrage. An over-enthusiastic publicist persuaded His Majesty's soldiery to escort the precious print from Southampton to Wardour Street!

British sensitivity changed the title of the next Chaney and Browning venture: *London After Midnight* (1927) became *The Hypnotist* in England. It was the first true American vampire movie despite the twist in its tail. Authentic vampire trappings abounded: twin punctures in the jugular, a hickory stick staked through the heart, pallid and dark-eyed lovelies at the window. Before the Browning version, Hollywood vampires had been pallid and dark-eyed lovelies of the Theda Bara breed: sucking their men dry but not of blood. Chaney had his

Phantom Poster: Claude Rains as *The Phantom of the Opera* (Universal 1943).

C. M. WOOLF
PRESENTS
BELA LUGOSI
SHIRLEY GREY
in
PICTUREDROME
The MYSTERY OF THE
MARY CELESTE
with ARTHUR MARGETSON
HAMMER PRODUCTION
Directed by DENISON CLIFT
GENERAL FILM DISTRIBUTORS LTD Temporary London Address 10, CORK ST. W.1. REGENT . . . 5354

Haunting Refrain: Music and monsters went well together, even in the silent cinema. *The Phantom of the Opera* (Universal 1925; *bottom right*) did the rounds with a special score for pit orchestra or pianist. Later versions had the music built in. In 1943 Susanna Foster sang 'The Melody of the Bells' to Claude Rains (*below*) and in 1962 Hammer's Herbert Lom serenaded with 'Saint Joan' (*bottom*).

expected unmasking scene, but in reverse. Swiftly divesting himself of frizzy fright-wig and fangs, the hideous vampire uncrooked to stand revealed as upright Inspector Burke of Scotland Yard, horn-rims and all! Outside the requisites of plot payoff, the make-up took a little longer: sharpened dentures made it painful for Chaney to speak, and wire loops in his eye-sockets were tightened before takes to bulge his eyes. The denouement was not, it appears, a cop-out. Claimed Browning:

> 'Mystery stories are tricky, for if they are too gruesome or horrible, if they exceed the average imagination by too much, the audience will laugh. *London After Midnight* is an example of how to get people to accept ghosts and other supernatural spirits by letting them turn out to be the machinations of a detective. Thereby the audience is not asked to believe the horrible impossible, but the horrible possible, and plausibility increased, rather than lessened, the thrills and chills.'

Within three years both Browning and his audience would have matured enough to accept the genuine vampire.

Carl Laemmle now sought a suitable follow-through to Chaney's Hunchback and Phantom. Looking to French literature again he discovered Victor Hugo's *The Man Who Laughs* (1928). This time MGM refused to let Chaney go. Undaunted, Laemmle turned to his native land and brought over the one other star who had carved a corner in

macabre characters. Conrad Veidt made Gwymplaine, the disfigured heir with the perpetual grin, a monstrous Pagliacci. His hideous laugh whilst under torture in the Iron Maiden was too much for the box office to bear. Veidt's cadaverous character made the skin crawl without the redeeming humanity inherent in even Chaney's most horrible creations.

The star of the most sensational American silent film of them all was less than human, less even than animal. It was a toy, a thing of rubbery stuff moulded around a jointed wire skeleton, all of twelve inches high. But when shown on the cinema screen, it became a monstrous brontosaurus that made Tower Bridge come falling down. The fair lady was Bessie Love, a box-office attraction not found in Sir Arthur Conan Doyle's original novel of *The Lost World* (1925).

Wallace Beery played Professor Challenger, leader of an expedition up the Amazon to find prehistoric life. Among the flora and fauna was Bull Montana, the well-known apeman. This time he was in the full, hirsute suit, as created by First National's wizard of the whiskers, Cecil Holland. Acting and direction (Harry O. Hoyt) were no great shakes, but the camerawork and effects were the best the Hollywood movie had yet produced. A team of three photographed: Arthur Edeson, Fred Jackman and Homer Scott used masking and double-exposure to combine men with models that had to be shot in stop-motion, two frames at a time.

The man behind the models was an ex-cartoonist from Oakland named Willis O'Brien. He became the special effects king of Hollywood horrors and as such finally won an Academy Award in 1949 (for, curiously, his worst work, *Mighty Joe Young*.) Yet always his horror was diluted by the light touch inherited from his previous profession. It showed in his first film, *The Dinosaur and the Baboon* (1917). This told the 500-foot tale of Stonejaw Steve and Theophilus Ivoryhead who try to catch a pterodactyl for lunch. Wild Willie, the missing link, encounters a monster. 'The dinosaur is some battler and Wild Willie meets his Waterloo and is sent on his way to baboon heaven.' Ivoryhead chances upon the body and claims it as his own, planting his foot upon the baboon's chest in a gesture of triumph that would become an O'Brien trademark. In this little puppet comedy can be found elements that O'Brien and his disciples would use through half a century of spectacular cinema. Two years later he made a slightly more serious single-reel dinosaur fantasy, *The Ghost of*

Slumber Mountain (1919). This caught the interest of the other missing link in the *Lost World* story, Watterson R. Rothacker.

Rothacker, West Coast manager of Billboard, saw the potential in films for publicity as early as 1911. Forming the Industrial Motion Picture Company he evolved many specialized techniques: he used animation to make movies of Gus Edson's newspaper comic strip, *Old Doc Yak*. O'Brien joined Rothacker and together they created the monsters of *The Lost World*. Although their flickery dinosaur was outclassed by the dragon Fritz Lang built in Germany for *Siegfried* (1924), the American epic had the showman's touch. The erupting volcanoes, stampeding monsters, and destruction of London thrilled a vast audience who would have been bored by the turgid Teuton legend. The film still thrills as Professor Challenger lowers his binoculars and mouths the immortal subtitle, 'This is the greatest moment of my life. I have seen a living pterodactyl!'

Roland West, who had directed Lon Chaney in *The*

Cats and Canaries: Forrest Stanley and Laura La Plante were *The Cat and the Canary* (Universal 1927; *above*), silent style. *Opposite:* Paulette Goddard and friend in the Paramount sound remake (1939).

Monster, now adapted *The Bat* (1926), a seminal mystery play that had broken Broadway records with 867 performances. He added a scary cinematic touch by magnifying a moth, trapped in an auto headlight, into the shadow of a monstrous bat against the ceiling. West also created a catchphrase that would become a cliché: 'we request spectators to keep the Bat's identity a secret.' Only now dare we reveal that the energetic thief behind the monstrous makeup was that least suspected person, Tullio Carminatti.

Through Chaney, the monster had become an established box-office ingredient. A unique example is *While London Sleeps* (1926). This Warner Brothers picture concerned Inspector Burke of Scotland Yard, his daughter Dale, the leader of Limehouse (a crook known as 'London Letter'), and his tool, a monster called 'the Monk'. At least, according to the American synopsis it did. When shown in London the film featured a warehouse owner, his daughter Edith, and a crook called 'the Hawk' who operated without a henchman, let alone a hirsute one! The American version ran 5,810 feet; the British ran 4,700. The wonder was that the star himself came through unscathed: he was Rin Tin Tin. This little programme picture, long forgotten, now stands alone in film history. It

was the first 'popular' picture to inject an element of horror as a box-office gimmick – and the first to be censored for that same horrific content. It also stands as an example of how the Silent film could be totally changed in shape and meaning by the application of scissors and subtitles.

The year 1927 opened with *The Monkey Talks*, filmed by Raoul Walsh from the French play by René Fauchois. Jacques Lerner, a small actor who had created the role on the London stage two years before, appeared as Jocko the dwarf. He defrauds circusgoers by posing as a talking monkey. Jocko loves lovely Olivette (Olive Borden), but so does the lion tamer. This villain kidnaps Jocko and rings in a real ape, but Jocko escapes in time to save the spangled beauty from that animal. He dies, Balaoo-like, in her arms. Wrote a critic, 'The fantastic apeman is an unusual conception and is invested partly with repulsiveness and partly with pity'. Thanks as much to M. Lerner as to Jack P. Pierce, the new makeup man out at the Fox lot.

By this time the influence of the German school of cinema was not simply confined to celluloid: Hollywood studios competed with cash to import actual Teutonic talent. From both sides of the camera they came: actors, directors, technicians. Carl Laemmle had the strongest connection with

Fixed Grins: The set smile of Gwymplaine *The Man Who Laughs* (Universal 1929; *left*) failed to amuse Mary Philbin. Conrad Veidt's laugh was catching: Sheldon Lewis smiles at Thelma Todd in *Seven Footprints to Satan* (First National 1929; *opposite*) and Lon Chaney laughs at Edna Tichenor in *London After Midnight* (MGM 1927; *below*).

his old country, of course, and among his many imports for Universal was Paul Leni. Handed the script of John Willard's Broadway success of 1922, Leni turned *The Cat and the Canary* (1927) into something more than the now standard comedy-thriller. The plot remained preposterous: one of the surviving relatives of an eccentric millionaire dons monstrous makeup to scare the heiress out of her pretty mind. But the trappings were superb: cobwebs, clocks, corridors down which camera and characters raced with uncanny speed, curtains billowing like spectral shrouds. Even the opening titles frightened, and the first shot symbolized shudders to come: the dying man, dwarfed by gigantic bottles and snarling cats, dissolves into his spiky old castle.

Leni's first sight of the crouching monster is, like Julian's Phantom, a double thrill. The Cat emerges from a shadowed panel in the background and slowly creeps towards unsuspecting Laura La Plante. He pops behind the door, then his claw comes clutching round, groping for her throat like a giant spider. When she finally sees his hideous face – the Cat bobs round and comes up at her – Leni cuts to a quick closeup, rushing his lens into Laura's face as she screams. Cut to an animated subtitle in towering, shivering letters: 'HELP!' As

a sly nod to his old school, Leni had his sinister little doctor made up to recall Caligari. Small wonder the New York Times called it 'the first time that a mystery melodrama has been lifted into the realms of art'. Smaller wonder that other studios rushed aboard the bandwagon.

The Gorilla (1927), like Ralph Spence's play, built up the comedy relief: Keystone comic Charlie Murray played the lead. His inept detection brought shrieks of both kinds when he confronted the killer, an eight-foot ape. It was really Walter Pidgeon all the time. More of a thriller was the gorilla in *The Wizard* (1927). This 'fiend-faced ape' was played by George Kotsonaros, the 'Monk' who had lost out to Rin Tin Tin. An updated, dressed-up version of *Balaoo*, Gustav von Seyffertitz was mad Professor Paul Coriolos, commanding his creature to kidnap a judge's daughter in revenge for sentencing his son. MGM's *The Thirteenth Hour* (1927) had Lionel Barrymore as Professor Leroy, whose houseful of sliding panels and sinister sofas was operated from a secret switchboard. At 1 a.m. he would go out on murderous prowl, returning home in time to don a wig and a benign expression.

Benjamin Christensen was one more Continental import whose creativity suffered in the cause of commercialism. This Dane had directed an imaginative documentary called *Witchcraft Through the Ages* (1921). He himself played naked Satan, presiding over a Black Mass depicted in a detail unsurpassed by the permissive cinemas of half a century on. Naturally, First National gave him their *Cat and the Canary* cash-in to do. *The Haunted House* (1928), from the Owen Davis play of scared heirs and hidden bonds, complete with mad doctor, weird caretaker, and sexy somnambulist, was so successful that the team of Christensen, scenarist Richard Bee, and title-writer William Irish, were told to do it all again. *Seven Footprints to Satan* (1929), Abraham Merritt's classic fantasy of Devil worship, was even given the same twist ending: all was eventually exposed as actors hired to hoax.

It was the last silent scream of the horror film. The voice of Jolson the Jazz Singer was heard in the land and to some the sound of horror had already begun. It was the end of an art form. To a world full of Chaney fans there was but one question. Would the Man of a Thousand Faces become the Man of a Thousand Voices?

Made-over Monsters: Horror movies are the hardy perennials of the cinema: when the originals are too old to revive, new versions are made, such as Hammer's *The Phantom of the Opera* (1962; *left*) and Fox's *The Gorilla* (1939).

KARLOFF AND LUGOSI, THE UNIVERSAL MONSTERS

In which Chaney talks, Lugosi bites, Karloff stomps, Jekyll changes, and Browning freaks out.

'I, Lon Chaney, being first duly sworn, depose and say: In the photoplay entitled *The Unholy Three* produced by Metro-Goldwyn-Mayer Corporation, all voice reproductions which purport to be reproductions of my voice, to wit, the ventriloquist's, the old woman's, the dummy's, the parrot's, and the girl's, are actual reproductions of my own voice, and in no place in said photoplay, was a "double" or substitute used for my voice.'

That affidavit, signed by Lon Chaney and sworn before F.L. Hendrickson, notary public in and for the County of Los Angeles on the 19th day of May 1930, was more than a good publicity stunt. It answered both cynical critics and mystified fans who were asking why the great silent star had held back from talkies for so long. The craze for sound had swept the world: everyone wanted to know what their favourite film star's voice was like. The disillusion ended more careers than the Hollywood scandals. Now of the great ones, only Chaney and Chaplin were holding out. Were they both devoted to the medium of mime – or was the old monster frightened of the new monster, the microphone? The real reason for Chaney's delays was kept secret – even from Chaney himself.

MGM boosted *Hollywood Revue* (1929) as their all-star show, but one star was unable to attend the revel. Instead Gus Edwards sang 'Lon Chaney will get you if you don't watch out!' while a parade of unnamed extras recreated Chaney's gallery of grotesques. Nor was he to be seen in the first talkie directed by his old partner in crime, Tod Browning. *The Thirteenth Chair* (1929), Bayard Veiller's stage mystery of a murderer unmasked by a medium, had been made as a silent in 1919. Now Margaret Wycherley replaced Marie Shotwell as Madame Rosalie LeGrange, but although the subject of spiritualism was close to Browning's heart, the film failed to thrill. There would come a consequence, for playing the suavely sinister Inspector Delzante

was a courteous Hungarian called Bela Lugosi.

Browning left MGM for Universal again. His timing was bad, for at last Lon Chaney was ready to meet the microphone. An all-talking version of their silent success, *The Unholy Three* (1930), was directed by Jack Conway. It was the ideal vehicle: it allowed Chaney to change his voice as often as his makeup. Proclaimed The New York Graphic, 'With the exception of Garbo no celebrity of Silent days has emerged with better advantage in Talkies.' A new career in horror seemed set, but on 26 August 1930, the cancer won. Chaney's last few days were grim; with his voice gone he had been forced to mime. Thus film and life mixed inextricably: he was truly a silent star.

Irving Thalberg, a key figure in Chaney's career, said:

'He was great, not only because of his God-given talent, but because he used that talent to illuminate certain dark corners of the human spirit. He showed the world the souls of people born different from the rest, because he himself was born of parents who were different.'

It was twenty-seven years before Universal offered their tribute. James Cagney played Chaney in *Man of a Thousand Faces* (1957). A sincere actor, Cagney recreated the man behind the makeup, but not the makeup. Bud Westmore's Technicolored rubber was no substitute for the living monsters Chaney made.

The sound of horror had begun in August 1928, in the second full-length talkie ever made: *The Terror*. For the first time movie audiences heard the howl of the wind, the beat of the rain, the creak of the door, and the scream upon scream of a girl in fear. There was also the pounding of the Terror at his

Definitive Dracula: Bela Lugosi as *Dracula* (Universal 1931).

underground organ, and the creepy croak of Squeegee the trained toad. It was the first and only total Talkie: even credit titles were taboo as the shadow of an unbilled Conrad Nagel intoned them from the screen.

Roy Del Ruth used Vitaphone to add a new dimension to pictorial fright. He took Edgar Wallace's melodrama of hooded madman, hidden loot, clutching hand and stormbound tavern, and salted it with cinematic shocks. With his cloaked killer whisking victims up flues, down trapdoors, and through catacombs, Del Ruth pointed his camera straight down at a table-top seance, slung it from a basket for an overhead travelling shot, and ran it on rollers into a screaming female face. More than enough movement to prove that sound did not need to kill the visual art of cinema.

Universal, not to be caught short, had Paul Leni put some sound sequences into *The Last Warning* (1928), his thriller which switched spooky house for spooky theatre, a sort of Cat and Canary of the Opera. Leni repeated his opening gambit, the mood-setting montage: the old theatre frontage formed into a monster's grimacing face. More original was Warner's follow-through, *Stark Mad* (1929). Lloyd Bacon directed his horrors in a ruined Mayan temple, where a giant ape was chained to the floor. Jacqueline Logan was abducted by 'a hairy, taloned monster', André Beranger played Simpson, 'a raving maniac', and Louise Fazenda screamed again. It made Christensen and Bee and Irish's third piece, *The House of Horror* (1929), look even more derivative than it was.

The tremendous success of the sound version of *The Unholy Three* had the result moviegoers had grown to expect. Speaking likenesses of other silent favourites were rushed into the cinemas. Paul Leni had suddenly died, so Universal gave *The Cat and the Canary* to Rupert Julian: he changed it to *The Cat Creeps* (1930). Neil Hamilton was the unsuspected heir who donned cloak and claw. Hal Mohr photographed, using the great camera crane he had designed for *Broadway*, a 50,000-dollar 'mechanical marvel' built by the Llewellyn Iron Works. Camera and man could be swung up, down, laterally, or in combination, whilst travelling forward or backward on a motorized truck. One thing it couldn't do was zoom: Charles Cline invented this effect for *The Bat Whispers* (1930), Roland West's revamping of *The Bat*. When a knife was thrown at a girl, Cline touched a trigger and shot photographer Robert Planck from longshot to closeup. Sudden expansion of the image in an early widescreen process doubled the impact. *The Gorilla* (1930) was redone by Bryan Foy, but the only difference was promotion for Walter Pidgeon from gorilla to red herring. And all in November; it was a good Hallowe'en.

Tod Browning was at Universal preparing a second vampire vehicle for Chaney. This time no holds were to be barred; the success of the stage play he had bought proved the public was ready for the real thing. The first American vampire was ready for takeoff when Lon Chaney died. Browning looked to the lead of the 1927 Broadway production: it was the actor he had used in *The Thirteenth Chair*. And this is where the story really starts.

Talkie Terrors: Original advertising for the first sound horror film *The Terror* (Warner 1928) and its remake *Return of the Terror* (First National 1934).
Evolution Revolution: *Island of Lost Souls* (Paramount 1932; *opposite top left*) inspired Fox's *The Fly* (1958; *opposite top right*) and *The Alligator People* (1959).

"The TERROR"

with
MAY McAVOY LOUISE FAZENDA
EDWARD EVERETT HORTON
ALEC FRANCIS
MATTHEW BETZ ••• HOLMES HERBERT
JOHN MILJAN
FROM THE PLAY BY
EDGAR WALLACE   DIRECTED BY   SCENARIO BY
HARVEY GATES
ROY DEL RUTH

A Warner Bros. Production

Based on the story "THE TERROR" by

EDGAR WALLACE

FIRST NATIONAL presents

"RETURN of THE TERROR"

with

Mary Astor · Lyle Talbot · John Halliday · Frank McHugh

Directed
Howard
Bretherton

TRADE SHOW
CAMBRIDGE
THEATRE
AUGUST 29th
at
3 P.M.

A FIRST NATIONAL & VITAPHONE PICTURE

'I am Dracula. I bid you welcome.' With these famous first words the horror film proper was born: yet even now the term did not exist. Only when Universal found their mid-budget picture building into their biggest money-maker of 1931 did they declare their intention of making 'another horror film'. Thus *Dracula* (1931) back-tracked into becoming the first horror film, and Bela Lugosi the first horror film star. No Chaney he, Lugosi forswore the makeup box for the smooth hair and black cloak favoured by Satan since 1908: the debut of 'The Devil' by Ferenc Molnar. His voice was laced with melodic menace; a natural aid was his native accent which, like his acting, was strictly from Hungary. Born Blasko in Lugos, the actor had fled from the Bela Kun uprising, abandoning a silent cinema career as Arisztid Olt. In New York he played the lead in 'The Red Poppy' without knowing English: he learned his part phonetically 'like the music of a song'. Ultimately a handicap, Lugosi's curious cadence added a queasy quality to the voice of the vampire.

A wolf howls hollowly. 'Listen to them . . . children of the night . . . what music they make.' The film is filled with memorable lines. Renfield (Dwight Frye's definitive performance) has taken his classic coach-ride to Castle Dracula. It is an opening sequence that more than visually recalls Murnau: 'It is Walpurgis night, the night of evil – Nosferatu!' His courtly host escorts him up the curving, crumbling stairway, leaving a vast spider's web curiously undisturbed. 'The spider spinning his web for the unwary fly. The blood is the life, Mr Renfield.' The Count does not share his guest's refreshment: 'I never drink . . . wine.'

The blood is the life. Renfield, bitten sufficiently to enslave, takes up the creed. Starting in a small way, he catches flies to eat alive, progressing to spiders. He escorts master and coffin aboard the *Vesta*, and when that ship sails into Whitby is the last man alive. His laugh as he comes creeping from his cabin is the most spine-chilling sound in the talkies.

Moving into Carfax Abbey ('It reminds me of the broken battlements of my own castle in Transylvania') the Count calls on his neighbour, Dr Seward. Mina, the daughter, is a gloomy lass given to sombre toasts: 'Hurrah for the next to die' she cries, prompting Dracula to muse, 'To die . . . to be really dead . . . that must be glorious!' Soon he is a bat flapping at her windows, materializing to stoop over her sleeping throat. But venerable Abraham Van Helsing (venerable Edward Van Sloan) is at hand, armed with wolfbane. 'The superstition of yesterday can become the scientific reality of today,' he declares, and soon the vampire is tastefully staked through the heart, off-screen and off-mike. Carl Laemmle Jr, who had been given Universal City as a 21st-birthday present, was playing it cool. He released the film on Valentine's Day as 'The Strangest Love a Man Has Ever Known!'

Stoker's novel had been dramatized for the London stage in 1924 by Hamilton Deane, as a vehicle for himself. John L. Balderston adapted it for Broadway, and Garrett Fort and Dudley Murphy had developed it further for the screen. Browning's only concession to cinema is his use of the camera in the opening scenes. It creeps through the crypt, watching the bowed glidings of Dracula's three wraith-like wives, the scurrying of rats around their coffins, then cutting-away as the Count rises from his, as if to spare his embarrassment. A moody piece due less to Browning than his gifted cameraman, the fabulous Karl Freund. Yet antique as *Dracula* undoubtedly is, it can still hold an audience in thrall. That it is the oldest talkie still playing commercially is due entirely to the hypnotic performance of its star.

> 'An evil expression in the eyes, a sinister arch to the brow or a leer on my lips – all of which take long practice in muscular control – are sufficient to hypnotize an audience into seeing what I want them to see, and what I myself see in my mind's eye.'

Lugosi's hypnosis was helped out by Browning aiming twin pencil-spots into his eyeballs. That one consistently missed its mark worried neither audience nor Warner Brothers, who quickly picked up the effect for John Barrymore's *Svengali* (1931). With a camera more mobile than the mesmerist's eyeballs, the film was successful enough to prompt a quick sequel. *The Mad Genius* (1931) cast Barrymore as Ivan Tzarakov, club-footed marionettist and mesmeric master of a ballet troupe. Playing Frankie Darro's father was an Englishman who got the job because of his Russian name. At the end of his few days' shooting, he went over to Universal to sign on as the murderer in a quick thriller called *Graft* (1931). His name was really William Henry Pratt, but he called himself Boris Karloff.

At Universal Bela Lugosi was the new star; Junior Laemmle hoped he would be the new Lon Chaney. It was Hollywood law that every success must have its successor: the standard contract was a two-picture deal. For Lugosi's follow-up Laemmle found *Frankenstein*. Peggy Webling's play of the Shelley book had opened in London on 10 February 1930. Miss Webling had successfully reduced the ancient epic to a cast of nine working in two sets; more, the actor who had played Dracula was the Monster in this one, Hamilton Deane. The connection was too obvious to miss. One snag: screen rights were held by Gaumont-British, who had announced a production in November 1930. Universal did a deal. John L. Balderston, the Anglophile responsible for the Americanization of *Dracula*, was hired to adapt the new one, and

Garrett Fort came back again for the screenplay. To direct, Laemmle chose Frenchman Robert Florey, one of the new breed of film-makers who had come up via experimental shorts. Florey shot two test reels with Lugosi as the Monster, striding around the sets of Castle Dracula, menacing

Late Night Line-ups: Leila Hyams, Bela Lugosi, Holmes Herbert, Margaret Wycherly, *The Thirteenth Chair* (MGM 1929; *below left*). Carol Borland, Herbert, Lugosi, *Mark of the Vampire* (MGM 1935; *below right*). Lila Lee, Walter Pidgeon, *The Gorilla* (First National 1930; *bottom left*). Paul Lukas, Marc Lawrence, Onslow Stevens, Joseph Calleia, Ellen Drew, *The Monster and the Girl* (Paramount 1940; *bottom right*).

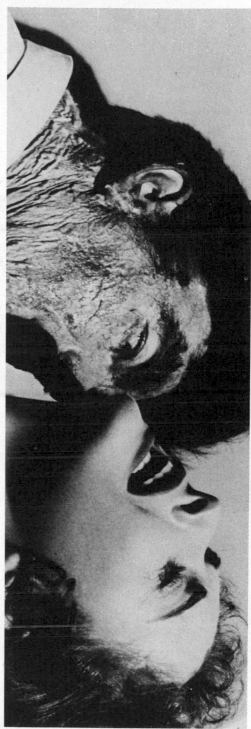

Blood Suckers: Vampire variation on the romantic necking scene. Bela Lugosi bares Helen Chandler's jugular in *Dracula* (Universal 1931; *above left*) and Christopher Lee seeks Veronica Carlson's in *Dracula Has Risen From the Grave* (Hammer 1968; *left*). John Beal prepares to bite Colleen Grey in *The Vampire* (UA 1957; *above*), while a Philippino vampire takes a bloodthirsty bite in *The Blood Drinkers* (Hemisphere 1966; *opposite*).

Edward Van Sloan. Jack Pierce created the make-up, and with Karl Freund at the camera it may come as no surprise that the Monster looked like the Golem. Lugosi wore a broad wig and had a polished, clay-like skin. Said Van Sloan, 'He looked like something out of *Babes in Toyland*!'

Lugosi rejected the role, Laemmle rejected the tests, Florey rejected the film. Actor and director began work on adapting Poe and the project was shelved. Meanwhile James Whale, an English stage producer, had exceeded Laemmle's expectations with the romantic *Waterloo Bridge* (1931). Offered his pick of thirty properties, Whale chose *Frankenstein*: 'I thought it would be amusing to try and make what everybody knows is a physical impossibility seem believable.' Whale rejected Leslie Howard, Universal's choice for the title role. He wanted Colin Clive, the friend who had given so tense a reading of Captain Stanhope in Whale's stage and screen versions of *Journey's End* (1930). But who to cast as the Monster?

Lunching daily in the studio commissary, Whale's eyes searched among the crowds of eating actors. One face stood out, lean and hungry even after meals: a character player from the *Graft* set. Whale, once a cartoonist, began to sketch that haunting, heavy head.

'Boris Karloff's face fascinated me. I made drawings of his head, added sharp bony ridges where I imagined the skull might have joined. His physique was weaker than I could wish, but that queer, penetrating personality of his, I felt, was more important than his shape, which could easily be altered.'

It was not that easy, particularly for Karloff. For a fortnight he sat still in the makeup chair, a guinea-pig for Jack P. Pierce. The derivative Golem concept was thrown out in favour of scientific plausibility. Said Pierce:

'I did some research in anatomy, surgery, criminology, ancient and modern burial customs, and electrodynamics. I discovered there are six ways a surgeon can cut the skull, and I figured Dr Frankenstein, who was not a practising surgeon, would take the easiest. That is, he would cut the top of the skull off, straight across like a pot lid, hinge it, pop the brain in, and clamp it tight. That's the reason I decided to make the Monster's head square and flat like a box, and dig that big scar across his forehead, and have metal clamps hold it together. The two metal studs that stick out the sides of his neck are inlets for electricity – plugs. The Monster is an electrical gadget and lightning is his life force.'

Pierce built Karloff an overhanging brow with layers of cotton and rubber. He coated his eyelids with wax and pulled his mouth out and down with invisible wire clamps. Combinations of grease-paint were applied until he found a blue-green blend that photographed grey as a corpse. The dead ends of the fingers were easiest: Pierce simply blackened them with boot polish. Then came the costume:

'I made his arms look longer by shortening the sleeves of his coat. His legs were stiffened by steel struts and two pairs of pants. His large feet were the boots asphalt-spreaders wear.'

The complete kit, including a steel spine, weighed forty-eight pounds. The makeup took three-and-a-half hours to put on in the morning, an hour-and-a-half to remove at night. Karloff was led to and from the set, his head under a cloth; he ate alone. The film was shot entirely in an enclosed studio, under lights, in the heat of summer. Said Laemmle,

Club Member: John Barrymore was hypnotic as *The Mad Genius* (Warner 1931; *above*).

Laughing Boy: *Son of Kong* (RKO 1933).

'Karloff's eyes mirrored the suffering we needed.'

Frankenstein (1931) took up where *Dracula* left off, and not just with confidence in its horrors. The first film ended with Edward Van Sloan stepping out of character and screen to deliver a sinister epilogue on the vampire: 'There are such things.' As the second film began he was back with a prologue.

'How do you do. Mr Carl Laemmle feels it would be a little unkind to present this picture without just a word of friendly warning. We are about to unfold the story of Frankenstein, a man of science, who sought to create a man after his own image without reckoning upon God. It is one of the strangest tales ever told. It deals with the two great mysteries of creation, life and death. I think it will thrill you. It may even shock you. It might even horrify you. So if any of you do not care to subject your nerves to such a strain, now's your chance to. . . . Well, we've warned you!'

Despite Mr Carl's friendly warning, an hysterical Christmas preview at Santa Barbara produced so many threatening letters that the studio considerably revised the film before release. They shortened a scene by a river where the Monster floats flowers with his first friend, a little girl, then tries to float her; he is saddened when she sinks. The abrupt cut made things worse, adding awful implication when the child next appears, dead and draggled in the arms of her father. (English censors let the scene stand, preferring to shorten the sequence where the Monster invades Mae Clarke's bedroom. The implication, again, was worse than the intention.) A new ending was added showing Frankenstein recovering from his fatal fall while his jovial father toasted, 'Here's to a son of the house of Frankenstein': a prophetic phrase foretelling two sequels unborn.

James Whale gave Karloff the greatest entrance an actor could hope for. From the grave-robbing prologue, all is literally build-up until the man-made man lies, bandaged and shrouded, waiting for life. Fervid Frankenstein, student of chemical galvanism and electro-biology, has stitched together a body from pieces hacked from coffin and gibbet. In its skull lies a brain stolen from medical university by his hunchbacked assistant. Little does Henry know that Fritz dropped the chosen brain and brought an abnormal one instead.

Roast Ghosties: Boris Karloff and Catherine Lacey in *The Sorcerers* (Tigon 1967).

'Think of it, Fritz. The brain of a dead man waiting to live again – in a body I made with my own hands!' Henry has gone beyond the ultraviolet to discover 'the great ray that first brought life into the world'. At the height of a storm he raises his man through the roof of the tower laboratory, bathing him with lightning. The table is lowered; one hand raises slowly: 'It's alive! It's alive!' Fadeout.

Audience tension, stretched to a peak, is stretched even further as Whale makes us wait through some 'light relief' for our first sight of the Monster. At last it comes. The set is darkened, silent save for the sound of heavy footfalls. A door opens and the Monster looms out of the darkness – backwards! Whale cuts in for a closeup of the back of his head. The Monster turns slowly, moving his face into the light. Then Whales cuts and cuts again, each time closer in on that awful face. Back he goes to longshot as the new-born man ('He's only a few days old') leans alarmingly towards his maker. Frankenstein's beckoning gestures, the Monster's lurching steps, recall Wegener and his Golem. But totally new, touchingly pathetic, are Karloff's hand movements as the scientist opens a trap in the roof to let his creation see daylight for the first time. Like the baby that he is, the Monster reaches out to grasp the sun. His cold grey body finds more than warmth in the fiery torch the hunchback uses to tame and torture him. The Monster has all our sympathy when, at the end, he hurls the creator who rejected him at the howling mob and dies, shrieking, pinned beneath a beam in a burning windmill.

Once in Karloff's long, lean years, he had hitched a lift from Lon Chaney. The star, no stranger to the hard grind of bit-part work, told Karloff his secret. 'Find something no one else can do and they'll begin to take notice of you.' Said Karloff, 'When I was offered the part of the Monster I knew that I'd found it at last. The part was what we call a "natural". Any actor who played it was destined for success.' Modest Boris, for not one of the actors who followed in his eighteen-pound boots achieved his stature.

Carl Laemmle had found his new Lon Chaney.

The Universal Monsters scared more than the audience and the censors: the other studios were frightened they might lose some of the action. Paramount got in first, timing *Murder by the Clock* (1931) to beat Frankenstein into the cinemas. Irving Pichel gibbered, and graveyards yawned: so did the audience. 'The blood-chilling mystery of a man who was murdered twice' lacked that new

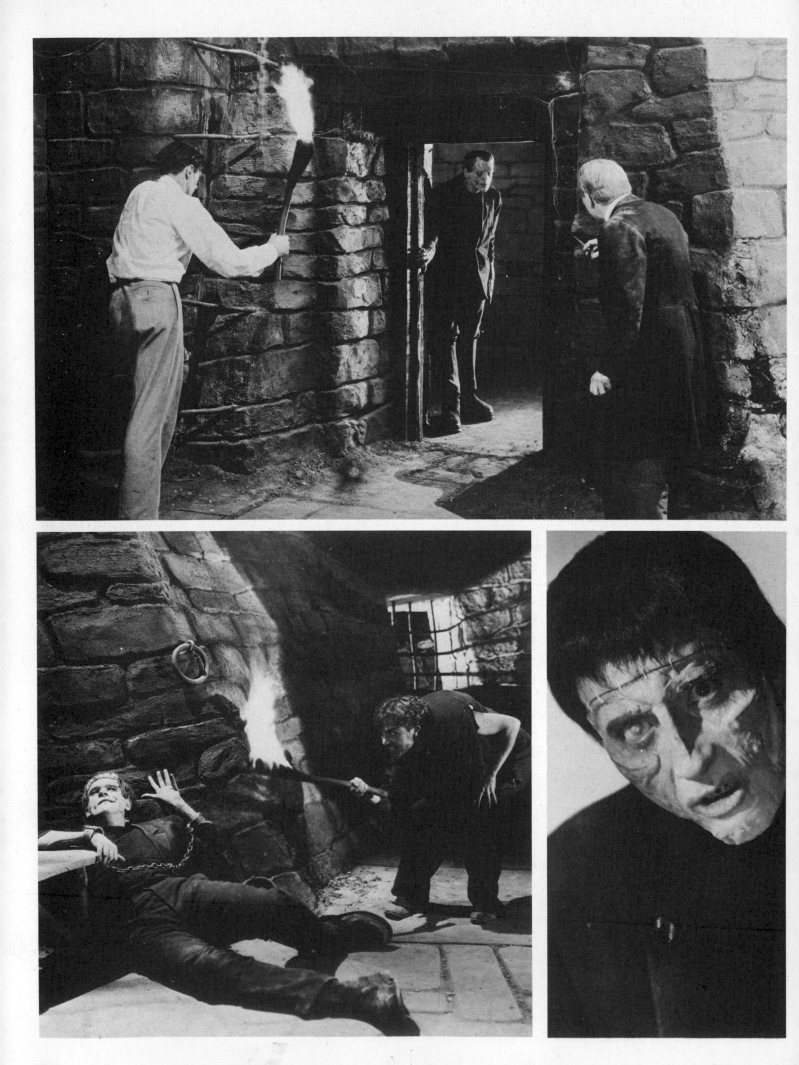

Classic Karloff: *Frankenstein* (Universal 1931) was billed as 'The Man Who Made a Monster'; it was the film that made a star, Boris Karloff, a long-standing small-part player, stomped to stardom as the synthetic yet soulful creation of Colin Clive (*opposite above*), unnatural victim of nature's freak, Dwight Frye (*opposite below left*). Karloff's creature was unique: often copied, never equalled. Christopher Lee in *The Curse of Frankenstein* (Hammer 1957; *opposite below right*) was forced to use new makeup (by Phil Leakey) as Jack P. Pierce's format was copyrighted by Universal.

touch of the supernatural that distinguished the true horror film. Pichel would find slightly steadier work as a director, but meanwhile his curious looks made him a convenient Karloff substitute. Paramount were pleased enough to revive for him their old success, *Dr Jekyll and Mr Hyde* (1931), but the poor man was instantly rejected by the director. Said Rouben Mamoulian, 'I wanted someone who could play Jekyll and Pichel could only play Hyde!' Mamoulian asked for Fredric March, a light comedian who was a ringer for the young Barrymore. Paramount objected; Mamoulian insisted; March won the Academy Award – the only Monster with an Oscar.

'For six weeks I had to arrive at the studios each morning at 6 a.m., so that Wally Westmore could spend four hours building pieces on my nose and cheeks, sticking fangs in my mouth, and pushing cotton wool up my nostrils.'

Rouben Mamoulian, Russian-born man of the theatre, was obsessed by that legendary full-view transformation by Richard Mansfield. He determined to devise a one-take change for his star. March was coated with successive layers of make-up, each more detailed than the last, each in a different colour. By holding colour transparencies in front of the camera and removing them one by one, the change from Jekyll to Hyde filtered through on to the film.

Mamoulian used the 'moving camera' subjectively to draw his audience into the picture and the very mind of his monster. In the beginning we are Jekyll, moving through his doctor's day, seeing our face only in his mirror. Later, as he raises the fatal phial to his lips, we again click into his eyes. The laboratory spins about us (Karl Struss tied to the top of his camera was revolved to secure this 360-degree pan); our blood pounds in our ears (Mamoulian ran up and down stairs recording his own heartbeats); until again we see our face, our new face, in the mirror. It is a moment of revenge for every movie monster: we who came to stare see only ourselves.

'Grimmer than *Dracula*, More Gruesome than *Frankenstein*!' Yardsticks already, the originals were used by Universal to boost their third entry, *Murders in the Rue Morgue* (1932). Lugosi, in fetching curls and overgrown eyebrows, was more evil than ever in costume (*Dracula* lost much of its mood by being set in the present), and Robert Florey emerged at last as a director of power. However, that Frenchman's conception of 1845 Paris was more like Gothic Holstenwall. Even Poe's plot came out like Dr Caligari, as Dr Mirakle, a sideshow hypnotist, commands Erik the gorilla to abduct frail Camille over the rooftops of Paris. Hunched Janos the Black One (Noble Johnson) aids Mirakle in his sadistic experiments, which involve strung-up prostitutes and transfusions of gorilla blood. The pioneer of demonic Darwinism is climactically strangled by his revolting pet.

The Hollywood pattern was ever one of cycles, and Universal had clearly started a new one. The British Board of Film Censors did not like it to start with and now that a new element, sex, was creeping in they liked it even less. The Soho erotics of Mamoulian's Mr Hyde were so explicit that in the British release print, Miriam Hopkins hardly appeared. But it was not sex that was the trouble with Tod Browning's latest picture. *Freaks* (1932) was banned outright in Britain. It even upset MGM, who produced it: after a spotty, press-protesting release they 'lost' it in their vaults. *Freaks* remains unique, the ultimate extension of the Quasimodo syndrome, the fascination of deformity taken to the nth degree – because there are such things.

Browning was back in his beloved world of sideshows and suckers. Upon the short story 'Spurs' by Clarence 'Tod' Robbins (he of *The Unholy Three*) Browning created a carnival of horrors. Harry Earles (again from *The Three*) is the midget who inherits a fortune. This makes him instantly

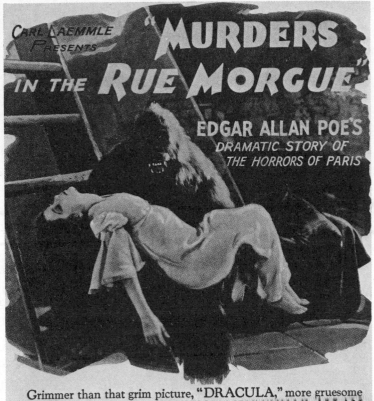

CARL LAEMMLE PRESENTS

MURDERS IN THE RUE MORGUE

EDGAR ALLAN POE'S
DRAMATIC STORY OF THE HORRORS OF PARIS

Grimmer than that grim picture, "DRACULA," more gruesome and awe-inspiring than "FRANKENSTEIN," EDGAR ALLAN POE'S remarkable mystery story "MURDERS IN THE RUE MORGUE," laid in the dark caverns of Paris, will thrill you to your finger-tips. Beautifully enacted by

BELA LUGOSI and SIDNEY FOX
The Original "DRACULA"   Star of "STRICTLY DISHONORABLE"
Directed by ROBERT FLOREY

Murders and Monkeys: Irving Pichel was Paramount's answer to Karloff in *Murder by the Clock* (1931; *opposite*). Universal already had their answer in Bela Lugosi. He objected to the Monster makeup, but not to the curls and eyebrows of *Murders in the Rue Morgue* (1931; *below*). Warner remade it in 3D as *Phantom of the Rue Morgue* (1954; *bottom*).

compatible in the eyes of Cleopatra, queen of the trapeze. The little man's fellows throw a banquet for the newly-weds. Present are his ex-fiancée, midget Daisy Earles, Raudian the Living Torso, Frances O'Connor the Armless Beauty, Pete Robinson the Living Skeleton. Johnny Eck the Man with Half a Body, Daisy and Violet Hilton the Siamese Twins, Olga Roderick the Bearded Lady, Coo-Koo the Bird Woman, and others less immediately identifiable. But once hitched to her moneyed midget, Cleopatra reveals her true and heartless nature. The mocked freaks gang up on her one storm-soaked night. Creeping and crawling through the mud, they exact their terrible revenge. The final shot is the final turn of the stomach: the freaks have skilfully enrolled a new member in their sideshow, Cleopatra the Human Chicken. So at the end, artifice makes the most monstrous monster of them all: a payoff which could be taken to justify the genre.

Browning had always created his films backwards, starting with a visual concept. In his days with Chaney the team had begun with a horrible makeup, and then devised a story-line to fit it. One of their experiments had been Chaney as a chicken. The concept, abandoned on Chaney's death, had now been revived with terrible success.

Horrible makeup played the major part in *Doctor X* (1932), this time with the added thrill of two-colour Technicolor. There have been six murders during six full moons, and somebody on Dr Xavier's staff is to blame. In every case the victim's left deltoid muscle has been torn from the base of the brain – and eaten. Preston Foster can hardly have been guilty of these cannibalistic stranglings, for he has but one hand. However, hanging in his locker are several spares. By welding one to his stump with electrical sparks he is able to throttle with ease. 'Synthetic flesh-h-h!' he hisses as he coats his face with molten muck, moulding himself into the Moon Monster and making for Fay Wray.

Dr Xavier, club-footed red-herring, marked the horror-film entrance of Lionel Atwill, starchy architect from Croydon. His brisk and British ways suited the genre. Clipped of speech and moustache,

Shrieks and Freaks: Suspected scientists strapped to strange devices observed a reconstructed moon murder in *Doctor X* (First National 1932; *opposite*) and Karloff conducted torture by super-science in *The Mask of Fu Manchu* (MGM 1932; *left*). Tod Browning never wasted an idea. He created a human chicken out of Chaney just for fun and later used the effect as the finale for *Freaks* (MGM 1932; *bottom*).

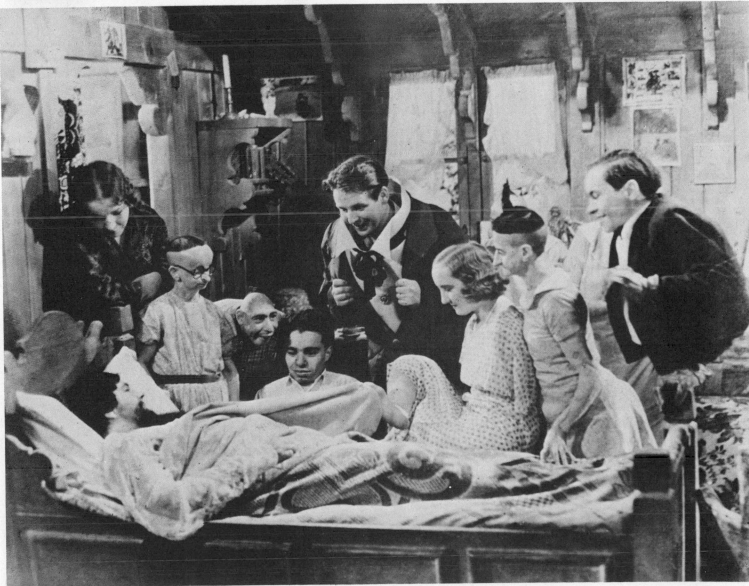

his fierce face and sly eyeballs bridged a curious gap between Mittel-European police inspectors and mad doctors. Atwill continued a tradition that had begun with Karloff: in Hollywood horror, British was best. Karloff, Clive, Atwill; shortly Banks and Rains and Rathbone; then Hardwicke and Zucco and even Skelton Knaggs. Was there something especially sinister built into the British accent – it even echoes in the speech of Vincent Price from Missouri – or was it that to German-born movie-makers English was 'foreign'?

The one great exception was Bela Lugosi. His chill lilt thrilled, but audiences found there was too much mystery in his movies: they couldn't understand what he was talking about. His early refusal to learn English, other than phonetically, was finally catching up with him. Only two major horror movies behind him and already he was working for the Halperin Brothers in their independent (i.e. cut-price) production, *White Zombie* (1932). This pictorial story of mesmerism and the walking dead was beautifully photographed (Arthur Martinelli), hauntingly scored (a Negro spiritual called 'Listen to the Lambs'), and atrociously acted. It was as moody a piece of visual mystery as the old days of silence ever wrought. Lugosi, talented when type-cast, played Legendre, a man known as Murder. Zombie-master to the trade, he supplied cut-price labour for the local sugar mills: corpses resurrected from recent graves and animated by his power of mind over matter. He went nowhere without his bodyguard, a crew for whom motley was hardly the word. 'Who are they?' shrilled the hero, and Lugosi replied, 'For you, my friend, they are the Angels of Death.'

After being thwarted in his plot to zombify Madge Bellamy, poisoned on her wedding day and held in his mountain eyrie, the Land of the Living Dead, Legendre and his eerie entourage go over the ramparts to end on the rocks. But while Lugosi was feeling the first chilly wind of change that blew less from the mountains of Transylvania than the Hills of Beverly, Karloff went from strength to strength. As the mute brute Morgan it took Melvyn Douglas, Raymond Massey and Charles Laughton to hold him down.

The Old Dark House (1932) was the full British horror bit, set in Universal's Wales. James Whale directed Yorkshire Laughton's Hollywood debut. The group that is forced to spend a stormbound night in the Femm family home is less ill-assorted than that family itself. Scion is Horace, played by Ernest Thesiger at his most nostrilled. A fugitive, he is a more feminine Femm than his sister, deaf and dirty Rebecca (Eva Moore), who cries 'No beds! They can't have beds!' as she serves up the black-eyed potatoes. Upstairs is the bedridden head of the family, Sir Roderick, age 102. His youthful excesses are responsible for the wrath now closing in, according to religious Rebecca. The old wretch was played by Elspeth Dudgeon under the more suitable pseudonym, John. Up another flight, behind a padlocked door, is yet a further Femm: Saul, 'the cleverest of us all'.

Morgan the mighty butler hits the bottle and unlocks Saul. A small white hand hovers on the banister. . . . The worst horror of them all turns out to be a little fellow, an old child, pathetic in his pleadings for freedom. Saul wins everybody's sympathy, but when nobody but us is looking his face slips into a snarl. Saul has a secret: he has discovered flame does not burn. It is cold, like ice, and cuts like a knife. He proves it by setting the house on fire.

Whale took his tale from J.B.Priestley's 1927 novel 'Benighted', bringing in Balderston, Benn Levy, and his old friend R.C.Sherriff from *Journey's End* to script. These literary intellects suited Whale, who liked to lighten his frights with twists of wit. Where his grotesque taste had leavened *Frankenstein* with the muttering scuttlings of Dwight Frye, hobbling along on a foot-high walking-stick, *The Old Dark House* was thick with eccentrics.

Karloff, scraggle-jowled and scarred, on no more dialogue than 'Grunt', again stirred a strange sympathy. He clasps his dead friend Saul to his chest, whimpering and rocking him like some awful baby. Karloff spoke for the first time in his second career in *The Mask of Fu Manchu* (1932). He played the devil doctor on loan-out to MGM, accentuating his natural lisp to achieve the snake-like hissing as prescribed by Sax Rohmer. In his mad bid to conquer the world for the yellow races, Fu used fiendish tortures lit with all MGM's gloss.

Camerawork was also a cornerstone of Karloff's Christmas box: Laemmle promoted Karl Freund. That photographer's debut as director was *The Mummy* (1932). Balderston opened his screenplay with a subtitle:

'This is the Scroll of Thoth. Herein are set down the magic words by which Isis raised Osiris from the dead. Oh! Amon-Ra. Oh! God of Gods. Death is but the doorway to new life. . . . We live today.

Beauties and Beasts: Fredric March and Miriam Hopkins in *Dr Jekyll and Mr Hyde* (Paramount 1931); Boris Karloff and Gloria Stuart in *The Old Dark House* (Universal 1932).

. . . We shall live again. In many forms shall we return, Oh Mighty One.'

As Bramwell Fletcher murmurs these words, the long-dead eyelids of an ancient mummy quiver open to reveal a Golem-like gleam of life. A breath, then silently the revived corpse crosses the room, takes the Scroll, and slips into the Egyptian night, trailing tatty bandages and leaving young Fletcher a laughing madman: 'He went for a little walk!' Ten years later, a dry old man called Ardath Bey helps David Manners uncover the lost tomb of Princess Anck-es-en-Amon. Bey and the mummy are the same man: Im-Ho-Tep, High Priest of the Temple of the Sun at Karnak, buried alive 3,700 years ago for daring to try to revive the dead Princess. 'Sentenced to death not only in this world, but the next.'

Zita Johann as the daughter of the Governor of Sudan becomes strangely possessed, speaking 'words not heard on this Earth for two thousand years'. The Mummy intends eternal reunion with his reincarnated princess, which can be achieved only by her death. Breaking free of his mesmeric thrall, she calls upon Isis for help. The statue of the Goddess comes to life and mystically reduces Im-Ho-Tep to ancient dust.

The Mummy consolidated Karloff as a character star in the Chaney mould. Ironically, the crumbling creature was created out of 'beauty clay', applied between layers of cotton by Jack P. Pierce. Once bandaged and caked, Karloff could scarcely move, and the effort to speak through the cracking clay helped him to create the grate of a 3,700-year-old throat. He was billed by surname alone, 'Karloff the Uncanny', a cinematic accolade hitherto confined to Garbo.

Lugosi, who had lost his chance of the Chaney crown, was now forced to take the makeup chair. As the Sayer of the Law in *The Island of Lost Souls* (1932), Lugosi said the Law: 'Not to spill blood. That is the Law. Are we not men?' He said it through a faceful of fur, for the Sayer was a humanized animal. The Law was that of Dr Moreau, Charles Laughton at his sweaty best. This sadistic vivisectionist rules his private Pacific isle with whip and knife. In his House of Pain he has bypassed a thousand years of evolution. His creations include faithful M'Ling (Tetsu Komai), a former dog; snouty Gola (Harry Ezekian), ex-pig; apish Ouran (Hans Steinke), once a monkey. His big success is Lota the Panther Woman, played by Kathleen Burke (winner of the Panther Woman of America contest). Lota's Achilles heel is her fingernails: they extrude under stress – 'The stub-

born beast-flesh creeping back.' This gives the game away when Moreau seeks to mate her with shipwrecked Richard Arlen. At the end the revolting creatures take their creator to his House of Pain. Like *Freaks*, but unlike Tod Browning, Erle C. Kenton leaves the screaming end-product to our imagination. Also like *Freaks*, the film was banned outright by the British censor, much to the delight of H.G.Wells (from whose novel 'The Island of Dr Moreau' it was adapted) and the fury of film fans.

Fay Wray's scream when used as bait to catch the Moon Monster of *Dr X*, made her the First Lady of the Horror Film. Born in Alberta in 1907, a grounding in Hal Roach comedies seemed unlikely training for her new career. She was teamed again twice with Lionel Atwill, first in *The Vampire Bat* (1933). Atwill played Dr Otto Von Niemann of Kleinschloss, who hypnotized his butler to supply fresh victims for his unconventional research. The vampire killings were cover-ups for something more horrid, and only Melvyn Douglas as Inspector Karl Breetschneider was able to save Fay Wray from a transfusion of Atwill's 'blood substitute'.

The Mystery of the Wax Museum (1933) saw Atwill and Fay Wray teamed in two-colour Technicolor. It brought the old Chaney style back to cinema, the horror of disfigurement. Atwill was Ivan Igor, waxworks sculptor, who lost both income and reason when his partner burned their museum for the insurance. The melting of the wax figures is an early touch of nastiness. Escaping the holocaust, seemingly unsinged but confined to a wheelchair, Igor sets up again. This time he snatches bodies and even murders to obtain models for his exhibition, coating the corpses with wax. Fay Wray exposes the mystery and Atwill, too, for as her fists flail at his face his whole head cracks away to reveal the burned, scarred and two-colour Technicolored mess beneath. The first great unmasking in modern horror movies, it remains a moment unequalled in the memories of millions, including Miss Wray.

'I was in his clutches and I had to hit him in the face. It was necessary for the audience to see this and be shocked. But when I struck him, and the moment I saw part of him, I just froze! I wanted to run; I just couldn't go on! So they had to make another mask and do it over when I recovered.'

But for Fay Wray the horror was only beginning. There were bigger things in store.

Monster's Mummy: Boris Karloff as *The Mummy* (Universal 1932).

THE KING OF KONGS

In which King Kong has a Son, Frankenstein has a Bride, Dracula has a Daughter, and the Devil has a Doll.

Fay Wray was at RKO-Radio as the title role in *The Most Dangerous Game* (1932): pursued through a foggy, boggy jungle by a Russian Count with a Tartar bow and *The Hounds of Zaroff* – which was the British title for this exciting expansion of Richard Connell's award-winning short story. Leslie Banks played the twisted sadistic aristocrat, a Hollywood debut for the British actor continuing the sinister tradition. Zaroff gave his pretty prey a head start in more ways than one. His trophy room was hung with stuffed souvenirs of similar hunts. This scene was too much for Britain: the censor, Zaroff-like, chopped it off. Fay Wray learned it had all been a dummy run when she was summoned by the producer.

'Mr Cooper said to me that he had an idea for a film in mind. The only thing he'd tell me was that I was going to have the tallest, darkest leading man in Hollywood. Naturally, I thought of Clark Gable.' What she got was King Kong.

Merian Coldwell Cooper, a Florida-born flier, soldier of fortune and journalist, had joined forces with an ex-Keystone Comedy cameraman named Ernest B. Schoedsack to create the American documentary. Their *Grass* (1925) and *Chang* (1927) are classics of authentic adventure – yet it is through their fantastic fiction of *King Kong* (1933) that they will be ever remembered in cinema history.

'Out of an uncharted, forgotten corner of the world, a monster . . . surviving seven million years of evolution . . . crashes into the haunts of civilization . . . on to the talking screen . . . to stagger the imagination of man!'

Those words in the Souvenir Programme hardly prepared audiences for the film that was about to unreel. 'The Strangest Story Ever Conceived by Man!' . . . 'The Greatest Film the World Will Ever See!' For once the catchlines were right. In the history of horror movies, indeed of movies, *King Kong* still towers above them all.

Kong, the fifty-foot King of Skull Island, somewhere south-west of Sumatra, had in reality a bigger build-up than even the fifty mist-wreathed minutes that precede the shock of his first in-film appearance. The movie was three years in the making, more if you include a pilot piece of pre-historic monster animation made for Harry O. Hoyt's abandoned project, *Creation*. This model work had been done by Willis O'Brien, man of *The Lost World*, and it caught the eye of David O. Selznick, newly arrived at RKO as vice-president in charge of production. He showed the reel to Merian C. Cooper, who had already come up with an idea about an outsize ape. Instead of expensive location shooting, could Cooper construct his giant gorilla idea entirely in the studio, using animation?

Edgar Wallace, whose play 'The Terror' had been the first horror Talkie, arrived from London on 5 December 1931. He had an eight-week contract with RKO to script a horror film. Three days later he wrote to his wife, 'I am also doing a story of prehistoric life!' For inspiration they ran him *Dracula* ('Crude horror stuff, but I must say it raised my hair a little bit') and *Murder by the Clock* ('The actor was the very man I want for my horror story'*), and on the 12th Cooper took him to see O'Brien making another test, a process shot.

'The camera shoots against a blue background lit up by about fifty orange arc lamps. It was two men making an attack upon a prehistoric beast. The beast, of course, was not there: he is put in afterwards, and every movement of the men is controlled by a man who is seeing the beast through a moviola, and signals by means of a bell every movement that the men make.'

* Irving Pichel. He did not, in the end, act in it; he directed it! (*Before Dawn*, 1933.)

King of Swing: *King Kong Versus Godzilla* (Toho 1962).

This was the Dunning Process in action. On 30 December Wallace saw the finished scenes: 'They were not particularly good, though there was one excellent sequence where a man is chased by a dinosaurus.' Wallace went into the animation room, a projection room converted into a workshop. O'Brien had completed the skeleton and framework of 'the giant monkey which appears in this play' (the King was as yet unchristened).

'I saw a woodcarver fashioning the skull on which the actual figure will be built. In another place was a great scale model of a gigantic gorilla, which had been made specially. One of the gorilla figures will be nearly thirty feet high. All round the walls are wooden models of prehistoric beasts. There are two miniature sets with real miniature trees, on which the prehistoric animals are made to gambol. Only fifty feet can be taken a day of the animating part. Every move of the animal had to be fixed by the artist, including the ripples of his muscles. Of course it is a tedious job.'

To anyone but a man of Willis O'Brien's devotion. Kong and the other models had to be separately photographed every time their position was changed a sixteenth of an inch. Said O'Brien, 'We worked ten hours a day – the fight between Kong and the pterodactyl took seven weeks to film!'

O'Brien had his work on *The Lost World* to guide him, but this time there was a brand-new problem. Since 1925 the movies had learned to talk: what did a prehistoric monster *sound* like? Murray Spivak of RKO's sound department built forty noise-making instruments in all. To vocalize an arsinotherium he blew a column of air through a vox humana pipe from an old organ. He next re-recorded this hiss at a subnormal speed: lowering it an octave added a note of terror. Then he reversed the soundtrack and slowed that down yet another octave. For other monsters he recorded the growls of cougars, leopards and lions, reversing them to obtain previously unknown noises. His biggest problem, of course, was Kong. The type of sound made by a prehistoric ape would naturally relate to its present-day descendant, but a gorilla's growl was less than effective: Kong was fifty feet tall. Recording gorilla cries backwards at a slow speed was part of the answer, the rest was a specially built sound-box 25 feet square. This came in handy for hollow thumps when the great ape beat his chest.

Cooper had key scenes sketched in detail before the film went on the floor, and no fewer than twenty-seven models of Kong were made, in different sizes but all to scale with the ape's official vital statistics:

Height	50 ft
Face	7 ft from hairline to chin
Nose	2 ft
Lips	6 ft from corner to corner
Brows	4 ft 3 in
Mouth	6 ft when stretched as in a smile
Eyes	Each 10 in long
Ears	1 ft long
Eye-teeth	10 in high, 7 in at base
Molars	14 in round, 4 in high
Chest	60 ft in repose
Legs	15 ft
Arms	23 ft
Reach	75 ft

When Kong reached for Fay Wray and examined her curiously, peeling off what was left of her clothes, the half-minute scene took twenty-three hours to film.

'They had a huge rubber arm with a steel cable inside large enough to hold me. The fingers were pressed around my waist and then, by leverage, they lifted me up into the air. All the closeups were done that way. There was a tiny little doll model used for when King Kong was holding me. It was about three inches long. I couldn't tell the difference when I would go to see the day's work, it was blended that well.'

Kong's name came from Cooper's fondness for mysterious monosyllables. Selznick liked the title, but the New York office objected: they thought it too much like his *Chang* and *Rango*. They publicized it as *The Beast*. Wallace suggested *King Ape* in January 1931, and although the completed picture was actually advertised as simply *Kong* in January 1933, it was finally combined with Wallace's title for copyright registration on 24 February 1933 as *King Kong*: exactly one year after Wallace's death.

King Kong had a monster première: it opened at the world's two largest theatres, the Radio City Music Hall and the Roxy in New York, simul-

Losing Face: "E's all eaten away!' screams Una O'Connor of Claude Rains, *The Invisible Man* (Universal 1933; *above*). Ilona Massey was touched by Jon Hall, *The Invisible Agent* (Universal 1942; *below*).

104

Monster's Mate: James Whale made the best modern horror movie, or the worst, according to your taste. Whale's taste was for the bizarre and in *Bride of Frankenstein* (Universal 1935) it ran as amok as his Monster. Whale mocked the crucifixion (*opposite above*) and the marriage ceremony (*below*) as well as the Hollywood Romantic Co-star Poster. He even overturned religious symbols (*left*). The Monster was Karloff, of course, and his Mate was Elsa Lanchester. A typical Whale twist was to cast her as the story's authoress Mary Wollstonecraft Shelley, as well: creator and created.

taneously: the only picture ever to do so. Ten thousand seats packed for ten shows a day: for escapist entertainment there was clearly no Depression. *King Kong* came in at 650,000 dollars: it is still making money. When unloosed on television for the first time, one New York station ran it sixteen times in seven days.

Film producer-cum-explorer Robert Armstrong charters *The Venture* and steams off for Skull Island, armed with a map, a camera, and Fay Wray. The natives are unfriendly until they see her. Soon Fay finds herself chained to two pillars while a witch-doctor, accompanied by Max Steiner's magnificent music, chants: 'Wa Saba ani mako, O Tar Vey, Rama Kong' . . . 'Thy bride is here, O mighty one, great Kong!' Crashing down the overgrown undergrowth comes her hairy husband, to bear Fay away to his primordial lair. Bruce Cabot braves many a monster before gassing the groom with grenades. The unconscious Kong is shipped to America and exhibited as the Eighth Wonder of the World.

'He was a King and a God in the world he knew, but now he comes to civilization merely a captive, a show to gratify your curiosity.' Dazzled by a thousand flashbulbs, Kong breaks his chains and rampages through New York. He finds his bride again and climbs to the top of the Empire State Building. Army planes swoop at him like mosquitoes; their machine-guns more than sting. Gently, the weakening King sets down his little Queen and falls, one hundred and two storeys, to his death. His captor speaks his epitaph: 'It was beauty killed the beast.'

The incredible success called for a sequel and Cooper and Schoedsack rushed *Son of Kong* (1933) into the cinemas for Christmas. Shorter by thirty minutes than the original's one hundred, the replay gave full rein to O'Brien's humour. Where he had given the father moments of charming humanity, he made the son such a clown that the film had to be subtitled 'A Serio-Comic Phantasy'.

Robert Armstrong, dunned for the damages caused by his discovery, flees to the South Seas in the good old *Venture*. His plan, to pay his debts with Kong's long-lost treasures. This time Helen Mack is the dark-eyed lovely taken along for the ride. Kong Junior, a white-haired ape, becomes attached to the explorers, following them around like a faithful dog, boxing a bear and otherwise coming in handy when prehistoric monsters threaten. The climatic earthquake is spectacular and touching: young Kong gives his life to hold the humans above the tidal wave.

Both Kongs were scripted by Ruth Rose (Mrs Merian C. Cooper) and directed by the ex-cameraman Ernest B. Schoedsack, but only the funny son was considered horrific enough to notify the Home Office. This was the current treatment given to the horror film by the British Board of Film Censors when they felt their 'A' for Adults Only certificate was insufficient warning. One other Kong spin-off upset them, too: *King Klunk* (1933) makes its niche in history by being the first cartoon film branded 'Horrific'. It starred Pooch the Pup.

With animated horror the latest craze, who in Hollywood needed the original stars? Neither Karloff nor Lugosi wanted to know about Laemmle's latest project, conceived as yet another field day for the Special Effects department. The star was to remain unseen until the final frame.

The Invisible Man (1933) again demonstrated the horror film's potential for creating new stars. Overnight Claude Rains, who had been knocking around in British films since the early twenties, became a world star: the little man who wasn't there. He played the entire movie swathed in bandages and black goggles. Only his voice, that soft-spoken English so essential to the genre, carried the thriller through to the final, death-bed materialization. He was helped by his dialogue, brilliantly adapted from H.G. Wells' 1897 novel by R.C. Sherriff. As he elaborates upon his projected reign of terror, the Invisible One (as he was billed) laughs: 'Even the moon is frightened of me, frightened to death! The whole world is frightened to death!'

James Whale directed, and peopled his snowbound village of Iping with the expected grotesques. Una O'Connor screamed at the drop of a tray as Mrs Jenny Hall, landlady of the Lion's Head, and E.E. Clive drooped a solemn walrus as P.C. Jaffers. When their strange visitor unpeels his bandaged face to reveal – nothing – stalwart Jaffers keeps his head. ''E's invisible, that's wot's the matter with 'im!' Only Whale would dare show his monster as a pair of disembodied trousers, skipping down the lane singing 'Here we come gathering nuts in May!' Or a farmer reporting the discovery of the transparent fugitive with an awed, 'There's breathin' in me barn!' Whale was the only director in the golden age of horror to realize the danger of the unwanted laugh. He gave his nervous audience relief from tension by letting them laugh with, instead of at, the film.

Jack Griffin was a dedicated research scientist. He had been experimenting with monocaine, a

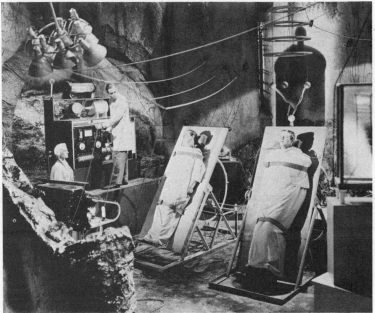

Locked in the Laboratory: No horror movie can be considered complete without a lab scene, and here is a selection of Universal's finest. Henry Frankenstein's original was enlarged and augmented for *Bride of Frankenstein* (1935; *left*), demolished and renovated for *Frankenstein Meets the Wolf Man* (1942; *top right*). Claude Rains' portable lab in *The Invisible Man* (1933; *top left*) was a do-it-yourself variation on Henry Hull's equipment for *Werewolf of London* (1935; *above*).

Battle Royal: King Kong squares up usually to Queensberry rules: Willis O'Brien, his animator, was a fight fan. Fay Wray is at the ringside in *King Kong* (RKO 1933; *right*), Robert Armstrong and Helen Mack in *Son of Kong* (RKO 1933; *opposite left*), but only the audience watches *King Kong Escapes* (Toho 1967; *opposite right*). One of the King's ringers was *Konga* (Cohen 1961; *below*).

drug from India. Tried on the dog it bleached the beast white and sent it raving mad. Griffin injected himself and became invisible. He went into hiding to work on an antidote, but, 'the drug seemed to light up my brain. Suddenly I realized the power I held, the power to rule, to make the world grovel at my feet.' He embarks on his Reign of Terror: murdering, robbing, derailing trains. But invisibility has its problems, as he explains to his unwilling associate, Kemp.

'I must always remain in hiding for an hour after meals. The food is visible inside me until it is digested. I can only work on fine, clear days. If I work in the rain the water can be seen on my head and shoulders. In fog you can see me like a bubble. In smoky cities, the soot settles on me like a dark outline. You must always be at hand to wipe off my feet, Kemp – even dirt under my fingernails would give me away.'

In the end Nature, as ever, abhors a vacuum: her snow shows his naked footfalls. A police inspector shoots – and suddenly there is a long dent in the smooth snow.

John P. Fulton, Universal's special effects man spent six months working out the several kinds of camera tricks. Some were done with 'invisible' wires (as when Griffin takes a cigarette or suddenly rocks a chair), others depended on an old conjurer's gimmick: a man completely clad in black is invisible against a black background. Details of the picture were painted out of the negative by retouchers working through microscopes with minute brushes, and there was double, triple, and more exposure, of course. Some tricks were new, others went back to the days of Georges Méliès, who had shown the way with *Siva the Invisible* in 1904. But whilst the whole hit a new high in an age of cinematic miracles, it was Rains' reading of the lines that made his the face the world most wanted to see. It was a triumph of man over machine. Besides, Rains gave horror-film heroes their most famous last words: 'I meddled in things that man must leave alone.'

The Hollywood family Laemmle, having fathered and grandfathered the horror film, could see their creation fading out under the weight of expensive special effects. They revived the corpse with a showmanlike shot in the arm: two monsters for the price of one.

'It's Tremonstrous!' screamed the posters: 'Frankenstein Karloff plus Dracula Lugosi plus Edgar Allan Poe!' Poor Poe, billed last, came off worst. By the time the British censor got through with it, *The Black Cat* (1934) itself, a supernatural reincarnation of female into feline, was seen so briefly that the film had to be retitled *The House of Doom*. Edgar G. Ulmer, the director, had been a set designer for Reinhardt in the theatre and Murnau in the movies, and much of the curious look of *The Black Cat* was his doing. Instead of the traditional trappings of cobwebby castle, Ulmer created an incredible, futuristic fort. The striking sets and way-out wardrobe caught Karloff's interest, for he had determined to play no more monsters. Karloff was cast as avant-garde architect Hjalmar Poelzig, whilst Lugosi bore the equally unlikely name of Vitus Verdegast. The co-stars' roles were weighted with care, for the first time siding Lugosi with the angels. Karloff, indeed, conducted a cult of devil-

Vampire Variants: The vampire remains the most indestructible of all movie monsters – there are more vampire films than any other genre-within-the-genre. Funny vampires include an encounter between Bela Lugosi and Old Mother Riley on one hand, and Roman Polanski's black satire *Dance of the Vampires* (Filmways 1967) on the other. Boxer Terry Downes made a particularly unpleasant apparition in the latter (*right*). Richard Matheson's vampiric variation 'I Am Legend' has been filmed twice with varying success. Vincent Price played *The Last Man On Earth* (Regina 1964; *below right*) and Charlton Heston *The Omega Man* (Seltzer 1971; *below left*). Rosalind Cash as a bleached Negress was perhaps a more alluring menace than the traditional clutching hand.

VINCENT PRICE in
"THE LAST MAN ON EARTH"
cert X
RELEASED BY GOLDEN ERA FILM DISTRIBUTORS

worshippers in his private chapel: or so the cock-eyed crucifixes would hint. In England, the censor switched Satanism to sun-worship.

David Manners, as ever, is the honeymooning hero *en route* to Budapest when a train crash injures his bride. Lugosi takes them along to Karloff's place, where the girl soon finds herself earmarked for sacrifice at the next session. Lugosi, fifteen years a prisoner of war, is seeking vengeance on his betrayer. In the interim Karloff has done more: he married Lugosi's wife, keeps her corpse under glass, and made a mistress of her daughter. Initial courtesy is thrown overboard as climaxes pile up. Karloff pumps his organ at a Black Mass; Lugosi saves the bride from sacrifice; Karloff is skinned alive; Lugosi is shot by the uncomprehending hero; the honeymooners escape as the dying Lugosi blows the minefield beneath the bizarre building; The End.

As if to atone, Universal produced a picture on a horror theme that was so serious in its approach that the British censor banned it outright. Of all horror films, *Life Returns* (1934) is the most 'lost'. Never seen in England, even in today's relaxed climate; never reprinted for television; unpreserved by archives, unmentioned by historians, unregistered even for copyright; yet it was the only 'documentary' horror film. It concluded with a sequence actually showing the dead restored to life. Dr Robert E. Cornish of the University of California revived a dead dog and filmed himself doing it. The rest of *Life Returns* was fiction, concocted by director Eugene Frenke with his writers James Hogan, John Goodrich, Arthur Homan, Wolfe Gilbert and Mary McCarthy.

Onslow Stevens, formerly the invisible scientist of Universal's science-fiction serial *The Vanishing Shadow* (1934), played John Kendrick, a doctor devoted to seeking a formula to restore life after death. He succeeds when his son's pet, called Lazarus of course, is gassed by the dog-catcher. The triumph also revives the boy's faith. Valerie Hobson played the doctor's wife: a dummy run for a bride to be.

'Alone you have created a man. Now, together, we will create his mate.'
'You mean . . . ?'
'Yes! A woman! That should be *really* interesting!'

The discussion between Dr Pretorius, eccentric experimenter, and Henry Frankenstein, reluctant collaborator, echoed an earlier discussion between two other, more real, monster-makers. Carl Laemmle Jr and James Whale were the Burke and Hare of the movie business. But these latter-day resurrectionists were not content with merely digging up the dead for money. They became the first men to bring the dead back to life (excluding, of course, Dr Robert E. Cornish).

'Who will be *The Bride of Frankenstein*? Who will dare?' The questions shouted by Universal Publicists were not answered by Whale's cast-list. It read 'The Monster's Mate . . . ????' A fuss had been made of testing both Phyllis Brooks and Brigitte Helm (the ex-robotrix of *Metropolis*) but in the end the part went to Elsa Lanchester. Or to Valerie Hobson, according to your interpretation of the title. The bride of Frankenstein was certainly Miss Hobson, while the mate of the Monster (Karloff) was undoubtedly Miss Lanchester. It is typical of Whale's turn of humour that he should see the part as a *doppelgänger*, both in title, and in concept: he had Elsa Lanchester play both the authoress, Mary Shelley, and her fictional creation. So pretty in the prologue, Miss Lanchester found herself built up on stilts from five-foot-four to a towering seven, and bound so tightly in bandages that she had to be carried about the studio and fed by tube. 'It was a horrible experience,' she said, 'It would have been easy to grow hysterical.'

The Bride's fantastic face was conceived by Whale and Ernest Thesiger, a refugee from *The Old Dark House*. Both men were artistic: Whale had cartooned for a London magazine and Thesiger was a crochet king. Using Queen Nefertiti as their inspiration, they designed 'a creature born of a thunderstorm, a wild jungle animal in captivity, with a suggestion of pride and dignity'. Their end-product, executed by Jack P. Pierce, enlivened by the Lanchester talent, made a memorable Mate.

Pierce had a busy time with two monsters to make up each day. Karloff alone took seven hours to construct, starting at 6 a.m. with the greasepaint, collodion and cotton, and ending at 1 p.m. with the steel braces, padded suit and boots. Then, at the end of a long day's shoot, would come the dismantling. He was lucky to be home by nine. There were modifications to makeup and costume: undying as the Monster had proved to be, he could hardly have survived the original climactic holocaust totally unscathed. His hair was now burned stubble, exposing unsightly skull-clips, and wrinkled scars marked his cheeks. His suit, shabbier than ever, gained an unaccountable fourteen

'Ware Wolves: Lycanthropy, the curse that brings out the beast in people, was a long time incubating. Universal made *The Werewolf* in 1913 and waited twenty-two years before making another. *Werewolf of London* (1935; *opposite, left*) starred Henry Hull. The makeup by Jack P. Pierce not only influenced that artist's later Chaney *Wolf Man*, but also Michael Landon's teenage version: *I Was a Teenage Werewolf* (American International 1957; *below left*), and Germany's *Lycanthropus* (Royal 1961; *below*). This one was known in England as *I Married a Werewolf* and in America as *Werewolf in a Girls' Dormitory*.

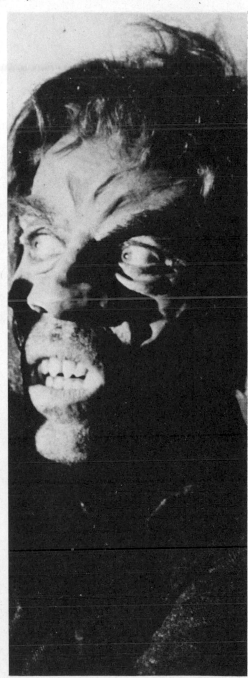

pounds in weight. In his first scene, the Monster's survival in an underground river beneath the ruined mill, Karloff broke a hip.

Bride of Frankenstein (1935) was a sequel, yet it came closer to the original novel than did the original film. It even opened with a prologue based on Mary Shelley's 1817 Preface. Lord Byron (Gavin Gordon) muses over Mary's morality of the Modern Prometheus: 'I relish each separate horror . . . I roll them over on my tongue.' (This allowed four-year-old memories to be refreshed by flashbacks.) He wishes for more and Mary obliges.

From the dying embers of the old mill comes one last belch of flame. 'His insides caught at last!' screeches old Minnie. This crone, a family retainer unseen in the original, is Una O'Connor, a Whale grotesque from *The Invisible Man*. Her mutterings

Living Dolls: Grace Ford was *The Devil Doll* (MGM 1936), looking small against scaled-up sets, an effect Laurel and Hardy pioneered in *Brats* (1930). Grant Williams achieved an atom-age equivalent by performing in front of a back projection screen: *The Incredible Shrinking Man* (Universal 1957; *left*).

and scuttlings replace those of Dwight Frye: when a great knocking comes upon the castle door, she scurries to answer with an 'All right, don't knock the castle over, we're not all dead yet!' The midnight caller is Dr Pretorius ('Pretorius? There's no sich name!'). This is Ernest Thesiger ('A very queer old gentleman') in a role evolved out of his effeminate Femm. He even says the same line: 'Do you like gin? It is my only weakness.' He brings Frankenstein the result of twenty years' experimentation, artificial life: 'I grew my creatures, like cultures. Grew them as nature does, from seed.' But Pretorius has a size problem: he can only create in miniature. Like a wicked old witch he displays his seven dwarfs in bottles. They range from a lusty Henry VIII (a Whale in-joke: his Bride's real husband – Charles Laughton – won the Oscar as bluff King Hal) to a mermaid ('An experiment with seaweed!').

Meanwhile the Monster seeks shelter in the hut of a blind hermit (O.P.Heggie). It is the burned, spurned brute's first encounter with something other than horror. Accepting him on equal terms as one of nature's cast-offs, the hermit gives the Monster food for body (bread and wine) and soul (Ave Maria on the violin). He teaches him simple words ('Bread, wine') and simple truths ('Friend good, fire bad'), but their fiddle-playing idyll is interrupted when huntsman John Carradine bursts in. In moments the hut is on fire. Whale's symbolism runs amok. Already brought in on a tree in mock crucifixion, now his Monster abandons his God-like friend in a hell of flames and overthrows the statue of a bishop. In the catacombs below, Dr Pretorius is dining off a coffin.

The Monster steps out of the shadows. The sudden sight provokes no fright in Pretorius. He raises a nostril. 'Oh,' he says offhandedly, 'I thought I was alone.' 'Friend?' queries the Monster, and Pretorius gives him the remains of his chicken carcase to crunch. To force Frankenstein's co-operation, Pretorius has the Monster kidnap Elizabeth. Karl (Dwight Frye) is dispatched to obtain a fresh female corpse. (Whale's original plan was to have him kill Elizabeth: the bride of Frankenstein would become the Bride of Frankenstein.) An artificial brain is inserted. The climax comes on a stormy night in a creation so creative that the original *Frankenstein* pales into a pilot. On a table raised on high as Karl flies kites in the lightning sky, the Mate is brought to life under the 'Cosmic Diffuser'. 'The bride of Frankenstein!' pronounces Pretorius as Whale treats us to his trick of curiously-cut closeups of the creature.

There is more mockery in the music: Franz Waxman's excellent score now chimes forth with wedding bells! The Monster reaches beseechingly for his bandaged bride. 'Friend?' he quavers. Her reaction is a sharp screech. 'She hate me, like others,' says the Monster, one tear rolling down one cheek. He pulls a lever and blows the laboratory to pieces, uttering his Famous Last Words: 'We belong dead.'

Bride of Frankenstein remains the biggest-budgeted, best dressed, highest-polished, finest-finished horror film in history; a first-class Hollywood product made with all the artistry and technology a top studio normally lavished upon only its most commercial ventures. It was Whale's best work – and his last in the genre; he felt he could not top it. With it he established himself as the master director of horror – although there are many who feel his sense of humour dilutes rather than enhances the whole. After a period of sad oblivion touched by alcohol and scandal, Whale was found drowned in his own swimming-pool on 29 May 1957.

Chaney was forgotten; Karloff was king; but who could replace Karloff? Laemmle needed a second-string monster; it was bad business to let a star have the whole field to himself. He thought he found one in Henry Hull, silent hero of D.W. Griffith's thriller *One Exciting Night* (1922). Laemmle had Jack Pierce make Hull look so Karloff-like as Magwitch that the posters for *Great Expectations* (1934) boosted that Dickens picture into the horror market. Stuart Walker directed, and when Whale declined further horrors, Laemmle reunited Walker and Hull on *Werewolf of London* (1935).

Valerie Hobson played Lisa to Hull's Wilfred, the unhappy Glendon. Warner Oland, a former Fu Manchu, was Dr Yogami of the University of Carpathia, who bit Dr Glendon one moonlight night. Both were in Tibet at the time, seeking the *mariphasa Lupino lumino*, a flower that blooms in the moon. Its other odd property was that it acted as an antidote to lycanthrobia. Glendon took a cutting back to London and nurtured it beneath a strange lamp, but both he and Yogami needed the prick of its pollen thorn. Yogami wins the race but loses his life, for Glendon grows hairy and kills him. Yogami had warned, 'The werewolf instinctively seeks to kill the thing it loves best.' Now Glendon stalks his wife. The head of Scotland Yard arrives in time to shoot him down and watch as the werewolf changes, in death, to the doctor.

Hull, in a six-hour makeup job (four to put on, two to take off) did well as the werewolf, but was

Fiery Pyres: Gloria Holden as Countess Marya Zaleska, better known as *Dracula's Daughter* (Universal 1936), presides over a private pyre for her father, the late Count (*below*). Kirsten Lindholm in *Twins of Evil* (Hammer 1971) is 'the innocent, beautiful woodman's daughter' who, continues the caption, 'writhes in terror as the flames leap when the fanatical Brotherhood burn her at the stake' (*right*). *Opposite:* Bela Lugosi, undead with a hole in his head to prove it, enfolds Elizabeth Allan in *Mark of the Vampire* (MGM 1935).

oo clipped of hair and speech as the hero. His harsh voice and brusque ways robbed the role of sympathy, spoiling Laemmle's hopes of a new Karloff to replace his new Chaney. Laemmle also tried to catch a little Whale: two old cockney biddies called Mrs Moncaster and Mrs Whack cackled eccentrically through the film, but instead of relief they were padding. Robert Harris wrote the story, grafting European folklore to Jekyll and Hyde. Jack Pierce's makeup also recalled that much-filmed monster, especially when, working with John P. Fulton, the dying change from wolf to man was shown as a series of overlapping dissolves.

Karloff, Lugosi and Poe, Universal's triple-threat, were teamed again in *The Raven* (1935). Walker had proved no Whale and this time Laemmle tried Louis Friedlander, who had directed *The Vanishing Shadow*. Lugosi, though as ever billed below, for once led the field as Richard Vollin, plastic surgeon with Poe on the Brain. His house on Hillview Heights was a torture-chamber shrine to the morbid poet. As Edmond Bateman, bearded fugitive from San Quentin, Karloff comes demanding a new face. Lugosi gives him one. He

unveils it in six long mirrors, all of which the snarling Karloff smashes. 'Maybe if a man looks ugly he does ugly things,' Karloff had said. Now he was more than ugly: Lugosi had tampered with his seventh cranial nerve. 'Your monstrous ugliness creates monstrous hate!' jibes Lugosi, 'I can use your hate.' Forced to assist in Lugosi's mad scheme to win Irene Ware by torturing Samuel S. Hinds, Karloff is shot saving her. He explodes the master switchboard and Lugosi dies screaming between in-crushing walls. His stuffed raven falls symbolically to the floor. 'Poe, you are avenged!' cried Lugosi at one climax; others would disagree.

Karloff and Lugosi were matched again in *The Invisible Ray* (1935). They co-starred as doctors Janos Rukh and Felix Benet, but this time Friedlander's serial-style science-fiction made way for Lambert Hillyer's fabulous futurism. The opening is breathtaking. In his laboratory-cum-observatory perched atop a Carpathian mountain, Karloff captures light rays from the past, reconstituting constellations within a great glass dome. A kind of time machine, it takes him beyond Andromeda to track the trajectory of a mysterious meteor. Enrolling Lugosi he treks to Africa to excavate the rock and harness its curious property, Radium-X. This ray cures blindness at short range, melts mountains at long range and makes Karloff glow in the dark. Only Lugosi can supply the antidote. Karloff's brain turns and he goes on a rampage of revenge. His very touch kills, and after each murder he melts a statue of one Deadly Sin (stone symbols surmounting that Universal edifice, Notre Dame). In the end his old mother (Violet Kemble Cooper) dashes the antidote from his fingers for 'breaking the first rule of science'. Karloff bursts into flames, leaps through the window, and goes up in smoke. A set-piece finale to a historic double-act: Karloff and Lugosi would ride again, but never as equal partners.

Universal brought the golden age of horror full circle with a sequel to the story that had started it. Lambert Hillyer directed Gloria Holden, an unknown from London, as Countess Marya Zaleska from Transylvania, otherwise *Dracula's Daughter* (1936). A moon-faced beauty, Hungarian of cheekbone, slumber-lidded of eye, Miss Holden played with sombre restraint as the cursed soul who sought only release. She intoned lines by John Balderston and Garrett Fort with sadness and belief, aided perhaps by some years in radio. Stealing the staked corpse of her father, she presides over his funeral pyre.

Ladies' Night: Women's Lib hits Transylvania. Barbara Shelley (*right*) bares her fangs and etceteras in *Dracula, Prince of Darkness* (Hammer 1965), setting a fashion followed by a female fiend in *The Return of Count Yorga* (American International 1971; *below right*). Ingrid Pitt as *Countess Dracula* (Hammer 1970; *below*) found an ideal cure for old age: virgin's blood. *Opposite page:* Nancy Barrett is crossed in *House of Dark Shadows* (MGM 1970; *top*). A vampire woman was but one horror in Bert I. Gordon's *Saint George and the Seven Curses* (UA 1961; *centre left*). Hammer also contributed Adrienne Corri, who bled Elizabeth Seal in *Vampire Circus* (1972; *bottom left*) and Barbara Shelley again as *The Gorgon* (1964; *bottom right*).

'Unto Adoni and Aseroth, into the keeping of the lords of the flame and lower pits, I consign this body, to be for evermore consumed in this purging fire. Let all baleful spirits that threaten the souls of men be banished by the sprinkling of this salt. Be thou exorcized, O Dracula, and thy body long undead, find destruction throughout eternity in the name of thy dark, unholy master. In the name of the all holiest, and through this cross, be the evil spirit cast out until the end of time.'

Her own epitaph is less wordy but more telling. Says old Von Helsing (old Van Sloan), 'She was beautiful when she died – a hundred years ago!' The Countess had expired at the hands of her jealous servant, Sandor (Irving Pichel in black hair and nostrils), shot through the heart by his wooden arrow. It was a fitting funeral for the first Universal epoch.

MGM continued to hold second place in the horror-film race. After three years they finally for-gave *Freaks* and let Tod Browning have his head. *Mark of the Vampire* (1935), a talking version of his *London After Midnight*, switched the locale to Mareka in Czechoslovakia, a more suitable venue for a revamp. One of his writers was Guy Endore, author of the best modern novel on lycanthropy, 'Werewolf of Paris'; his photographer was James Wong Howe; his stars were Lionel Barrymore, Bela Lugosi and Lionel Atwill. Clearly only the best would do. The original Lon Chaney double role was doubled up: Barrymore as the investigator and Lugosi as the vampire. An additional twist was that Barrymore played in a realistic variation of Chaney's original vampire makeup, a shaggy old scientist called Professor Zelen, while Lugosi played straight Dracula in black cloak and eyeballs as Count Mora. Boosting the cast was the Vampire Girl, blood-sister to America's Panther Woman. Carol Borland, winner of the role of Luna, daughter of Mora, had an unfair edge in that she played with Lugosi on a *Dracula* tour. This had prepared her for almost anything, except Tod Browning. He wanted her

Double Feature: Boris Karloff and Bela Lugosi, the first great stars of horror, became partners in crime. Less the Abbott and Costello of horror films, more your Laurel and Hardy: like those latter-day laughter-makers Lugosi and Karloff were actors of equal weight. However, Karloff quickly took the lead, and by the time of *The Body Snatcher* (RKO 1945; *above*) Lugosi was reduced to small-part support – except in the billing. He fared better in the Universal team-ups, flaying Karloff alive in *The Black Cat* (1934; *opposite*), released in England as *House of Doom*, and tampering with his nerve ends in *The Raven* (1935; *left*).

121

Karloff before him), serenading a wax figure of Orlac's wife (an echo of Atwill). His pet cockatoo (a familiar in the tradition of Lugosi's vulture of *White Zombie*) exposes her when she takes the place of the statue, by drawing blood with its claws. 'Each man should kill the thing he loves,' expounds Gogol (*après* Yogami) as he strangles Frances Drake with her own hair.

There was a familiarity about the credits, too: Karl Freund directed (sadly his last such exercise; he returned to his old love, the camera), and John L. Balderston and Guy Endore worked on the screenplay. Unfamiliar, and horridly so, was the star. Peter Lorre from Hungary, the child-like child-killer of *M* (1931), Fritz Lang's first talkie. Lorre's ogling Gogol was the original egg-head with eyes poached to match. His Hollywood debut brought a new face, style and thrill to the horror film.

The Devil Doll (1936) was the last horror film from MGM, and from Tod Browning. It was a tremendous farewell for him, totally fantastic yet completely characteristic. Lionel Barrymore, Devil's Island escapee, donning drag as Madame Mandelip, proprietress of a Montmartre doll shop, was familiar Chaney stuff; novelty lay in making the dolls miniaturized humans. Marcel and Malita, eccentric scientists, devised their diminisher as an answer to the over-population problem, but the cracked ex-con sees wider possibilities. He dispatches his eight-inch automata to wreak revenge on the men who framed him. A brilliant sequence showed Grace Ford as little Lachna, stirring to life in the crook of sleeping Juanita Quigley's arm, climbing down the eiderdown, squeezing through an ajar door, shinning up a chair-leg, tossing pearls down to the waiting Barrymore, and running a poisoned stiletto into the outflung arm of snoring Robert Greig.

Browning took his plot from 'Burn Witch Burn', a novel by Abraham Merritt. He threw out the author's alchemy and had Guy Endore, Garrett Fort and Erich Von Stroheim switch the script to science-fiction. Learning from his last over-explained vampires, Browning let his pictures carry conviction by simply looking real. It was an incredible climax to an incredible career. When Browning died in 1962, he had been so long in the wilderness that Hollywood was surprised to learn he had still been alive.

to swoop bat-like at the window. First they had to design and build a flying harness that would hide beneath her Adrian-designed gowns. A jockey hired as her stand-in got airsick. Her springed bat-wings sprang in instead of out. She had a bar from the back of her neck to her ankles to hold her stiff: when they forgot to lower the tail-wires first her swoop turned into a belly-flop. It took three weeks to shoot a shot that lasted ten seconds; a stunt which, according to the plot, was quickly rigged by actors to scare a murderer. This ultimate exposition was more preposterous than the proposition that 'there are such things'.

Mad Love (1935) was released in England under the title of the novel from which it was taken, *The Hands of Orlac*. Colin Clive continued in nerve-wracked vein as Stephen Orlac, concert pianist, whose famous hands have to be amputated after a train smash. Dr Gogol, bald, bulb-eyed, brilliant, sews on some new ones: hands cut from the corpse of Rollo, a murderous knife-thrower. Gogol dies from a knife thrown by those hands, but not before he has framed Orlac for killing his father and frightened him with an horrendous apparition. Orlac follows a beckoning figure to the Inn of the Three Feathers. It throws back its cloak: its hands are steel. 'I have no hands. Your hands were mine once.' Then it pulls back its cape. 'They cut off my head, but Gogol put it back!': a bloated white face, fixed in place with a leather brace.

There are other joys, some familiar. Orlac's wife is branded nightly in *Grand Guignol* at 'Le Théâtre des Horreurs' (just as the Judge's daughter danced 'The Spirit of Poe' in *The Raven*). Gogol pumps a private organ (as did the Phantom, the Terror, and

Hands Down: Colin Clive in *Mad Love* (MGM 1935; *above*); Lon Chaney Jr as *The Wolf Man* (Universal 1941).

A CHIP OFF THE OLD HUMP

In which even a man who is pure in heart and says his prayers by night may become Lon Chaney Junior when the wolfbane blooms and the autumn moon is bright.

'My son. If you burn with desire to pursue my work, carry on. Even though the path be cruel and tortuous, carry on. You have inherited the secrets of the Frankensteins, my son. I trust you will not inherit their fate.' [Extract from the letters of Baron Heinrich Von Frankenstein (deceased).]

The new men at Universal had inherited the secrets of the Laemmles. They, too, trusted they would not inherit their fate, for the old firm was no longer a family concern. The new faction needed money fast, and won it on a dare: 'We dare you to book these two pictures and show them in one programme!' *Frankenstein* and *Dracula*, disinterred from the studio vaults, were reissued in one monster show. It was the first ever double bill of horror: a novelty then, standard practice today. The inspiration and presentation – 'Can your patrons take it?' – was worthy of the Laemmles, and Universal were quick to cash in on their cash-in. With the stars restored to their former gory glory, Karloff, Lugosi and the New Universal (as they liked to call it) initiated a New Age of Horror with the logical consequence of *Bride of Frankenstein*.

Son of Frankenstein (1938), Wolf, in the elegant yet coiled-steel style of Basil Rathbone, entrains from England to claim his heritage. This, far from the remembered ruin, has become a castle vaster than either yet seen, a Baronetcy, a 'Von', and a box containing his father's 'faiths, beliefs and unfoldments'. Even the village (Ingoldstadt in the novel, Goldstadt in the play, Oldstadt in the first film) is now called Frankenstein. He is greeted by Inspector Krogh of the District Police: Lionel Atwill, stiffer than ever, thanks to a wooden arm – result of a childhood encounter with the Monster. There have been mysterious murders in the village. The answer lies in Frankenstein's laboratory (the exploded watch-tower is now 'that weird-looking structure across the ravine'). It is the Monster, preserved by an unsuspected sulphur pit beneath the floorboards. Nurse to the brute is Ygor (Lugosi), a scruffy shepherd who once escaped the gallows with nothing worse than a broken neck.

'Make him well, Frankenstein. Your father made him and he was your father, too.' Unable to resist this call of the blood, Wolf, with his butler at the generators, revives the Monster. Karloff, fuller in face, bulkier in body, wears a sheepskin bodice (presumably fashioned by friend Ygor). He can do no more than grunt or snarl: an intellectual diminution explicable only by Karloff's personal objections to his previous articulation. He publicly protested against Whale's dialogue, feeling it weakened his weirdness. The Monster makes Wolf stand beside him before a mirror: in this odd echo from Edison 1910, he compares their reflections. Ygor comes at Frankenstein with a pick, but Wolf fires his pistol. In another echo, this time from Whale, the Monster cradles the corpse of his only friend and howls in anguish. Then he makes for the bedroom of Wolf's little son. He leads the lad towards the steaming sulphur pit. Krogh shoots, Wolf swings down on a chain, and the Monster is kicked into the pit. Screaming, he sinks beneath the bubbles.

The first of the new horror films, the last of the great ones: Karloff would play the monster no more. He turned in his eighteen-pound boots; he was fifty-one years old. *Son* was made as a top-budget epic, excelling *Bride* in expense and length: ninety-six minutes of terrific entertainment. Rowland V. Lee directed with expertise, but Whale would have seen the funny side of the servants' saying:

If the house is filled with dread,
Place the beds at head to head.

First Love: Lon Chaney Jr and Carole Landis in *One Million BC* (Roach 1940).

The great wonder of the film is its styling: huge, crazy, obviously studio, the sets overshadow the actors in a way hardly seen on the screen since the German Expressionists. Jack Otterson, the art director, called them 'Psychological Sets'.

> 'I departed entirely from any known style of architecture. The sets were an orderly array of planes and masses which, at first glance, resemble a castle interior. But the angles and masses were calculated to force an impression of a weird locale without intruding too strongly into the consciousness.'

The Frankenstein rehash had a backwash that came in an onrush: remakes of other old favourites, but by different studios. *The Cat and the Canary* (1939) came from Paramount as a brilliant comedy-thriller: laughs from Bob Hope and his cowardly quips, thrills from Douglass Montgomery as the unsuspected Cat. Director Elliott Nugent cheated by having another actor play the monster in every scene except the unmasking. Next year they all did it again as *The Ghost Breakers* (1940). Fox took over *The Gorilla* (1939) and tripled the fun by casting the Ritz Brothers in the lead. Lionel Atwill and Bela Lugosi lent the weight of their names to the proceedings, but they were mere red herrings. *The Hunchback of Notre Dame* (1939) came this time from RKO. Chaney was outdone at last; Laughton was an actor. His Quasimodo is unsurpassed, a frog-hopping, tongue-lolling, eye-rolling gargoyle, yet human enough to break your heart. 'My makeup was horrible, simply horrible. I looked vicious enough to make anyone scream. You have never seen anything as hideous,' he said. The film took three months to shoot. Sixty days in makeup that took two and a half hours to apply, half an hour to remove: twenty-two working days just getting in and out of disguise. Against this the other major statistics of the film – the employment of 3,500 actors, 2,500 wigs, and 1,500 flaming torches – seem small.

More original was *Dr Cyclops* (1940), except to those who remembered *Devil Doll*. Albert Dekker, bald and pebble-lensed, was mad Dr Thorkel up the Amazon without a scruple, shrinking a troupe of small-part actors even smaller. With Ernest B. Schoedsack directing, domed Dekker, a tiny Janice Logan in his hand, more than resembled a clean-shaven Kong. But he goes down in horror history as the first monster in full, glorious Technicolor.

There were more remakes to come. MGM did *Dr Jekyll and Mr Hyde* (1941) with style, as befitted the man who directed *Gone With the Wind*. Victor Fleming showed Spencer Tracy's transformation through a symbolic, surrealistic montage created by Peter Ballbusch. Universal composed a new *Phantom of the Opera* (1943) with Claude Rains disfigured in Technicolor, a process which came in as a surprise climax to MGM's *The Picture of Dorian Gray* (1945): handsome Hurd Hatfield corrupted to match his portrait as painted by the Albright Brothers. Accelerated ageing, once the prerogative of *She*, put an end to Nils Asther and his dreams of eternity: a familiar finale to the otherwise unfamiliar *The Man in Half Moon Street* (1944).

The British Board of Film Censors, long bothered by the horror film, had finally introduced a new category. Their certification system was changed for the first time since 1913. It became three-tier: 'U' for Universal (children alone), 'A' for Adult (children and adults), 'H' for Horrific (over-sixteens only). Ironically, the 'H' came in just as horror films went out. Beginning 1 January 1937, all Lord Tyrell of Avon could find fit to certify was Dame May Whitty in MGM's straight remake of *The Thirteenth Chair* (1937). But should a new age dawn, the BBFC would not be found wanting. And dawn it duly did; yet studios found the 'H' was no escape clause. Horror films were out, gone by the Board for the duration as liable to cause alarm and despondency. Those that did slip on to the circuits were mutilated beyond the dreams of their own mad doctors.

At Universal, history was repeating itself in a more personal way. Under the old regime, the studio had been a home-from-home for German film-makers. Now it was proving a haven again. But this time the refugees chose the studio rather than the other way round. They were driven out by Hitler, not lured forth by Laemmle. Curt, sometimes Kurt, occasionally Curtis, Siodmak was a Dresden-born writer of science-fiction films. In time he would become the most prolific scripter in Hollywood horror. Joe May, Viennese veteran, had been making pictures since 1911 (he had directed Fritz Lang's first scenario, it will be recalled). May's first Universal assignment was a remake of Leni's *Last Warning*, adapted by Peter Milne as *The House of Fear* (1939). Now May and Siodmak were brought together in typical Hollywood fashion: they were given a story set in provincial England. It was Universal's second

Family Likeness: *Son of Frankenstein* (Universal 1938) was Basil Rathbone as the offspring of Colin Clive and Mae Clarke, or possibly Valerie Hobson, both of whom had played Elizabeth Frankenstein. Karloff remained the Monster, in care of Ygor (Bela Lugosi, *below*). This crooked shepherd presumably provided Karloff's sheepskin liberty-bodice. Ygor cared for the Monster like a brother, which relationship was claimed by Karloff to Rathbone (*left*).

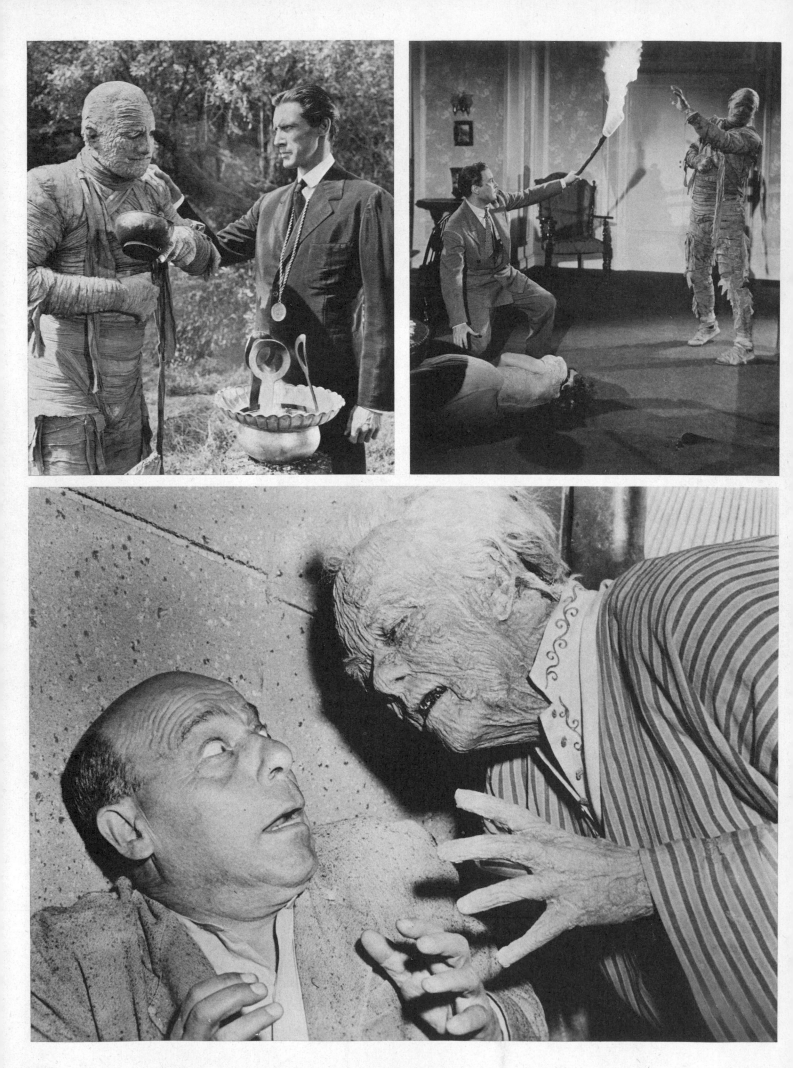

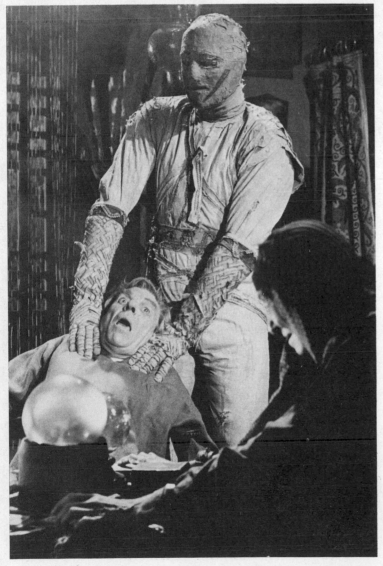

Mummy's Boys: From out of the archives of ancient Egypt and ancient Universal came Karloff's *The Mummy*. This 1932 classic sparked off a saga, beginning in 1940 with *The Mummy's Hand* (*above*). Ageing cowboy hero Tom Tyler was unrecognizable to his fans as 3,000-year-old Kharis. Lon Chaney Jr took over as the series unwound with *The Mummy's Tomb* (1942; *opposite top right*) and *The Mummy's Ghost* (1944; *opposite top left*). As a handy monster the mummy continues to thrill. *Pharaoh's Curse* (Bel-Air 1956; *opposite below*) introduced ancient Alvaro Guilliot, and Eddie Powell bore bandages bravely in *The Mummy's Shroud* (Hammer 1967; *left*).

129

Monster Made Man: *Man Made Monster* (Universal 1941; *opposite left and right*) made Lon Chaney Jr. Lionel Atwill turned him into *The Electric Man*, which was the British release title of the film. (Censors disapproved of the word 'monster'.) Chaney was given a glow by effects specialist John P. Fulton, and by Universal's contracts department. Billed as 'The Master Character Creator' he went into *The Wolf Man* (1941) and *The Ghost of Frankenstein* (1942; *right*). Bela Lugosi returned as Ygor and Sir Cedric Hardwicke turned up as a surprising second son of the original experimenter (*below*). Outside the Universal saga was *Lady Frankenstein* (Condor 1971; *below right*) in which the Baron's daughter makes her own Monster to kill her father's creation.

130

exhumation of the second wave of horror, *The Invisible Man Returns* (1939).

Jack Griffin had well and truly died; death had been the antidote to his invisibility. No man-made creation he, there could be no possible resurrection beyond the cheat of the title. Following the family formula of the Frankensteins, Curt Siodmak created for Griffin a brother. Frank has continued the experiments of John, gone these nine (!) years. Indeed, he has so improved upon monocaine that it is now called duocaine! However, the film is still the mixture as before. The Invisible One dons bandages and black goggles, then peels them off to scare a confession from Sir Cedric Hardwicke, the man who framed him for murder. There are comical cockneys, posses of police, and the traditional hint of unhinged opportunism. John P. Fulton was back at the Special Effects, adding to his triumphs of old by showing what had only been talked of before: the Invisible Man outlined by a puff of pipe-smoke or shining in the rain.

History repeated indeed, and in other ways: the rehashed plot was a box-office burster and the sinister tones of the Invisible One, with his climactic materialization, created a new star. It was Vincent Price's initiation into a field he would finally dominate. His christening had been in a butt of malmsey: club-footed Karloff drowned him therein in Rowland Lee's historical horror, *Tower of London* (1939). But Price's ambition as an actor went beyond monster makeup; and when Universal spun the Man into a series, Jon Hall took over.

Invisible Agent (1942) was Curt Siodmak's contribution to the war effort. Incensed by the bombing of Pearl Harbor, Frank Griffin (Hall) offers his invisible abilities to the nation. Parachuting into Berlin he foils Sir Cedric Hardwicke's plan to invade America, escapes from Peter Lorre's net of fish-hooks, and materializes in the arms of Ilona Massey. *The Invisible Man's Revenge* (1944) had no visible continuity save Hall and his surname of Griffin. He played Robert of that ilk, usurped from his inheritance by one Sir Jasper. In the woods lives John Carradine, who has discovered the secret of invisibility and has a transparent Great Dane to prove it. The invisible Griffin terrorizes Sir Jasper, scares Evelyn Ankers, and materializes by draining Carradine's blood into his own veins. The Great Dane kills him before he can drain Alan Curtis, too.

What the New Universal really needed was the New Karloff, the New Chaney. He was around; currently he was over at the Hal Roach studio, fighting a dinosaur.

One Million BC (1940) was an epic affair for the hitherto chronicler of Laurel and Hardy. Although both Roach and son shared directorial credit on the finished picture, it was actually the work of an illustrious other. D.W. Griffith, the architect of American cinema, had been first in the field of animated monsters back in 1913. His experimental *Wars of the Primal Tribes* was eventually released by Biograph as *The Primitive Man*. Neglected by Hollywood since the failure of *The Struggle* (1931),

Griffith was encouraged out of alcoholic oblivion by Roach's plan to adapt Eugene Roche's novel of prehistoric life. Griffith's treatment, called 'When Man Began', created a complete language for the cavemen. Perhaps the idea of using living monsters instead of animated models was Griffith's too. Did he prefer the reality of photographically enlarged, fancy-dressed animals to the *King Kong* concept – or was it an inspiration of the economy-minded Roach? At any rate, these battling beasts, blown-up and slowed-down by Roy Seawright and Frank Young, were real enough in their gore to upset the American Society for the Prevention of Cruelty to Animals – which included dinosaurs when they were dressed-up lizards. With a new ban upon

Dinosaur or Dynamation? Less than an aeon separated *One Million BC* (Roach 1940; *below*) from its remake, *One Million Years BC* (Hammer 1966; *left*), yet its technique differed vastly. Griffith made live monsters by sticking fins on lizards. Chaffey used models animated by Ray Harryhausen.

similar goings-on, producers plundered this prehistoric piece, renting the monsters by the yard to back-project behind their own actors. It became the most-seen sequence in movie history, turning up in *Two Lost Worlds* (1950), *Untamed Women* (1952), *Robot Monster* (1953), *King Dinosaur* (1954), *Valley of the Dragons* (1961), to name but a few. The original picture had several titles, too: Britain saw it as *Man and his Mate* and a reissue, shorn of the present-day prologue, was called *The Cave Dwellers*. But more importantly, *One Million BC* gave the world a new Lon Chaney: Lon Chaney Jr.

The dying star beckoned his young son to his side. He reached out for his battered makeup box, took up a stick of greasepaint, and shakily scrawled something on the lid. He fell back dead. The son looked at the box. After the engraved name, 'Lon Chaney', was written 'junior'. Tears came; music swelled; 'The End'. Thus the legend of Hollywood as laid down by Universal's *Man of a Thousand Faces* (1957). The reality was somewhat different.

In 1922 the sixteen-year-old Creighton Tull Chaney told his father he wanted to become an actor. The star not only refused, he took the boy out of Hollywood High and packed him off to business college. When Lon Chaney died eight years later, he was happy in the knowledge that his son was on his way to becoming boss of the General Water Heater Corporation. 'But', as Junior said, 'the ham was there.' In 1932 Radio Pictures tested him, then signed him. When Selznick asked him to change his name to Lon Chaney Jr (it was the time of the horror boom) he refused, and it was as Creighton Chaney, that he starred in a Western serial, *The Last Frontier* (1932). The career of the smiling young husky with the Brylcreemed hair and teeth to match followed his father's in the wrong way: in the same way. For years he played whatever came along: heavies and heroes, characters and bits, even extra work. In 1937 he did change his name to Lon Chaney Jr – 'They starved me into it' – but still the big break did not come. He tested for his father's part in RKO's *Hunchback* but, fortunately, lost out to Laughton.

In 1939 John Steinbeck's 'Of Mice and Men' moved from Broadway to Los Angeles. Broderick Crawford left the play to make a film, leaving the part of Lennie open to comers. Chaney auditioned and thus made his debut in the theatre; he was tremendous. When Lewis Milestone came to make the movie, Chaney was tested and won again. His hulking simpleton was the definitive, murderous moron: like Victor McLaglen's *Informer*, Lon's Lennie stands alone – a limited actor's finest hour. Hal Roach produced and quickly signed Chaney for *One Million BC*. As Akhoba, leader of the Rock People, Junior truly proved worthy of his name. Bearded and bloodied, gored by a prehistoric musk-ox, he snarled and stomped and stole the film from the stars, pretty Carole Landis and prettier Victor Mature. But there was one major change from the Chaney of old. Where the elder had created his own characters, the younger did not. Even were Universal's biography true, Lon Jr could not have used Lon Sr's old box of tricks. For now the makeup men had a union; and Ben Madsen did the job.

Meanwhile Jack Pierce, the Universal monster-maker, was looking out the bandages. The studio, continuing its revivalist mission, had excavated Im-Ho-Tep. A run-through of Freund's moody *Mummy* had revealed a romance unsuited to the fast-paced taste of the forties. It also revealed a waste: Karloff's mummified monster had walked in but one short scene. Griffin Jay, a writer of radio mysteries, elaborated that single sequence into a whole new mythos.

The Mummy's Hand (1940) was economical yet looked expensive, thanks to its use of the temple set from *Green Hell*. It also used the entire foggy flashback of Karloff's incarceration, filtering it through the Waters of Khar as Eduardo Cianelli, High Priest of Karnak, quaveringly indoctrinated acolyte George Zucco. Im-Ho-Tep has changed his name to Kharis. No longer a High Priest, he is a Prince in love with Princess Ananka. When she dies he steals not the Scroll of Thoth, but the forbidden tana leaves, the juice of which will revive the dead. Caught, he is buried alive as ever, but with one refinement –

'they cut out his tongue so the ears of the Gods would not be assailed by his unholy curses.'

There is more: the awful responsibility borne by each successive High Priest is to keep Kharis alive. The fluid brewed from three tana leaves must be fed to him once a night during the cycle of the full moon. Should unbelievers seek to desecrate Ananka's tomb, the dose must be tripled. This will give her guardian power to move, to obey, to avenge. As howls echo round the Hill of the Seven Jackals ('Children of the night' smiles Cianelli; another echo), Zucco is sworn in. In no time he is

RDIGAN'S
NS OUTFITTERS

Chaney's Baby: 'He was my baby' is how Lon Chaney Jr affectionately refers to Lawrence Stewart Talbot the unlucky Llanwellyan. This lycanthrope loped through five films, from *The Wolf Man* (Universal 1941; *opposite top left and right*) to a fatal encounter with Abbott and Costello. *Above*, he appears in *Frankenstein Meets the Wolf Man* (Universal 1943), also *opposite below*, where he is seen between full moons, thawing out Bela Lugosi. That ageing Hungarian had been tested for the original monster in the original *Frankenstein*, but had turned it down. Now a decade later he was happy to take on the heavy makeup as long as stunt-man Eddie Parker took on the heavy duties.

brewing up as unbelievers come a-desecrating in the shape of Dick Foran and Peggy Moran.

The horrible ragbag of rot that limped and groped and bore away into the night was a handsome man called Tom Tyler, a cowboy star from the silent days. No name now, he filled the bill by his uncanny resemblance to the cadaverous Karloff of eight years before. But Tyler was no new Karloff in the star sense. Nor could ever be. There was horrible truth in his crippled Kharis: once athletic, Tyler was in the grip of arthritis.

Universal's second generation of monsters was making money; what they needed was a second-generation star. At last the Old Gods of Universal City smiled on Lon Chaney Jr, and he was signed to a five-year contract, back on the lot where he saw his father star. Down from the shelf came a script written for Karloff and Lugosi. It had never been used: it was too much like *The Invisible Ray*. Now with Chaney as Karloff as Big Dan McCormick, and Atwill as Lugosi as mad Dr Rigas, *Man Made Monster* (1941) came stomping into the cinemas (except in England, where it proved too much of a title: censorship switched it to *The Electric Man*, its far-back original).

Sole survivor when a bus crashes into an electric pylon is Dynamo Dan the Electrical Man. This cheery carnival exhibit intrigues Dr Rigas, eccentric electro-biologist, whose theory is that ever-increasing charges of electricity will both preserve and motivate life, and thus create a race of controllable supermen. Duly dosed, Dan glows in the dark. A walking shell, he bears Anne Nagel into the night. His rubber suit catches on a barbed-wire fence, the electricity leaks out, and he shrinks to smouldering ash.

Good, typical stuff, but Jack Pierce's makeup was considered insufficiently monstrous. He had wrinkled Chaney's face by applying cotton to his stretched skin, then letting it relax into wrinkles. John P. Fulton took the completed film and put a pulsing glow on. It was the finishing touch, and Chaney emerged as a truly man-made monster. As if to seal his career, on 11 December 1940 he attended a ceremony. On the great set of the Paris Opéra, five survivors of the original crew unveiled a plaque. It read: 'Dedicated to the memory of Lon Chaney, for whose picture *The Phantom of the Opera* this stage was erected in 1924.' Chaney was dead, yet Chaney lived. From his very next picture Universal dropped Junior's 'Jr': only in movies could the dead truly come back to life.

'Even a man who is pure in heart,
And says his prayers by night,
May become a wolf when the wolfbane blooms
And the Autumn moon is bright.'

It wasn't so much the moon that turned Lon Chaney into *The Wolf Man* (1941), or even a bite from Bela Lugosi. It was a six-hour sit in the make-up chair while Jack Pierce painstakingly pasted him over with yak-hair and stranded kelp. Wearing a T-shaped nosepiece of moulded rubber, fangs on his teeth, hair in his palms, and feet tippy-toed into padded paws, Chaney knew what it was to suffer the curse of the pentagram. Small wonder Evelyn Ankers screamed at the sight, so frightfully well that this Chile-born English lass became the second First Lady of Horror, finally tucking more monster movies under her girdle than even Fay Wray. But Pierce's processing was only the beginning of Chaney's ordeal. Worse even than the nightly eat-off with acetone was the great transformation scene organized by Pierce, Fulton, and Joseph Valentine the photographer.

'The day we did the transformations I came in at two a.m. When I hit that position they would take little nails and drive them through the skin at the edge of my fingers, on both hands, so that I wouldn't move them any more. While I was in this position they would build a plaster cast of the back of my head. Then they would take the drapes from behind me and starch them, and while they were drying them, they would take the camera and weigh it down with one ton, so that it wouldn't quiver when people walked. They had targets for my eyes up there. Then, while I'm still in this position, they would shoot five or ten frames of film in the camera. They'd take that film out and send it to the lab. While it was there the makeup man would come and take the whole thing off my face, and put on a new one, only less. I'm still immobile. When the film came back from the lab they'd put it back in the camera and then they'd check me. They'd say, "Your eyes have moved a little bit, move them to the right . . . now your shoulder is up. . . ." Then they'd roll it again and shoot another ten frames. Well, we did twenty-one changes of makeup and it took twenty-two hours. I won't discuss about the bathroom!'

Yet for all that, Chaney loved his Wolf Man: 'He was my baby!' Although an unlikely choice for an English heir (he plays Lawrence Stewart, son of Sir John Talbot of Llanwelly, Wales), with an unlikely star for a father (Chaney towered a good foot over Claude Rains), he did the double in the best Jekyll and Hyde tradition. *The Wolf Man*, a title originally announced for Karloff in 1932, sprang from the monster makeup of *Werewolf of London*. It also had that film's plot twist of the two werewolves. Lugosi, aptly cast as Bela, played the biter, but Chaney soon killed him with his silver-handled cane. Maleva the mother who crooned the rune had more to say, over her son's corpse, and over Larry's later. 'The way you walk is thorny through no fault of your own. For as the rain enters the soil, and evil enters the sea, so tears run to their predestined end. Your suffering is over. Now find peace for eternity, my son.' Fine words, written by Curt Siodmak, intoned by an ex-star of the Moscow Art Theatre, Madame Maria Ouspenskaya. But they still failed to end Chaney's suffering.

'They cast me as the Frankenstein Monster. It took four hours to make me up. Then they led me to the set. They dug a hole in the cliff and put me in. They stuck a straw in my mouth and covered me up with cement. It took till twelve o'clock to

Rise and Shine: Charles Laughton in *The Hunchback of Notre Dame* (RKO 1939; *above*); *The Mummy* (Universal 1932).

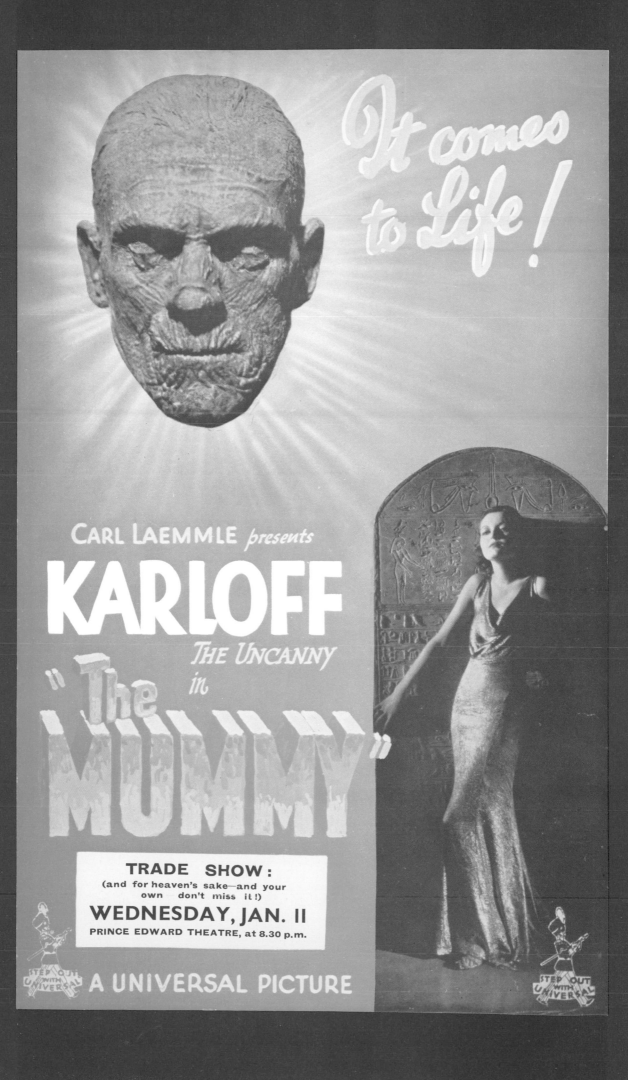

The story starts where *Son* leaves off as Dwight Frye dynamites the Frankenstein castle. Rising from the ruins comes, inexplicably, Ygor (Lugosi). He excavates the Monster from his pit of sulphur. Last seen bubbling at 800 degrees, the stuff is now as dry as dust. In a splendid scene the stumbling Monster renews his strength in a storm: his mother, the lightning, strikes at his neck electrodes. Then it's off for Vasaria and Dr Ludwig, whose determination to dissect the Monster is undone by a visitation from his father's ghost: 'Would you destroy that which I dedicated my life to creating? Unknowingly I gave it a criminal brain. With your knowledge of science you can cure that.' Inspired, Ludwig plans to transplant the brain of the late kindly Dr Kettering. But he reckons without Ygor, who has found an evil soulmate in Ludwig's assistant, Lionel Atwill. When the Monster revives on the operating table he speaks with Ygor's voice: 'I have the strength of a hundred men! I, Ygor, will live for ever!' Ludwig is horrified: 'The crime of my father is now mine, but a thousandfold!' he cries as the Monster thrashes around the laboratory. But nature prevails: the Monster goes blind. 'What good is a brain without eyes?' he screams, flinging Atwill into a generator. The lab roars into flames, a beam falls on the Monster, his face begins to blister, and Ralph Bellamy speedily escorts Evelyn Ankers towards the rising sun.

'The New Master Character Creator', as Chaney was billed, was promptly put under wraps: the 400 yards of tattered gauze vacated by Tom Tyler. Chaney was so painted over by Pierce with liquidized Fuller's Earth, so caked with cracked beauty clay, that even a High Priest of Karnak would have been hard put to tell the difference. Kharis, who last went to blazes in overturned oil, limped unsinged in *The Mummy's Tomb* (1942), animated as much by the call of the box office as by the juice of the tana leaves. The film was short on thrills but long on economy: Pierce fashioned a mask that saved a deal of makeup time. It also helped stuntman Edwin Parker look like Chaney look like Tyler look like Karloff, for once again the Waters of Khar unfold with their flashbacks. This time they take in clips from *The Mummy's Hand*, too, as George Zucco passes on the tana leaves to Turhan Bey. Thirty years have elapsed since that last outing, and this time Kharis turns up in Mapleton, Massachusetts, to bring the anger of the Ancient Gods upon the greying Dick Foran. Turhan Bey's plan to enrol lovely Elyse Knox as his Priestess is foiled by fire: the village mob with

get me sealed in. Then everybody went to lunch!'

The Ghost of Frankenstein (1942) was released on Friday the 13th, a lucky day for Universal. The picture had been a great gamble. Karloff had forsworn the Monster for mad doctor roles more in keeping with his advancing dignity; Basil Rathbone was now totally identified as the movies' Sherlock Holmes. Rathbone's role of Wolf was rewritten for Sir Cedric Hardwicke and called Ludwig, Frankenstein's second son and Doctor of the Mind.

Karloff's Monster remained unchanged, except by Chaney. Jack Pierce tried to mould him into a Karloff, but the taller, thicker, jowlier man remained a hulking Lennie, a flat-topped, jutbrowed brute of a mute. His performance has robotic power, but lacks soul, even a man-made one.

Monster Posters: *King Kong* was still called *Kong* when RKO first advertised it in January 1933, and was still the mighty yardstick when Nikkatsu advertised *Gappa* in 1967. *Above*, the first coupling of *Dracula* and *Frankenstein* in 1938.

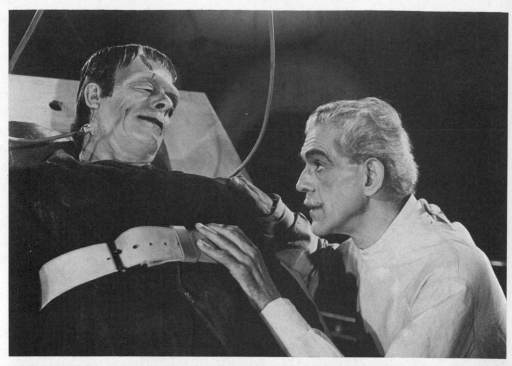

Monsters Meet: Boris Karloff, too old to wear the makeup, came face to face with himself in *House of Frankenstein* (Universal 1944; *right*). Glenn Strange, a B-western 'heavy', wore an adaptation of Jack Pierce's original Karloffian conception. Found frozen (*below*), Strange later survived a climatic quicksand to be revived again in *House of Dracula* (Universal 1945; *below right*). He failed to survive his obligatory encounter with Abbott and Costello.

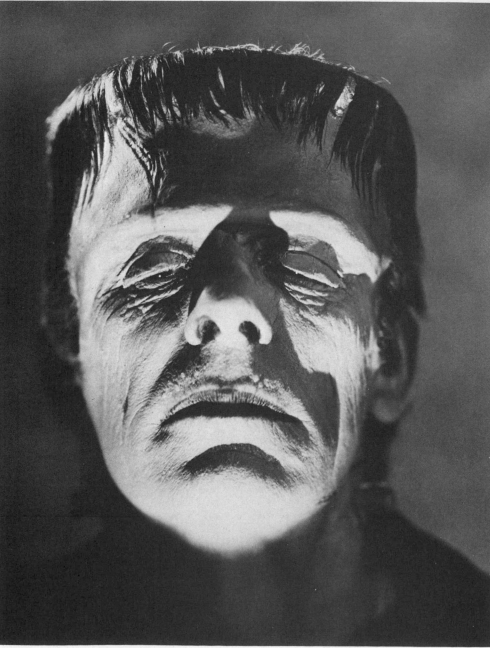

their flaming torches is a familiar climax – spliced in from *Frankenstein*! Chaney, who hated his Mummy as much as he loved his Baby, unwound by playing Larry Talbot again.

Frankenstein Meets the Wolf Man (1942) was conceived as a battle of the giants. The idea was vintage Laemmle: instead of teaming stars, team monsters. But Universal had set themselves a problem; both the Frankenstein Monster and the Wolf Man had last been played by the same actor, Lon Chaney. Chaney would let no one else play his Baby, so who to cast for the Monster? The problem was soon solved. Lugosi's part in the saga, Ygor, was now dead, his brain in the Monster's head, his voice in the Monster's mouth. What more natural than have Lugosi play the Monster? If he was still recognizable under Pierce's makeup, then that was simply Ygor showing through! Besides, there was an element of destiny that the fans would not have forgotten. Lugosi had rejected the original role twelve years earlier. Lugosi could no longer afford to be so choosy. He brought to the Monster his own curious interpretation, a hissing evil that snarled through the makeup. His stretch-armed strutting seems senseless in context, yet was not so in shooting. For as filmed Lugosi's Monster is blind as a bat. Pre-release shortening by the studio removed the reason for Lugosi's climactic close-upped smile: Patric Knowles has not only restored the Monster's strength, but his sight, too!

Larry Talbot finds the Monster entombed in ice beneath the ruins of Frankenstein's home in Vasaria. The Wolf Man has wended from Wales in care of old Maleva, hopeful that the late scientist's records may reveal a release. His curse has apparently overcome the permanent death dealt him by Claude Rains and his silver-headed cane. Baroness Elsa (Ilona Massey replacing Evelyn Ankers), to thwart Patric Knowles' plan, pulls a well-remembered lever. The apparatus explodes, the Monster goes berserk, the werewolf changes, the villagers blast the dam, the young couple flee, the water crashes down, and the castle caves in. That left Chaney, the Universal Monster, one to go for full house.

Son of Dracula (1943) saw Chaney with no make-up other than a moustache, a relaxing change. But his well-fed face was out of place in an undead vampire who lived on blood. Quick-witted J. Edward Bromberg unravels the anagrammatical Anthony Alucard, newly arrived from Budapest as guest of Louise Allbritton, heiress to the Louisiana plantation of Dark Oaks. Metaphysic-ally minded, she is soon under his spell, and if it hadn't been for Robert Paige finding the Count's coffin down a drain, Evelyn Ankers would have been bitten, too. Curt Siodmak, who had fathered Chaney's Baby, wrote this one, and brought along his brother to direct. In his three-week schedule, Robert Siodmak found time to visualize one nice touch: Alucard's coffin bobs to the surface of a lagoon, the vampire materializes from smoke within, and glides to shore in this spooky punt.

For Chaney the vacation was over. In 1944 it was back to the bandages, twice. *The Mummy's Ghost* had Zucco back with the flashbacks as John Carradine took over the High Priesthood of Arkan (anagrams were in fashion). The mummy of Princess Ananka is on show at the Mapleton Museum. One touch from her devoted Kharis and she crumbles away. Her soul has been reincarnated in Amina El Harun, a local girl. Kharis abducts her for embalming, but Carradine tries to tempt her into tasting the tana leaves. Kharis kills Carradine and stomps off with his girl. Ananka, like Ayesha of old, ages rapidly and the eternal lovers sink blissfully into a swamp.

The Mummy's Curse (1944) was released eight months later yet begins '25 years later!' Peter Coe is the new High Priest and he has a familiar tale to tell Martin Kosleck. The swamp has been drained and Kharis is back on the tana leaves. Ananka has also emerged, this time as Virginia Christine. Kharis carries her off to an abandoned monastery, which he promptly brings down upon everybody's heads. It was the end of a saga, if not of an era. Yet that, too, was closer than either Chaney or Universal thought.

'All Together! The Screen's Titans of Terror!' There could be no complaints about that catchline for *House of Frankenstein* (1944). Curt Siodmak's script reunited the Monster and the Wolf Man, revived Dracula, and more: it brought back Boris Karloff. With other stalwarts of the form in smaller roles, J. Carrol Naish as an evil hunch-back, Lionel Atwill as Inspector Arnz, even George Zucco, the film only missed on one count: Bela Lugosi. Dracula went to long John Carradine, a superbly spoken fellow far more cadaverous than his 'son'. Continuity went astray for him, for when last seen Dracula was being cremated at Whitby. Now he materialized upon his skeleton in Zucco's Chamber of Horrors, in top hat, white tie and tails. He also flapped into an outsize bat, animated by John P. Fulton, and died at dawn, reaching for his coffin as the sun dissolved the flesh from his bones.

Monster Funsters: The Frankenstein Monster was created by Universal, survived because of Universal, and continues to survive despite Universal. Edwin Parker first played him for laughs in *Hellzapoppin'* (1941; *opposite top left*), and Glenn Strange caught mermaid Ann Blyth (*opposite below*) on the set of *Abbott and Costello Meet Frankenstein* (1948; *opposite top right*). Lou Costello met both Monster and Dracula in *Abbott and Costello Meet Dr Jekyll and Mr Hyde* (1953), and ultimately Universal cast Fred Gwynne in the Karloff mould for *Munster Go Home* (1966). Yvonne De Carlo was Lily to Fred's Herman (*right*).

Bud **ABBOTT** & Lou **COSTELLO**
MEET DR. JEKYLL & MR. HYDE
CO-STARRING
BORIS KARLOFF CERT. X
A UNIVERSAL-INTERNATIONAL PICTURE   G.F.D. RELEASE

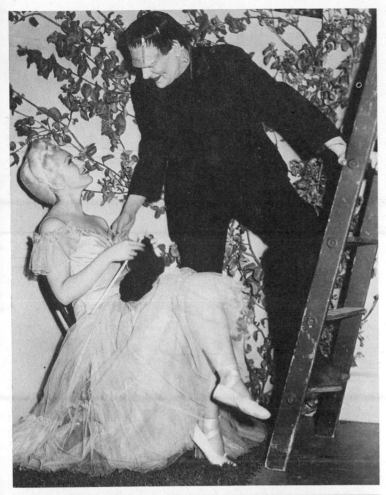

Karloff was the prime mover as Dr Gustav Niemann, animal experimenter, escaping from Neustadt jail to find Wolf Man and Monster ('Triumphant climax of Frankenstein's genius!') deep-frozen beneath the ruins. First to be thawed is an ungrateful Chaney. 'Neath the light of the full moon he changes again and is suitably shot with a silver bullet 'fired by the hand of one who loves him' (Elena Verdugo). The Monster is climactically revived by Niemann and his 100,000 mega-volts. The flashing this requires brings the villagers out with their flaming torches, and they chase him into a handy bog.

The new Monster, the fourth, might have been Lane Chandler, a Western heavy on the Universal payroll. Instead his pardner got the job when Jack Pierce found a more suitable facial contour on Glenn Strange. This big fellow, once a wolfman himself in *The Mad Monster* (1941), had little to offer the role beyond his contour. But he had the world's best teacher by his side.

'Nobody ever helped anybody as much as Boris Karloff helped me. I never forget that. I asked him for advice because I wanted to do this thing as near as he did. He would stay on the set and coach me on the walk and the movements and so forth.'

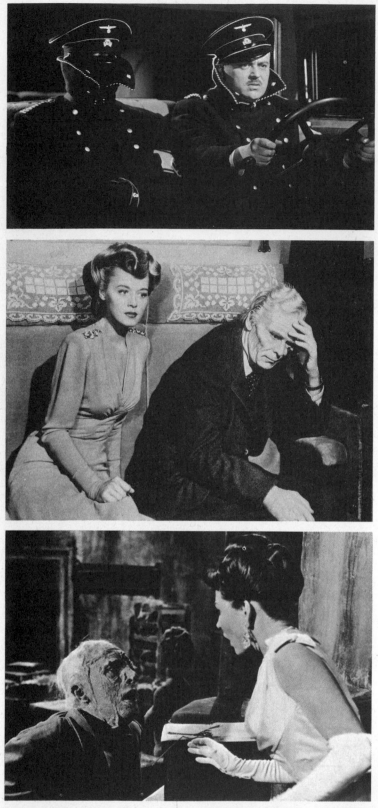

'His physical processes give way to self-hypnotism. His glands generate certain hormones which bring about the physical changes. There is a crowding of the brain because the cranial cavity failed to enlarge sufficiently.'

Edelmann cures Larry's lycanthropy by using a home-grown mould to soften and reshape his cranium. Edelmann had a cure for vampirism, too, an antibody to consume the strange parasites he isolated in Dracula's blood. Carradine was back for the Count in *House of Dracula* (1945), his coffin secreted in Edelmann's cellar. Unfortunately Edelmann's blood-transfusion backfires and he gets a dose of the parasites. Unlike the gentlemanly Dracula (who becomes bones in the sun again) Edelmann turns into a fiendish vampire, laughing as he revives the Monster, found dormant in the Devil's Hole. Larry shoots Edelmann, the lab catches fire, and the Monster is hit on the head by his third beam. Tighter scripted than the previous pot-pourri, Edward T. Lowe intertwining the devil's brood where Curt Siodmak had opted for episodes, the film created an excellent new character in the Jekyll/Hyde fiend of Onslow Stevens. Yet it missed something: sincerity perhaps? love perhaps? Karloff perhaps?

Glenn Strange strode again in what proved to be Jack Pierce's last monster makeup.

'When I had the makeup on I had trouble seeing, because the Monster's eyelids hung over my eyes. The makeup made my face raw. The skull cap I wore was so tight it wouldn't let the perspiration out. After a couple of hours I could shake my head and the water would rattle round inside.'

The rattle Strange heard was a death rattle. *House of Dracula* was the last of its line, the end of the Second Generation of the horror film. Not a Golden Age, perhaps a Silver Bullet Age, certainly a Universal Age. The Old Gods put their unholy five out to pasture, Dracula, Monster, Mummy, Wolfman, Invisible Man: Chaney had played them all but one. Like true immortals they would rise again, but as shadows of their former glory. The comeback would come, but it would be just for fun.

Side By Side: Jon Hall took a day off when this still was shot for *Invisible Agent* (Universal 1942; *top*). *The Man In Half Moon Street* (Paramount 1944; *centre*) was Nils Asther, whose age suddenly caught up with him. The surprise of Helen Walker was nothing to the shock of Hazel Court when the same thing happened to Anton Diffring (*bottom*): *The Man Who Could Cheat Death* (1959) was a Hammer film. *Opposite:* corruption keeps Hurd Hatfield young but ages his portrait: *The Picture of Dorian Gray* (MGM 1945).

Have pity for Lawrence Stewart Talbot, reluctant werewolf. He sought blessed rest and found none. Universal legend decreed that holy silver would bring death, but Universal Studio legend was a law unto itself. Dr Franz Edelmann was summoned to Vasaria Prison by Inspector Holz (Lionel Atwill). There in a cell stood mad Larry, moonlight in his eyes, yak-hair on his cheeks. Edelmann, whose creed was 'Science against sorcery', took Talbot to his castle laboratory for examination.

THE CURSE OF THE 'B' PEOPLE

In which Karloff takes his mad doctorate, Lugosi takes the money, Cat People take over, and Katzman takes the cake.

The German horror film had been cursed by the *doppelgänger*; the American horror film was cursed by the Double Bill. Every big picture had to have a little picture in support. Every 'A' must have its 'B': it was a Hollywood law as immutable as any of Amon-Ra's. And when the major studios couldn't make enough 'B's of their own, the minors rushed in and filled the bill. Soon the horror film became as regular on the release roster as the mystery or the Western, with characters as predictable as Charlie Chan or the Bowery Boys.

'Greater than *Frankenstein* say the critics!' They said it, apparently, of *The Monster Walks* (1932), but Mayfair Pictures carefully named no names. The first of the 'B's, this was also the first of the 'H''B's: blue-pencilled by the British Censor until he had introduced his Horror Certificate. Dated in style to start with, by then the poor little picture was so passé that the conscience-stricken distributor retitled it *The Monster Walked*. Hanns Krug, maniac, binding a scientist's daughter to a post, lashing Yogi the Ape to a fury, and strangling his own mother by mistake, brought laughs, some of them unwitting. Clutching Hanns was played by Mischa Auer, who in the years between had changed his line to mad Russians of a different bent.

Bela Lugosi had been the first modern horror star, and he was the first to be cursed by the 'B' people. In 1933 Harry Cohn's Columbia studio was less than major. They made their 'A' pictures in three weeks, and a *Night of Terror* (1933) was scarcely 'A'. Still, it had Lugosi, which is more than Columbia could say for their next, *The Ninth Guest* (1934).

Boris Karloff, too, felt the sting of the 'B's, but by the time he clocked in at Columbia there was a little more honey to be had. *The Black Room* (1935) was almost an 'A', by Columbia's standards at any rate. Karloff in costume played good-and-bad twins, which stretched his talent but not the budget. It was at Columbia, later, that Karloff starred as *The Man They Could Not Hang* (1939), a quickie more significant than it sounds.

Karloff played Dr Henryk Savaard, inventor of a mechanical heart. This was an elaboration on the genuine invention of Charles A. Lindbergh and Alexis Carrell, which had already been improved upon by Edmund Gwenn. Gwenn had revived Karloff with it in *The Walking Dead* (1936). Now Karloff himself was having a go. Unable to lay his hands on a convenient corpse, he dispatches a volunteer. Unhappily the resurrection is interrupted by police, and in consequence Karloff is hanged. However, his assistant has his instructions, and soon Karloff is up and about again. Unfortunately, but not perhaps unexpectedly, the experience has unhinged his mind and he can think only of electrical vengeance. The crackling climax kills his daughter, but he revives her, proving it all worthwhile. Then Karloff dies again, taking his secret with him.

Nick Grinde, a brisk man with a 'B', and Karl Brown, a once-famed director turned writer, here found a formula of their own. Like that of Lindbergh-Carrell, the Grinde-Brown formula injected new life into the horror film at a period when, save for the time-to-time extravaganza, the big studios were letting it die. The Columbia Karloffs were so similar that they became known in the trade as the Mad Doctor Series. For no matter how outlandish a name they gave him, how bizarre a line of research, or how grand a finale, by the next 'B' picture Karloff was back in business, all eyebrows and British lisp, raising the dead, tampering with nature, injecting serums, switching switches, pulling fatal levers, and generally meddling with that which man should leave alone. In short, Karloff was Karloff: the continuity was not in the character, but in the star.

Karloff practised next as Dr Leon Kravaal, *The Man With Nine Lives* (1940). In England he lost six

The Brute Man Cometh: Rondo Hatton as *The Brute Man* (Universal 1946).

Present Arms: Jean Cocteau's fantastic image of living limbs, used in *Beauty and the Beast* (1945), is handed down through the horror film. The clutching hands of Karloff's *Bedlam* (RKO 1946; *below*) match the sawn-off sword-arms of *Jack the Giant Killer* (Small 1961; *right*).

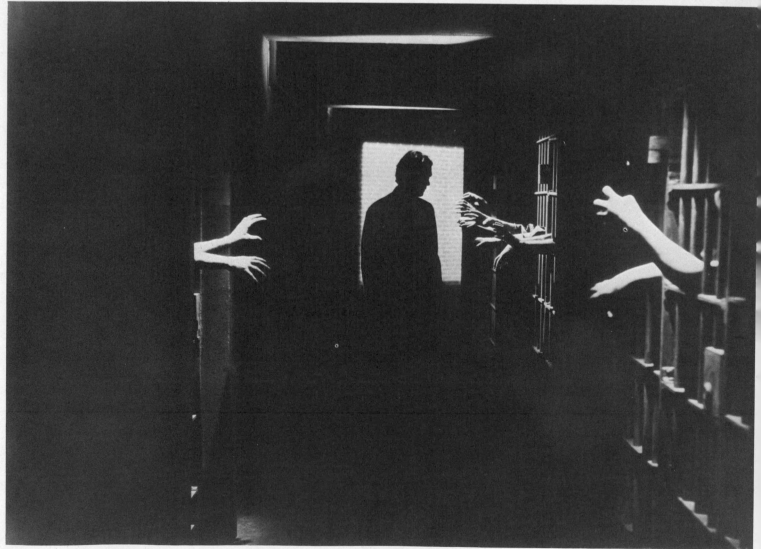

minutes of them at the hands of the censor. Then they sent it out as *Behind the Door*. Found frozen in an ice chamber on Crater Island, Karloff is thawed from his ten-year deep-freeze, living proof that 'frozen therapy' cures cancer. Unhappily, unbelievers unhinge him and he has to be shot. Karloff turns his notes over to Roger Pryor and dies, 'happy in the consciousness that his great labour will be carried on'. But it was a case of carry on Karloff. As Dr John Garth he was back in the Columbia laboratory, seeking a 'cure for death'. This time the title was *Before I Hang* (1940). A serum of human blood, injected direct into the heart, restores the twinkle to Karloff's rheumy eye. Unfortunately it was murderer's blood, so Karloff becomes not only younger, but a strangler to boot. Luckily, Bruce Bennett arrives in time to save Evelyn Keyes for better things.

The Devil Commands (1941) had better things for Karloff: a new director, Edward Dmytryk, and a good book as a basis, 'The Edge of Running Water' by William Sloane. Karloff was Dr Julian Blair who, stormbound in his private power-station, harnessed the living to link with the dead. He failed, but not so badly as the censor's scissors led the British to believe. *The Boogie Man Will Get You* (1942) teamed Karloff with Peter Lorre as Nathaniel Billings and Dr Lorentz. They sent up the series by failing to create an electrical superman out of Slapsie Maxie Rosenbloom. Karloff ended his contract with a smile. It was the last of the medicos.

The Return of the Vampire (1943) was the return of Lugosi. Columbia did the old Count well by casting him as Armand Tesla of Rumania, revived in the London Blitz when Nazi bombs disturb his grave. Workmen mistake the stake in his heart for shrapnel and extract it. Soon he is back in action, fanging Nina Foch, turning Matt Willis into a hairy werewolf, and generally bedevilling Frieda Inescort. Willis rebels and drags the vampire into the sun. A waxen image of Lugosi, moulded over a skeleton, gradually melted: a careful climax completely cut from the British print, despite the censor's award of an 'H'. He had less problems with *Cry of the Werewolf* (1944), in which Nina Foch switched sides. As Celeste La Tour, Queen of the Trioga gypsies, she inherited the crown and the curse from her mother. No shape in wolf's clothing, Miss Foch turned into the real thing: an off-screen transformation upon which film fan frowned but censor smiled. He gave it an 'A'.

So Columbia finished with monsters; but the corpse of the horror film, revived in their laboratory, went

stomping on. In a new direction, down Poverty Row. With a Mad Doctor in charge, all a small studio needed was a little sparky spectacle in the way of stock electrical gadgetry and some low-key lighting (an appealing economy in itself).

Karloff still had his standards: Monogram, yes; PRC no. When Karloff turned down a script from the smaller studios, there was always Lugosi. 'Ecksss-ellent!' he would invariably exclaim as he went about his, and their, fiendish work, happy to take the money and lope.

Karloff was happy enough to make *The Ape* (1940) for Monogram, an Adam Hull Shirk play the firm had filmed as *The House of Mystery* (1934). William Nigh had directed then, and directed again, but could hardly have recognized Curt Siodmak's adaptation. Karloff killed an escaped ape, skinned it, and hid in the hide to ambush villagers and extract their spinal fluid. It was all in a good cause: a cure for paralysis. It was easy work for Karloff, too. Not only could he act mad doctors on his head, once in the ape-suit a double took over! Lugosi clearly took over in the case of *The Devil Bat* (1940): his Dracula tones and suspect sneer hardly fitted the role of 'kindly physician, Paul Carruthers'. In the rushed world of the B-picture there was seldom time for a re-write. This PRC piece had Lugosi creating electrically-enlarged bats, trained to attack anyone wearing Lugosi's lotion, a sinister after-shave. He died by his own bat. Yet for all that, six years later when Rosemary La Planche came to town as *Devil Bat's Daughter* (1946), her fears of 'inherited vampirism' were exposed as the mere machination of a jealous psychiatrist. Worse, she cleared her father's name in as blatant a whitewash job as was ever conceived by Tom Sawyer.

Lugosi made nine 'B's for Monogram, all of them for a kind of sub-section called Banner Pictures, a 'B' studio's 'B' unit. It was run by Sam Katzman, an ex-prop boy. The films made money, but little sense. *The Invisible Ghost* (1941) had Lugosi as Charles Kessler, who had only to see his wife's face at the window to turn into a stalking strangler. Why was never explained; nor was there a ghost – unless it was truly invisible. *Spooks Run Wild* (1941) put Lugosi among the East Side Kids: juvenile capers written by a young Carl Foreman. *Black Dragons* (1942) had Lugosi giving plastic surgery to Japanese spies. *The Corpse Vanishes* (1942) was shown in England as *The Case of the Missing Brides*. Lugosi was Dr Lorentz, luring ladies from the altar with a whiff of his orchid, and keeping the corpse of his wife alive with their virgin blood.

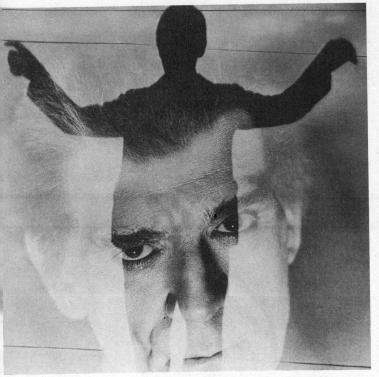

Bowery at Midnight (1942) saw Lugosi doubling up. By day he is Professor Brenner, slum missioner; by night, Karl Wagner, with a more sinister mission: crime. He is duly done away with by a cellarful of living dead.

The Ape Man (1943), called *Lock Your Doors* in England, had Lugosi as Karloff: or so internal evidence would suggest. It was scripted from an original called 'They Creep in the Dark' by Karl Brown, who had written the Columbia Karloffs. It was made at a time when Karloff was too busy on stage in 'Arsenic and Old Lace' to complete his Columbia contract. Odder: in that play Karloff played Jonathan Brewster, and in this film Lugosi played James Brewster – a pretty strange name for a Hungarian. The plot itself is uncommonly like *The Ape*, which Karloff had appeared in for Monogram. Lugosi kills people to obtain supplies of fresh spinal fluid, the only antidote to his apishness. The twist is that instead of donning a gorilla skin, Lugosi is half-gorilla himself.

Ghosts on the Loose (1943) was Lugosi and the East Side Kids again. This time the British called it *Ghosts in the Night*: a rare case of trying to make a film sound more horrific than it was. *The Voodoo Man* (1944) was an all-star movie by Monogram standards: Lugosi, Zucco and Carradine as Marlow, Nicholas and Job, zombie-makers. The unwholesome three were reunited in *Return of the Ape Man* (1944). This catch-penny piece had nothing at all to do with the previous year's success. It justified its title by being about the return of an apeman. Lugosi as Professor Dexter revives prehistoric Frank Moran from an Arctic iceberg. He inserts John Carradine's brain and the apeman turns into George Zucco! The logic was frightening if the film was not.

Of all the 'B' movie monsters, the zombie was favourite. The walking dead looked pretty much like the walking quick, particularly if you used the less expressive, hence less expensive actors. Besides, a zombie cannot talk and that was another saving: the union scale was lower for a non-speaking part!

The Halperin Brothers, who had started things off with *White Zombie* (1932), dug them up again four years later for *Revolt of the Zombies* (1936). Whilst steamy Cambodia stood in nicely for shadowy Haiti, keen Dean Jagger was no replacement for Lugosi. Nor were his squad of zombie soldiers dead ringers for Legendre's Angels of Death, even if they did march implacably through shot and shell: truly impenetrable Orientals. Yet they were better by far than Dr Sangre and his Caribbean corpses in Monogram's *King of the Zombies* (1941). Henry Victor, once a hero in British silent films, played the Voodoo sorcerer in a style that, at least, proved his consistency. *Revenge of the Zombies* (1943) starred John Carradine as Dr Von Altmann, Nazi scientist, operating out of a Louisiana manse. Here he is building a zombie army for the Führer, starting with his wife. Lila the lady

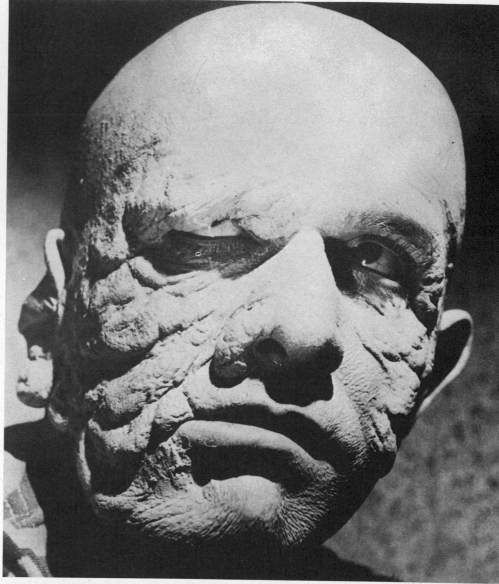

Face to Face: Rondo Hatton was the only horror film star to play monsters without makeup. Cast as 'The Creeper' he appeared in *House of Horrors* (Universal 1946; *above*). Hatton suffered from acromegaly, a distorting disease simulated by Ralph Morgan in *The Monster Maker* (PRC 1944; *opposite above*), Leo G. Carroll in *Tarantula* (Universal 1955; *right*) and Michael Brennan in *Doomwatch* (Tigon 1972; *page 155*). Even more frightening were the faces worn by George Sawaya in *The Black Sleep* (Bel Air 1956; *above right*), Herbert Lom in *Murders in the Rue Morgue* (American International 1971; *opposite below left*), and Philip Coolidge in William Castle's *The Tingler* (Columbia 1959; *opposite below right*).

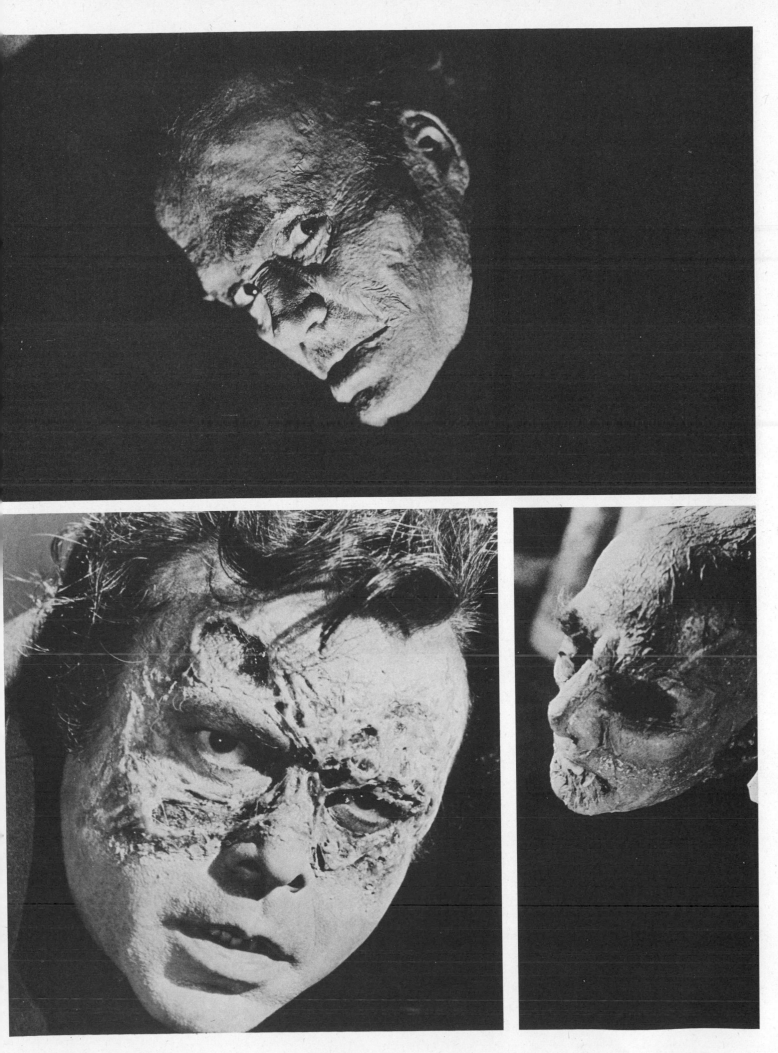

zombie was played in the manner born by Veda Ann Borg. The British distributor, having called *The Corpse Vanishes – The Case of the Missing Brides*, called *Revenge of the Zombies – The Corpse Vanished*! Carradine, borne into a bayou by Miss Borg, was back in a trice as Professor Randolph. In *Face of Marble* (1945) he restored life of a kind to a drowned sailor, his own deranged wife, and a Great Dane. They kill him. It was the last of the Monograms.

PRC, or to give them their due, the Producers Releasing Corporation, was to Monogram what Monogram was to Columbia. PRC's Sam Katzman was called Sigmund Neufeld, who formed a curiously harmonious partnership with Sam Newfield. Together this team found time between Westerns to produce and direct a field of four. George Zucco was their biggest name. He played in three but made up for it by playing in one twice. A star on the PRC lot, Zucco was a small-part fellow elsewhere, lending his Manchester lip-roll and his marbly eyeballs to many a creepy cameo. In *The Mad Monster* (1942) he was Dr Lorenzo Cameron, growing hair on his handyman with transfusions of wolf's blood. Pedro the simpleton was an initiation into horror for Glenn Strange, former wrestler,

would-be Monster. Zucco's preposterous proposition that infusions of living wolf's blood could create an invincible army was scoffed at by the ghostly conclave of scientists summoned up in his crazed brain. Yet someone did take him seriously: the British censor. *The Mad Monster* was banned for twelve years and only then allowed out with an 'X' Certificate, the Adults Only ticket that ultimately replaced the 'H'. Even then they insisted that every cinema exhibiting the film must also exhibit this notice: 'The public would be quite mistaken to think that any personal characteristics could be passed on by blood transfusion. Animal blood is never used for transfusions in the treatment of disease.' So there.

Dead Men Walk (1942) was Zucco's *doppelgänger*. He appeared as Dr Harold Clayton and disappeared as his twin brother Elwyn. This vampire was assisted by Zolarr, a hunchbacked comeback for Dwight Frye, who promptly went away again. *The Monster Maker* (1944) was Dr Igor Markov, played by J. Carrol Naish for a change. Not a nice one, for in order to wreak his will upon Wanda McKay he injected her father with acromegaly. As he was a concert pianist the resultant swellings hurt his career as much as they did him. A nasty piece by any standards, even PRC's. Zucco returned for a less than grand finale, *The Flying Serpent* (1946). As Professor André Forbes, archaeologist, he stumbles upon Montezuma's treasure. It is guarded by a fierce feathered reptile, so Zucco trains it to kill. It drinks the blood of anyone upon whom Zucco plants its feather. And if the proceedings sound familiar, remember Lugosi and his Devil Bat.

Republic Pictures came first in the minor league studios, but last in the horror field. Herbert J. Yates had more interest in Rogers and Trigger than Boris and Bela. He had even more interest in Vera Hruba Ralston, his regular star. He married her, but not before he had starred her in one of the title roles of *The Lady and the Monster* (1944). The British censor, shocked, changed that to *The Lady and the Doctor*. Later Republic changed it to *The Tiger Man*. Playing the role of Monster/Doctor/Tiger Man was Erich Von Stroheim, 'The Man you Love to Hate'. As Professor Franz Mueller, 'a diabolical and self-centred scientist', he extracted the brain of a fresh-dead financier and kept it alive in a bowl. It grew to dominate Richard Arlen. Curt

Bat Trick: Bela Lugosi in *The Devil Bat* (PRC 1940; *above*); *Doomwatch* (Tigon 1972).

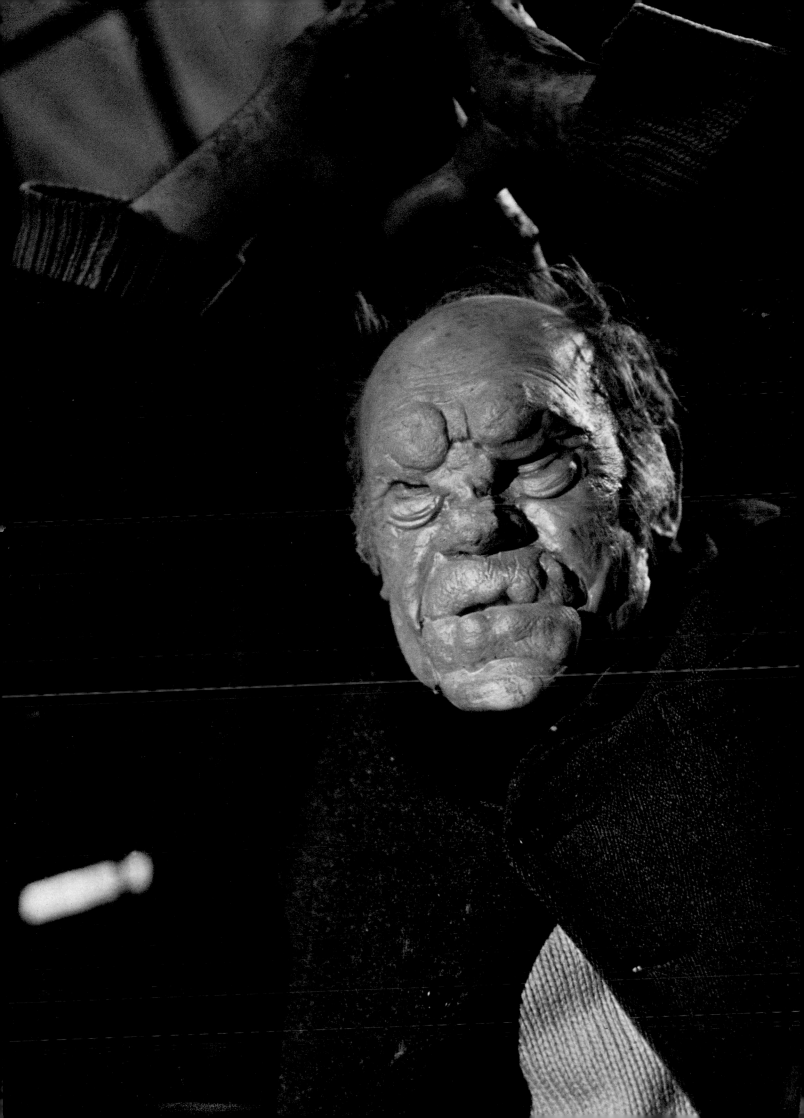

Siodmak's novel 'Donovan's Brain', was more sincerely served by later remakes.

The Phantom Speaks (1945) was similar stuff: Richard Arlen was in it, but he was not the one possessed. Stanley Ridges was the psycho-scientist taken over by the vengeful soul of an executed killer. Tom Powers was seen in double-exposure, but not in Britain, where the film was banned. *The Vampire's Ghost* (1945) meant brief stardom for John Abbott, a sad-eyed, bag-eyed soul from the small-part ranks. He played Webb Fallon, who ran the honky-tonk in Bakunda, West Africa, and turned out to be a vampire, cursed in the days of Queen Elizabeth. *Valley of the Zombies* (1946) was another promotion: Ian Keith, needing fresh blood to maintain his immortality, rejoiced under the name of Ormand Murks. *The Catman of Paris* (1945) was Robert Wilke in whiskers, but despite a starrier support (Carl Esmond and Leonore Aubert), like Ormand Murks he, too, failed to make it to England.

Of the major studios who ran their own 'B' picture units, Warner Brothers-First National were quick off the mark with *The Return of the Terror* (1934), a rejig of that very first horror talkie. They used the same gimmick for *The Return of Dr X* (1939), but Humphrey Bogart could hardly be considered a dead ringer for Lionel Atwill, even with a becoming white stripe in his hair. The film itself seemed in need of a transfusion: it was shown in sepia. *Sh! The Octopus* (1937) was a comedy workover for *The Gorilla* – which had been a comedy to start with – but the British censor failed to see anything funny in *The Mysterious Doctor* (1943), and gave it an 'H' for its headless ghost. Perhaps the final disclosure that it was actually a Nazi, trying to stop our brave Cornish villagers from working a tin mine, proved too much to bear.

Paramount's only 'B'-class horror was *The Monster and the Girl* (1941), a rescoring of a 1920 silent called *Go and Get It*. This time Philip Terry was the executed murderer whose brain, inserted into an ape by George Zucco, impelled the beast's vengeful rampage.

Twentieth Century-Fox scored but two, but two good ones. The better came first. *The Undying Monster* (1942) was directed by John Brahm, a Hamburger who had changed his name from Hans. Taken from Jessie Douglas Kerruish's good 1936 novel, the tale of a family cursed since the Crusades

was moody stuff, quite spoilt by the British censor's scissors. Not only did he remove the carefully-photographed final metamorphosis, leaving audiences to wonder why the dim thing that the police shot should suddenly look like John Howard, but he also insisted on the title being changed to *The Hammond Mystery*. Fortunately enough of Brahm's brilliance was devoted to less shocking sequences so that most of his mood remained. Lucien Ballard swung his camera round an ancient room, alighting on odd objects at each dour bong of midnight. Casting and Cornish atmosphere were both good, too, perhaps because Brahm did his first film work at Twickenham studios. Only one thing spoiled the script. The rune, obligatory to any werewolf film, ran:

'When the stars are bright on a frosty night,
Beware the baying in the rocky lane.'

To film fans there was only one Rocky Lane: the Republic Western star!

Fox's other film was *Dr Renault's Secret* (1942). Fox's secret was that this was really *The Wizard* all over again (and that had been *Balaoo*). George Zucco played the French doctor who proved Darwin was right by operating upon an ape. J. Carrol Naish was the end-product, alias Noel the handyman from Java. He died, as did they all, saving the doctor's daughter from abductive Mike Mazurki. The director was artistic Harry Lachman.

RKO Radio had a 'B' picture unit that was a different belfry of bats: Charles Koerner, production chief, organized it purely to produce horror films. In charge he placed a Russian-born journalist who

Hands Up: *The Return of Count Yorga* (AIP 1971; *opposite above*); *Dracula AD 1972* (Hammer 1972). *Right:* Bela Lugosi in *Black Dragons* (PRC 1942).

'B' Beings: J. Carrol Naish came in handy as the apeman-servant of *Dr Renault's Secret* (Twentieth Century-Fox 1942; *right*), and that latter-day Frankenstein Glenn Strange had a dry run as *The Mad Monster* (PRC 1941; *below*). Bela Lugosi and John Carradine seem as bewildered as neanderthal George Zucco in *Return of the Ape Man* (PRC 1944; *opposite centre*), a sequel in name only to *The Ape Man* (PRC 1943; *opposite below left*). Lugosi alone was in that, while Carradine made a lady out of Acquanetta the Ape Woman in *Captive Wild Woman* (Universal 1943; *opposite top and bottom right*), with a little help from Jack P. Pierce and his yak-hair.

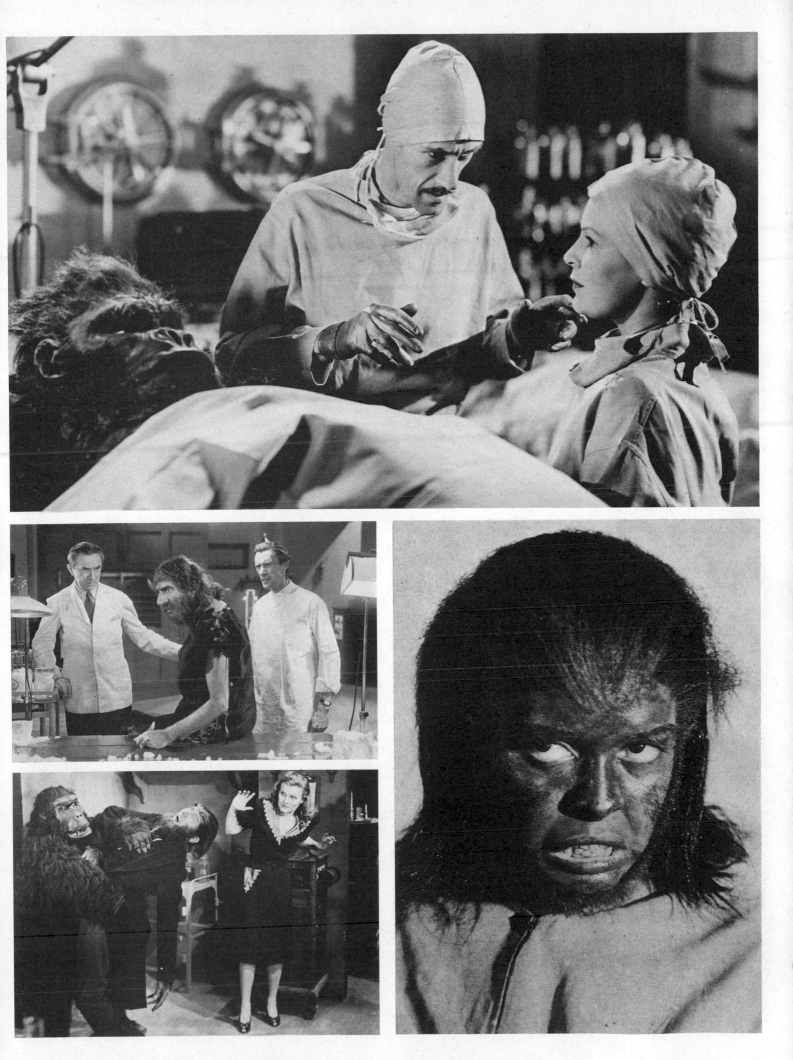

Cheap Horrors: The cheapest horror pictures not only skimped on budgets, they cheated on chills, too. *The Strange Case of Dr RX* (Universal 1942) billed top monster Lionel Atwill (*below*) but he was only a red herring called Dr Fish. The ape and girl still (*opposite*) was featured big in the publicity but never appeared in the film. *The Return of Dr X* (Warner 1939) had as much to do with their well-remembered monstrosity *Dr X* as *The Return of the Ape Man* had to do with *The Ape Man*. But it did have Humphrey Bogart (*left*).

had been David O. Selznick's story editor. Vladimir Ivan Lewton, who called himself Val, was given his first assignment, a title created by Koerner, pretested and found audience-appealing. Out of *Cat People* (1942) Lewton wrought a minor masterpiece that changed the face of horror films. It did not change the face of Simone Simon, however, and that was its secret. As Irena Dubrovna, a Yugoslavian dress designer, she suffers the curse of her race, but turns into a black panther off-screen. Lewton, a man of taste, abhorred the obvious. His belief was that it was not the thing seen but the thing unseen that truly frightened. This was terrifyingly translated into pictures by Jacques Tourneur, who had inherited no little of his father Maurice's pictorial talent. The taut, short, shadowy film worried Koerner, who had hoped for hairier stuff: but the $134,000 'B' finally brought in over four million dollars! Lewton was anything but pleased with his reward: a new title – *The Curse of the Cat People*! This sequel arrived in 1944, co-directed by Gunther Von Fritsch and Robert Wise. Simone Simon, killed as a panther, returns as a smiling ghost to aid and comfort her lonely little daughter. A brilliant piece of supernatural cinema, but a long way from horror.

I Walked With a Zombie (1943) was a long way, too, from those regular walking dead at the Monogram lot. The title was given Lewton by Koerner again, who had bought a series of articles by Inez Wallace, run under that heading in the Hearst

The Quickie and the Dead: Fast-buck flicks were churned out at top speed and the easiest-to-make monsters were zombies. The walking dead were easy to come by at the Hollywood extras' agencies. Height and eyeballs were all that was required from Darby Jones in *I Walked With a Zombie* (RKO 1943; *right*); the girls in *Voodoo Man* (Monogram 1944; *below right*) did not even need to have height. John Carradine had enough of that. Henry Victor was as wooden as his victims in *King of the Zombies* (Monogram 1941; *below left*). *Opposite:* George Zucco and Bela Lugosi put their heads together for *Voodoo Man* (Monogram 1944).

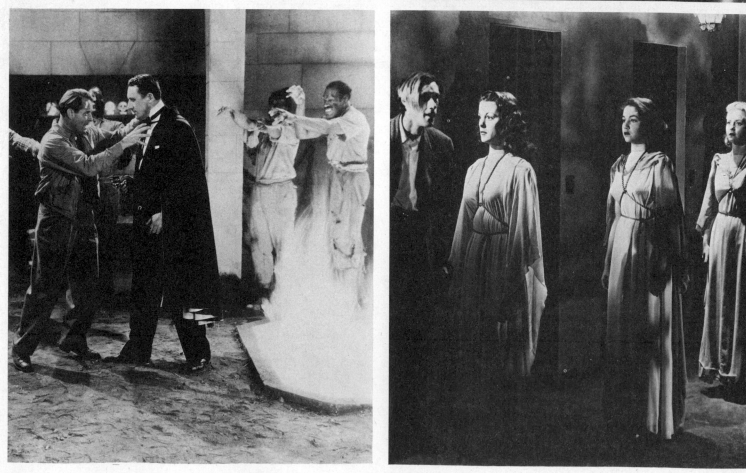

Sunday supplements. What Lewton gave Koerner back was 'Jane Eyre in the West Indies' (Lewton's phrase), even though Curt Siodmak wrote the screenplay. Tall Darby Jones played Carre Four, the zombie who towered over Frances Dee. She was the nurse who finds happiness with Tom Conway, a sugar planter whose wandering wife has been zombified by his mother. The title certainly didn't cheat the way *The Leopard Man* (1943) did. The third in a row from the Lewton-Tourneur team, it was mystery without horror or monsters, taken from Cornell Woolrich's thriller 'Black Alibi'. Mark Robson, who had edited all three, was now promoted to director and made *The Seventh Victim* (1943). This was also a debut for Kim Hunter as an orphan girl involved with Devil-worshippers in Greenwich Village. Robson's *The Ghost Ship* (1943) had no ghost, of course, unless it was that of Jack London who may have recognized his 'Sea Wolf' in Richard Dix.

Boris Karloff and Bela Lugosi now signed on at RKO. Koorner had suddenly died and the new man, Jack J. Gross, wanted a more traditional horror movie. *The Body Snatcher* (1945), a solo from Robert Wise, gave Karloff one of his finest roles. He played the grave Gray, cabman and specimen supplier to the medical trade. Robert Louis Stevenson's story of nineteenth-century Edinburgh provided a splendid role for neglected Henry Daniell (Dr MacFarlane) but a minor one for doomed Lugosi (Joseph). Everything built to a terrifying climax on a runaway coach. It went over the heads of the British audience: the censor cut it out.

Lugosi went over to RKO's other 'B' unit to put the wind up Brown and Carney in two frightening comedies, while Karloff stayed with Lewton for two very different frights, both with Mark Robson. *Isle of the Dead* (1945) continued Lewton's studio-built globe-trotting by setting itself off the coast of Greece. Karloff was General Nikolas Pherides, weakened by plague and bothered by vrykolakas, the local vampires. Banned in Britain for a while, the film was at least seen; more than can be said for *Bedlam* (1946), which the censor found beyond bearing. It was set in the infamous eighteenth-century institution for the insane, St Mary's of Bethlehem, inspired by William Hogarth's eighth painting in his series 'The Rake's Progress'. Karloff was Master George Sims, who put his patients to perform strange plays for the pleasure of the rich. This was the authentic horror of history, a use of the genre's star and style to illustrate truth. It was Karloff's last for Lewton and Lewton's last for RKO. He abandoned the 'B' hive

for 'A' features that were worth more in money but less in while. He died very suddenly in 1951. He was forty-six.

Universal, when they weren't making class 'A' horrors, made class 'B' ones instead. Sometimes as well! *The Mad Doctor of Market Street* (1941) was type-casting for Lionel Atwill. With him at the helm the audience knew what they were in for. Only the title cheated: one moment's madness in Market Street and Atwill spent the rest of the sixty minutes shipwrecked on a South Sea Island. There lay Princess Tanao, comatose. A swift jab with the old adrenalin and she is up and about, while natives fall on their knees and worship Atwill as their God of Life. Atwill returned in *The Strange Case of Dr RX* (1942). He played Dr Fish but was merely a red herring. The masked man determined to exchange the brain of his ape with that of Patric Knowles was none other than Samuel S. Hinds. Atwill lurked again in *The Night Monster* (1942), this time in company with Bela Lugosi. Both were red herrings in a *House of Mystery* (the British title) that demonstrated the power of mind over matter. Nils Asther's mind gave Ralph Morgan matter. This rich cripple grew new legs at will and

Females of the Species: Girls, more usually the done-to, as in *The Neanderthal Man* (Global 1953; *opposite left*), are occasionally the doers. A pioneer in the cause of Women's Lib was Nina Foch in *Cry of the Werewolf* (Columbia 1944; *below*). Her Queen Celeste of the Trioga Tribe was followed, duly if belatedly, by Deidre Biddulph (Ursula Howells) in *Dr Terror's House of Horrors* (Amicus 1964; *right*). Carol Thurston was the disfigured victim of a disfigured female who used *The Hypnotic Eye* (Allied Artists 1960; *opposite above right*), and Greek vrykolakas beset Ellen Drew in *Isle of the Dead* (RKO 1945; *opposite below right*).

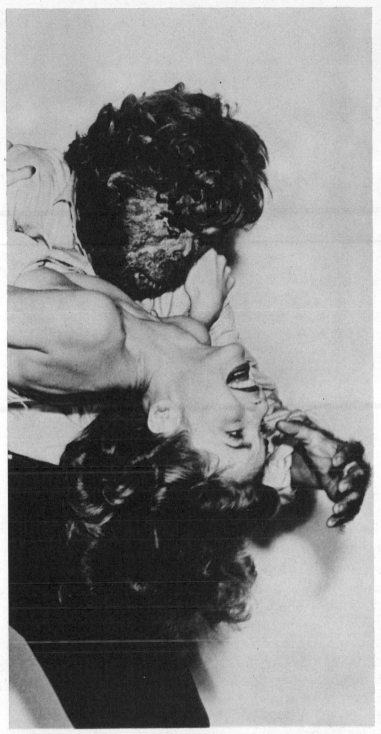

thus wreaked surprising vengeance upon his more hidebound medical advisers. *The Mad Ghoul* (1943) was David Bruce, who took one whiff of George Zucco's gas and wrinkled alarmingly. Only a fresh heart would restore the youth to his cheeks and Evelyn Ankers to his arms.

The success of their *Mummy* saga inspired Universal to initiate an original 'B' movie monster series. The twist was, instead of the traditional plot of the monster and the girl, this time the monster *was* the girl: *Captive Wild Woman* (1943). John Carradine as Dr Sigmund Walters treated Cheela the orang-outang with glandular extractions from Martha MacVicar, and named the result Paula Dupree. But like the Panther Woman of America,

that stubborn old beast flesh comes creeping back. Under moments of emotional stress – she discovers Milburn Stone prefers the company of Evelyn Ankers – Paula goes ape. The gorilla girl saves her beloved from a circus stampede but is shot by mistake. Yet Acquanetta, who played her, was soon back in Jack Pierce's makeup as *Jungle Woman* (1944), revived from the dead by J. Carrol Naish, otherwise Dr Fletcher. He turned her into a girl again, but once more jealousy reared its, and Paula's, ugly head. Undaunted, Otto Kruger as Dr Stendhal set about reviving her corpse once more. In *Jungle Captive* (1944) Paula's changeover was indeed a change: the ape metamorphosed into Vicky Lane. Even this did not satisfy Kruger, how-

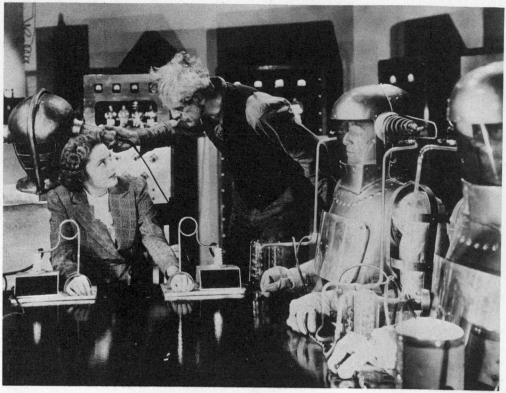

Brain Drain: The human brain is a key prop in many a horror movie, generally as a transplant, often with an ape's. Boris Karloff was a handy man with a brain, and here is seen tapping into Amanda Duff's in a misguided but spectacular attempt to communicate with his dead wife: *The Devil Commands* (Columbia 1941; *right*). Curt Siodmak's classic novel 'Donovan's Brain' has been filmed thrice. *Opposite:* Anne Heywood, previously known as Violet Pretty, contemplates the convolutions in her husband's Anglo-German production, *Vengeance* (Stross-CCC 1962).

ever, who determined to give her Amelita Ward's brain. The gorilla girl reverts to type in time to stop the operation by strangling Kruger. It was the end of the ape-woman. Poor Paula, she never even met Abbott and Costello. But she left behind her, if not an interesting body of work, an interesting body.

Lurking around the background of *Jungle Captive* was Moloch the outsize handyman. His outsize hands were, like his outsize head, due to acromegaly, that distorting disease of the pituitary which J. Carrol Naish, *The Monster Maker*, had used on Ralph Morgan. But that actor, at the end of the picture, could peel off the putty and go home. Not so Rondo Hatton. When Moloch's work was done, he went home looking like Moloch: Hatton actually *did* have acromegaly. His horrendous looks had supported him through many a minor movie. Whenever an ugly convict was needed around the Big House, casting directors sent for Hatton. In *Pearl of Death* (1944) he had been cast to type as the Hoxton Creeper, strangling about the Universal London in a foredoomed attempt to prevent Sherlock Holmes (Basil Rathbone) from saving the Six Napoleons. Another Holmes piece, *Spider Woman* (1944), became cash-in inspiration for *Spider Woman Strikes Back* (1946), wherein Gale Sondergard as Zenobia Dollard (ex Adrea Spedding) raised carnivorous plants to do away with Kirby Grant's cows. Her deaf mute henchman was Hatton, billed as Mario the Monster Man.

Universal raised Rondo Hatton to a stardom of sorts with *House of Horrors* (1946). Back in form as the Creeper, he comes crawling out of a river just as Martin Kosleck is committing suicide. One look at the Creeper and Kosleck changes his mind, taking him back to his studio to pose for a sculpture. Kosleck has but to express dislike for an art critic for that critic to be found with his spine snapped: the Creeper paying back a kindness in the only way he knows. The British censor showed his disapproval by forbidding the title. It went on release as *Joan Medford Is Missing*! The end of the story came in *The Brute Man* (1946). The Creeper, last seen shot dead, returned Golem-like in a tale of how he came into the world. It seems that he is really Hal Moffatt (Fred Coby), football hero, class of 1930 at Hampton University. An explosion in the Chemistry Lab turns him into the back-breaking Creeper (Hatton). His one soft spot is for piano-playing Jan Wiley – who is blind. Totally unable to give the Creeper a fraction of the Chaney-like pathos the character required, totally unable, indeed, to act, Rondo Hatton nevertheless carved a unique niche in the history of the horror film. The only genuine monster star because he was a monster. The glorification of the Quasimodo syndrome and of Browning's freaks, yet the ultimate proof that it is the actor behind the makeup that is the key to the art of horror.

Rondo Hatton and his Creeper brought the age of Universal horror to an end. He died. His miserable film shocked even the studio that had made it. They disowned it, giving it to the lowest of the low to distribute. It went out on release as a PRC picture: the ultimate horror.

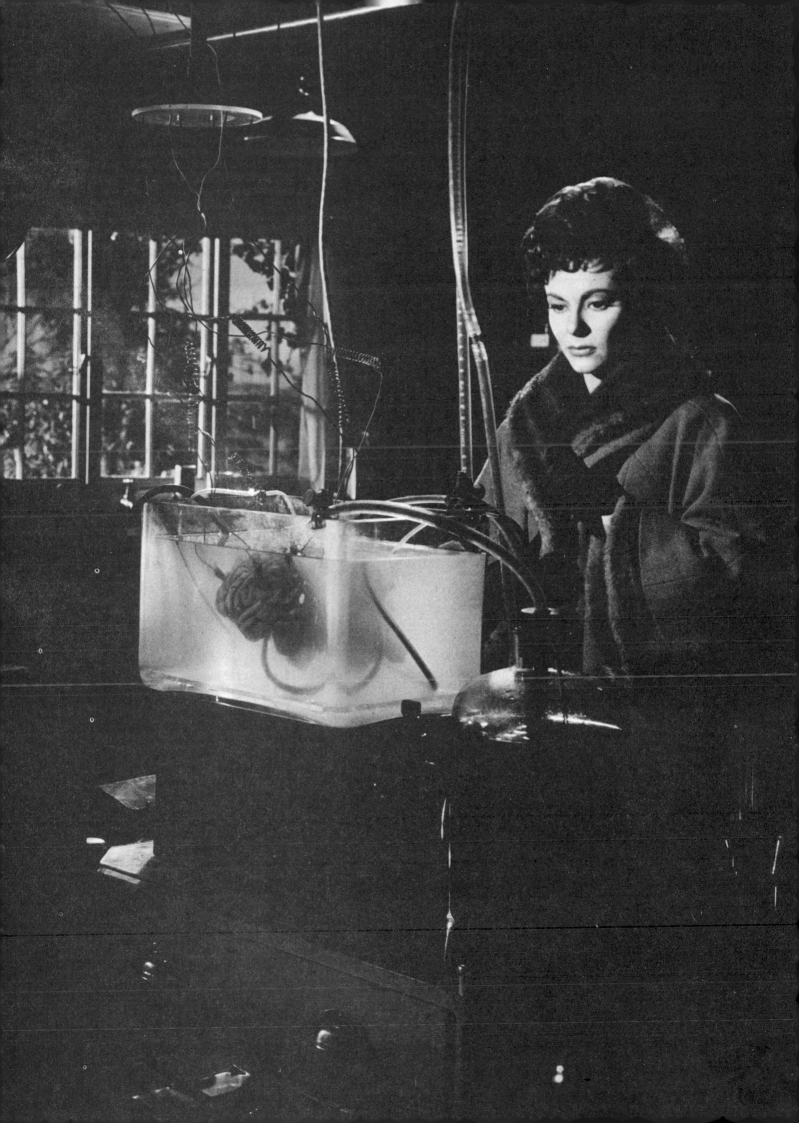

A THING IN YOUR LAP

In which there is a Thing from Outer Space, a Beast from 20,000 Fathoms, a Creature in the 3-D Lagoon, a Skeleton in the auditorium, and Roger Corman is a Teenage E. A. Poe for A.I.P.

The Thing was eight feet tall. It was hairless and mewed like a cat. It had no nerve endings and bled green. It flew through unfathomable space at unbelievable speed and survived a crash at the North Pole. Frozen solid, it defrosted by chance and revived alive. It was hacked by axes, set on fire, and had one arm torn off by dogs. It grew another arm; the severed arm came to life, too. The Thing reproduced itself asexually by podding, drank human blood, and was a vegetable. It was more intelligent than any man, stronger than ten, and was unshootable. And it looked like Boris Karloff.

The Thing (1951), semi-subtitled *from another world*, was the first entry in the new wave of horror: a shock wave born from Bikini. The old horror films, which had been twentieth-century rationalizations of medieval legends, could now be interpreted as apocalyptic warnings, forebodings of doom should single-minded science be allowed a full, free hand in the pursuit of knowledge. Unheeding real-life Frankensteins had created an unstoppable monster, and for millions the Atomic Bomb meant the end of the world. It had killed the horror movie, too; none had been made for six years.

The Thing, for all its dazzling direction, fast-paced cutting, overlapping acting and authentic setting, was beneath its cinematic surface set securely in the mould of Universal Gothic. Howard Hawks and Christian Nyby used the classic horror film formula: a tight society cut off from the real world without, caught up by an unreal menace within. Their Arctic research base is the village of Vasaria; its icy boundaries are the ghetto roofs of Prague; the bright pool of home-made light in the night is the splashed paint of Holstenwall. Dr Carrington is Dr Frankenstein, willing to sacrifice all to make contact with an alien in the furtherance of man's knowledge, while Captain Pat Hendry is a keen young Van Helsing, realizing the danger and determined to destroy. The Thing is, of course, the Monster: in looks, in power, yet not in soul. There is no spark of even man-made humanity in this man-shaped monster: it is a creature of fury, of violence, of hate.

'Who Goes There?', John W. Campbell Jr's novel, from which Charles Lederer took his screenplay, recorded the visitation of an utterly alien creature. Contemporary critics protested against the film's obvious humanoid, but time soon proved Hawks right. For the hundred tentacled, barnacled, blubber and rubber monstrosities that have since oozed, squelched and slithered across the screen, there is still only one Thing. Lee Greenway sculpted him eighteen times before Hawks was satisfied. Then he got to work on a tall, rangy young actor called James Arness, and built him into a space-suited Karloff.

The frightening flashes of the Thing, half-glimpsed behind a suddenly flung door, half-seen in a splash of light, won high praise in England for their reticent shock value. But the fact was that only in England was the Thing quite so unseen. The climactic trap where the Thing, caught by an electric arc, cooked into shrivelling smoke, recalled the fate of Dynamo Dan the Electric Man. The Thing shrank, but in England in more ways than one. The censor, not content with the award of his new 'X' for Adults Only certificate, used his scissors too: perhaps the only time a censor's cutting actually added to a film's artistic reputation.

The Thing naturally sparked off a cycle: indeed, its successor actually arrived first. *The Man from Planet X* (1951) achieved this by a process somewhat simpler than a time-warp: a lower budget. Edgar G. Ulmer, that old hand at horror, did well with his misty moors. Again that classic setting, the cut-off community (a small Scots island), and that classic confrontation, the monster and the girl. The new twist is that mad doctor and monster are combined into one: the X-Man, hideously

Gill-Man: *City Under the Sea* (American International 1965), shown in USA as *War-Gods of the Deep*.

168

This and That: The atomic mushroom bore strange fruit. Science-fiction films could do no wrong, provided they provided a monster of one kind or another. *Them* (Warner 1953; *right*) were ants, fifteen feet long: the unexpected outcome of A-bomb tests. *The Green Slime* (1969) slithered through Richard Jaekel's space station in a co-production between MGM and Japan's Toei (*above*). *Opposite:* Kim Parker has her brain sucked out of the back of her neck by materialized thought: *Fiend Without a Face* (Eros 1958).

humanoid, super-weaponed, the ultimate egghead. Something else was new: the shoot-up finale with the monster mown down by army bullets. Gone are the dooms, as decreed by supernature: the crucifix, the silver bullet, the wolfbane. Gone is even the natural justice of fire and water and swamp. The Universal mob, who never turned out without first lighting their torches, never thought to carry anything more lethal than a knobkerrie. If blood was shed, it bled off-screen. From here on in, man would make war on monsters the modern way, as he did on his fellow-men.

The spectacular battling reached a crackling climax with *The War of the Worlds* (1953), George Pal's Technicolored transplant of H.G. Wells' novel of invasion by Martians. Pal moved it from the Woking of 1898 to the Los Angeles of 1953, and threw everything into it including the A-Bomb. But in the end, as the commentator concluded, 'after all that man could do had failed, the Earth and humanity were saved by the littlest things which God in His wisdom had put upon Earth': it was the Common Cold that killed the Martians. And for all the super spectacle (Gordon Jennings died before he knew he had won the Academy Award for his special effects), for all the ultrabright Technicolor, Byron Haskin's direction touched on tradition. Over the very American action intoned the English accent of Sir Cedric Hardwicke, and inside the monstrous Martian was that old-time apeman, Charles Gemora.

Edwin Parker was secretly Universal's only true universal monster. He had been the stunt-man double for the Wolf Man, the Mummy, the Monster, and Mr Hyde. Now he was encased in an exposed brain and claws as the Mutant of Metaluna, extraterrestrial menace of *This Island Earth* (1955). MGM joined the space race, too, but their Monster of the Id of Altair 4, title place of *Forbidden Planet* (1956), was materialized through cartoon animation. Not, as you might expect, by the studio's own *Tom and Jerry* men, but by designers from Disney.

Less inspired, but sometimes more monstrous, were the Things that came from that other Beyond – the pale of the major studios. *Phantom From Space* (1953) was a muscleman in jockey shorts and bald dome; *Killers From Space* (1954) wore celluloid eyeballs; *It! The Terror From Beyond Space* (1958) was paunchy ex-Rangebuster Ray 'Crash' Corrigan in a rubber suit; *The Cosmic Man* (1959) was John Carradine in negative. Best of the independents was Walter Wanger's *Invasion of the Body Snatchers* (1956). Don Siegel directed documentary-style, his real locations adding awful authenticity to Jack Finney's frightening novel of pods from space that bloom into duplicated humans. Worst of the independents was the cutprice series of double-bill thrillers churned out by a former bellboy from Twentieth Century-Fox.

With the collapse of the minor studios, small-town exhibitors were having trouble filling their schedules with low-rental products. First to fill their bill was Robert L. Lippert, who distributed independently-made quickies by such reliable old firms as the Neufeld-Newfield combo. Their *Lost Continent* (1951) starred Cesar Romero who turned green when he met a man in a tyrannosaurus suit. Yet it was a masterpiece when set beside *Monster From the Ocean Floor* (1954), wet jetsam that drifted Lippert's way from a director called Wyott Ordung. Even so, when two gentlemen of venture decided to call themselves the American Releasing Corporation, they hired the producer of Ordung's monstrosity, not only as their producer, but as their writer and director, too. Thus Roger Corman left bell-hopping behind for good and launched into a quickie career that would make even William 'One-Shot' Beaudine and B. Reeves 'Breezy' Eason look like Cecil B. DeMille.

The Day the World Ended (1955) was the day the future began – for Corman as a director, for Paul Blaisdell as a monster, for Samuel Z. Arkoff and James H. Nicholson as ARC (soon it would be

Atomic Boom: Outsize oddities bedevilled the world. In America there was *Tarantula* (Universal 1955; *opposite left*), *The Deadly Mantis* (Universal 1957; *opposite right*) and *The Black Scorpion* (Warner 1957; *left*). In Japan, which had known the other end of the atom, there was *Godzilla Versus the Thing* (Toho 1964; *opposite below*). The Thing was Mothra from the film of the same name. Then came *Space Amoeba* (1970; *bottom left*), *Gamera Versus Jiger* (1971; *bottom right*), and the celebratory monster party, *Destroy All Monsters* (1968; *below*).

173

changed to AIP – American International Pictures), and for the Corman formula. This was a sixty-minute running time, a ten-day shooting schedule, a minimal crew, an even more minimal cast (once he got it down to three!), a monster in a rubber suit, and a twist in the tail. Soon he was shooting his films in tandem, using the same sets, actors, crews: instant double bills. His casting was cut-price, fading 'B' players or young beginners, and this accidentally helped his horrors touch a new nerve. Corman's unknowns communicated with the teenagers in the drive-ins. AIP had tapped a new audience area. Young people liked Corman's throw-away movies and ultimately, ironically, made a cult hero of a director who was so cynical of the take-anything crowd that he even came to dispense with his monsters. *Beast With a Million Eyes* (1956) was an economically invisible force, while *Not Of This Earth* (1957) was Paul Birch in business suit and sunglasses! Except in the advertising; AIP were not that stupid. If anyone complained, Arkoff and Nicholson claimed their posters gave an 'artist's impression' of the films.

Nothing accelerates scientific progress like a war. In 1952 cinema itself went to war. The enemy: television. The secret weapon: a pair of spectacles. Arch Oboler, of all people, launched the attack. He was a man of words, a radio writer, creator of mental images of horror in 'Lights Out'. Now he whipped up an assault on the eyeballs called *Bwana Devil* (1952), which had as its slogan 'A Lion in your Lap!' Shot in polarized Natural Vision, it brought back the eye-blinking shock of George Barnes and his 1903 six-gun, with the added realism of three-dimensional Anscocolor. A cheap piece, it was not so much a spectacle, more a bespectacle, as audiences squinted behind obligatory glasses. More spectacular were its profits, and the big studios were quick to leap aboard the stereoscopical roller-coaster.

Warners, who had pioneered the sound wave, were first in the van of the new revolution. Once again Hollywood history repeated itself: the second 3-D movie was a horror film, and, of course, it was a remake. *House of Wax* (1953) was a full colour, full dimension rehash of *The Mystery of the Wax Museum*. The late Lionel Atwill's part went to velvet-toned Vincent Price, wearing a Warner-colorful new makeup by Gordon Bau. It re-established the star in the genre from which he had vanished long before, but the added dimension diminished the horror. Stereo separated the actors from the backgrounds but polished them into shimmery waxworks that worked in a rounded reality that was curiously unreal. The shocks came not from tangible horror but from a small ball, ping-ponged out of the screen directly at your nose.

André de Toth directed *House of Wax* with a surprising eye for 3-D detail. Even in polaroid specs de Toth saw everything 'flat'; he had only one eye. But as he pointed out, 'Beethoven couldn't hear music either, could he?' Roy Del Ruth, who had pioneered the dimension of sound with *The Terror*, now followed through in depth with *The Phantom of the Rue Morgue* (1954). This reworking of the Poe piece cast Karl Malden, a method man, as Dr Marais the Darwinian, but although he rolled his steroscopical eyeballs he was no Lugosi. Fox, busy with Cinemascope, let a subsidiary called Panoramic Productions try 3-D. They dusted off an old plot and an ape-suit and called it *Gorilla At Large* (1954). 'He's in the aisles! He's in the balcony! He's everywhere!' lied the posters, for inside the skin was a she, Anne Bancroft.

Robot Monster (1953) was the first science-fiction film in stereo, but whilst the hairy Ro-Man blew 3-D bubbles, the monsters remained stubbornly 2-D: they were stock shots from *One Million BC*! The same producer, Al Zimbalist, sent Sonny Tufts into space to confront *Cat-Women of the Moon* (1954), a telepathic tribe played by the stereoscopic 'Hollywood Cover Girls'. The surprise of both movies comes only in retrospect: their music was written by Elmer Bernstein.

Universal, home of horror, took naturally to Natural Vision, but where Warners had looked back to vintage monsters, the old firm took an unexpected look into the future. Combining the trend towards science-fiction with the fashionable fad for location filming, Jack Arnold directed *It*

Space Race: The inhuman race from outer space ranged from the tentacled head of the *Invaders From Mars* (Twentieth Century-Fox 1953; *opposite*) to Ray 'Crash' Corrigan in a baggy suit as *It! The Terror From Beyond Space* (UA 1958; *right*). Somewhere between comes the po-faced big-head *The Man From Planet X* (UA 1951; *below left*) and his muscle-bound contemporary *Phantom From Space* (UA 1953; *below right*).

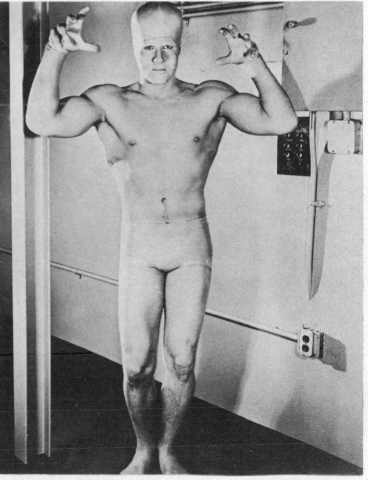

Swinging Poe: Edgar Allan Poe has proved inspirational to the American horror movie from the days of D. W. Griffith. Unhappily, the master poet of the macabre mood does not transpose well to the cinema screen, beyond the mere illustration of his classic devices. *The Pit and the Pendulum,* first filmed in the silent period, popped up in *The Raven* (Universal 1935; *right*), which was more Boris and Bela than Edgar Allan. Roger Corman filmed it with Vincent Price in 1961, then sent it, him, and themselves up in *Dr Goldfoot and the Bikini Machine* (American International 1965; *below*).

Came From Outer Space (1953). Ray Bradbury's story of wandering Xenomorphs, aliens of misty aspect, was futuristic stuff, yet behind it the old horrors lurked. The small town in the Arizona desert stood in for the cut-off community of European yore; the glamour-gowned girl, possessed in mind in the wind-blown night, was a bride of Dracula; the stolid citizens, mindless zombies in the dark, were somnambulists straight from Caligari's Cabinet.

Universal and Arnold manufactured a brand new monster specifically for stereo. The Gill-Man was an Amazonian throw-back, but he acted pretty much like the old monsters. *Creature From the Black Lagoon* (1954) was Ben Chapman, a swimmer in a rubber suit that made him a literal frogman. Designers Bud Westmore and Jack Kevan gave him a fierce fish-face, fins and flippers, but no visible reason for abducting swimsuited Julia Adams. The underwater sequences stood out in an otherwise damp entry. But the box office warranted a return, and there duly came *Revenge of the Creature* (1955), which brought the Gill-Man to Florida. Neither Arnold, Chapman, nor the third dimension were involved in the last of the series, *The Creature Walks Among Us* (1956). Ricou Browning was the Gill-Man until Dr Jeff Morrow operated upon him; then he became Don Megowan. The sinuous swimmer, elegant in his own element, turns into a shambling, clumsy hulk, pathetic as he harks to the strange call of the oceans, ugly in his sackcloth Frankenstein suit. For once, man is the monster, the monster his victim. Last seen the Gill-Man was heading out to sea, preserving sufficient natural instinct to steer clear of Abbott and Costello.

The men who made the decision to drop the Bomb have much to answer for, in life and in movies. The fall-out was far-flung. The Atomic Age began, for Hollywood, eight years after Hiroshima. The Army is A-testing in the Arctic.

'Every time we let one off I feel like I'm writing the first chapter of the new Genesis.'
'Let's hope we're not writing the last chapter of the old!'

The conscience is ignored, the button is pressed, and the fury let loose upon the world. But this time it takes physical form in the prehistoric person of a rhedosaur, aroused from its hundred-million-year deepfreeze. *The Beast From 20,000 Fathoms* (1953) burst an iceberg, crashed down Coney Island, and bowled over the box office. It set a behaviour pattern for countless followers: re-awakened creatures, magnified monstrosities, intergalactic invaders. An atomic test, an initial sighting ignored, a climactical rampage, and an ultimate extinction by radioactive weaponry, a variation of the force that gave the menace life.

Although the Beast is credited to a Ray Bradbury tale, 'The Fog Horn', its true parent is undoubtedly the dinosaur that destroyed London in Willis O'Brien's original *Lost World*. Ray Harryhausen, O'Brien's youthful disciple (he reckons to have seen *King Kong* more times than its animator), built and operated the Beast, which at 25,000 dollars was the main item on the movie's 180,000 dollar budget. The producers were two old Monogram men: Jack Dietz, who with Sam Katzman had run the East Side Kids series, and Hal E. Chester, who had been one of those very Kids. Chester it was who, producing *Night of the Demon* (1958) in England, insisted on showing the materialized monster. Critics complained, but Chester knew the box-office potential of full-frontal crudity.

Ray Harryhausen took up where O'Brien left off and did it all again with an octopus in *It Came From Beneath the Sea* (1955), extra-terrestrials in *Earth Versus the Flying Saucers* (1956), and an Ymir from Venus in *Twenty Million Miles to Earth* (1957). Along with his producer, Charles Schneer, Harryhausen switched to fantasy. He shot the first Technicolor confrontation between man and model monster in *The Seventh Voyage of Sinbad* (1957). His system, a unique mixture of earlier methods, is called Dynamation (when it isn't called Superdynamation).

A second side-effect of the nuclear explosion was enlargement. *Them!* (1953) were ants, atomically expanded to fifteen-foot lengths, who came jingling out of the New Mexico desert with lethal injections of formic acid at the ready. *Monster From the Ocean Floor* (1954) was a magnified protozoon; *It Came From Beneath the Sea* (1955) an outsize octopus; *The Phantom From 10,000 Leagues* (1955) a marine mutation; *Monster From Green Hell* (1956) a thirty-foot queen wasp; and *Monster That Challenged the World* (1957) a colossal caterpillar. Self-explanatory were *Tarantula* (1955), *Attack of the Crab Monsters* (1957), *The Deadly Mantis* (1957), *The Giant Claw* (1957), *The Black Scorpion* (1957), *The Spider* (1958), *The Killer Shrews* (1959), *The Giant Gila Monster* (1959), and *Attack of the Giant Leeches* (1959). The monsters were proportionate to their budgets, not so much in size as in concept. If Harryhausen animated his magnified

Insanity Claws: The old 'Clutching Hand' of silent serial days still grabs them where it counts. Ann Robinson is tapped on the shoulder by a Martian in *The War of the Worlds* (Paramount 1953; *above left*), and Yvette Mimieux meets a Morlock in *The Time Machine* (MGM 1960; *above right*). *The Return of the Fly* (Twentieth Century-Fox 1959) came as a surprise to Danielle De Metz (*right*), as did the emergent *Gorgo* (King 1960; *opposite*) to two torchlight fishermen.

monsters, chances were the film would be good. At the other end of the scale was Bert I. Gordon and his back-projected insects.

Bert Gordon was the man who, when Universal and Jack Arnold reversed the expanding trend with *The Incredible Shrinking Man* (1957), an atomic variation of Browning's old *Devil Doll*, came up with a reversed reverse: *The Amazing Colossal Man* (1957). Glenn Langan played a bald colonel who grew ten feet a day, thanks to the power of a plutonium explosion and a back-projection screen. The army mowed him down on the Boulder Dam, yet he returned a year later for *War of the Colossal Beast* (1958). Still seventy feet tall and bald, he looked slightly different: he had a hole in his head and was played by Dean Parkin. When a rival producer nipped in with *Attack of the Fifty Foot Woman* (1958), Gordon was undaunted. Remembering the Universal picture that had inspired it all, Gordon struck back with *Attack of the Puppet People* (1958), which was released in England as *Six Inches Tall*.

Meanwhile your common or garden dinosaur was undergoing a revival of interest, and nuclear tests were often the cause of its revival, too. Willis O'Brien was behind *The Beast of Hollow Mountain* (1956), the first monster movie made both in Regiscope and Mexico. O'Brien and Eugene Lourie,

who had directed *The Beast From 20,000 Fathoms*, came to London on location to knock down the docks for *The Giant Behemoth* (1959), and Lourie did it again on his own with *Gorgo* (1960). O'Brien returned home for *The Lost World* (1960) in colour (this time he used live monsters – reptiles in costume), but his influence remained: *Konga* (1961) was a British piece about, of course, an outsize ape. O'Brien died in 1962. Seven years later his protégé Ray Harryhausen completed a prehistoric piece O'Brien had begun for RKO back in 1942. *The Valley of Gwangi* (1969) had its dynamated dinosaur burn to death in a Spanish cathedral, but no room in its credits for O'Brien.

O'Brien's Kong remains the giant of them all, the fifty-foot yardstick against which all monsters are measured. Even *Godzilla, King of the Monsters* (1955) was billed as 'Makes King Kong look like a Midget!' – but only in actual inches. This 400-foot dragon who took on Tokyo (Tokyo lost!) was but an actor in creature's clothing compared to the animated ape. He stomped around a model city, breathing fire and fury, pushing down skyscrapers, chomping up railway trains, tromping on ocean liners, laughing off the mere tickle of high-voltage shocks. Big spectacle but on a miniature scale, engineered in the painstaking tradition of the

Head for the Hills! Scarcely a city was left standing under the onslaught of outsize monsters during the Atomic Age of Cinema. New York was knocked down by *The Beast From 20,000 Fathoms* (Warner 1953; *opposite top left*), Stockholm by *Reptilicus* (Cinemagic 1962; *opposite top right*), Tokyo by *Godzilla, King of the Monsters* (Toho 1954; *left and opposite below*) and again by *King Kong Versus Godzilla* (Toho 1962; *below left*), and London by *Gorgo* (King 1960; *below*).

Fish School: The underwater world still holds a few surprises. Lionel Barrymore discovered a whole race of fishmen as far back as 1929: *The Mysterious Island* (MGM; *right*). Julia Adams discovered the prehistoric Gill-Man up the Amazon and got carried away: *Creature From the Black Lagoon* (Universal 1954; *below left*). Miss Adams and he were in 3-D. Ricou Browning swam the part again in *Revenge of the Creature* (Universal 1955; *opposite*) but after his operation Don Megowan took the part: *The Creature Walks Among Us* (Universal 1956; *below right*). A later Gill-Man appeared briefly in *City Under the Sea* (*page 169*), known in America as *War-Gods of the Deep*.

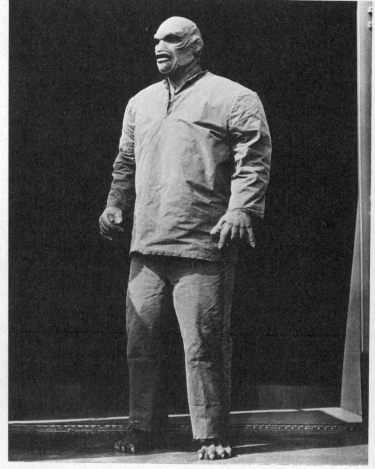

Japanese craftsman by Eiji Tsuburuya.

Gojira was Japan's first international success. Directed by Inoshiro Honda in 1954, the Toho company sold it to America where new scenes were inserted by Terry Morse, with Raymond Burr as reporter Steve Martin. He finds Tokyo in the same kind of panic that had gripped New York the year before when attacked by that Beast from 20,000 Fathoms. The Bikini Bomb has awakened a monster who is on the loose. Being a Japanese monster, Godzilla is mythic. He breathes fire like all true dragons, but with a modern touch: Godzilla's fire is radioactive. Ancient islanders have been appeasing their local legend, Kong-like, with the annual gift of a girl on a raft. Scientists now send Godzilla a depth-bomb instead. In return the outraged dragon razes Tokyo and is finally killed when a Dr Seriza destroys all the oxygen in the sea. The awful responsibility of this deadly decision makes the doctor commit hara-kiri.

Godzilla, an atomic allegory created by the victims to shock the conscience of the victors, backfired. It was a victory for commercialization over contamination, and despite his definitive death Godzilla came roaring back. There was *Godzilla's Counterattack* (1955), *Godzilla Versus the Thing* (1964), *Son of Godzilla* (1966), *Godzilla Versus Hedorah* (1971), and even *King Kong Versus Godzilla* (1962). O'Brien's old ape proved truly immortal: Honda and Tsuburaya revived him yet again in *King Kong Escapes* (1967). Godzilla also turned up in *Ebirah, Horror of the Deep* (1966). This time on 'our' side, he saved the world from an incredible crab.

Godzilla was one of the many 'guest stars' in *Destroy All Monsters* (1968), Toho's celebratory twentieth monster movie rally. Most of the Japanese creatures came, a role which by now includes *Half-Human* (1955), an abominable snowman; *Rodan* (1956), a terrible pterodactyl; *Varan the Unbelievable* (1958), a fire-breathing bat; *Mothra* (1961), a monster moth; *Gorath* (1962), a prehistoric reptile; *Matanga, Fungus of Terror* (1963); *Dogora the Space Monster* (1964), a giant

Same Name: *Frankenstein 1970* (Allied Artists 1958; *below*) and *Frankenstein Conquers the World* (Toho 1965; *right*) are but two of the modern-made horror films to cash-in on the non-cop title. Universal's monster makeup remains in copyright, however, which makes other studios' monsters but pale imitations. Other name-droppers include *Frankenstein Meets the Space Monster* and *Jesse James Meets Frankenstein's Daughter*.

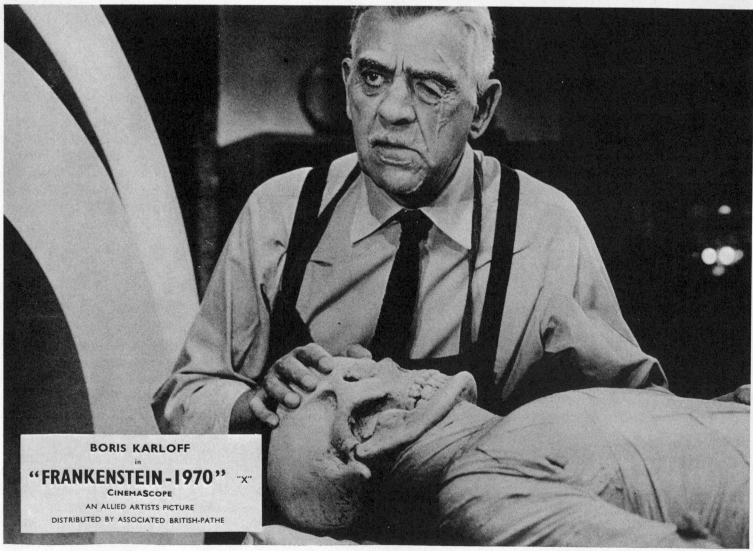

BORIS KARLOFF
in
"FRANKENSTEIN-1970" "X"
CinemaScope
AN ALLIED ARTISTS PICTURE
DISTRIBUTED BY ASSOCIATED BRITISH-PATHE

jellyfish; *Ghidrah the Three-Headed Monster* (1964), a three-headed monster; *Gamera* (1965), a turtle with teeth; *Majin* (1966), a walking statue; *Ebirah, Horror of the Deep* (1966), a colossal crab; *Gappa the Triphibian Monster* (1967), a beaky lizard; *The X From Outer Space* (1967), an X from outer space; *Gyaos* (1967), a fanged and flying fox; *Viras* (1967), a squid from space; *Goke, Bodysnatcher From Hell* (1968), a vampire jelly; *Jiger* (1969); *Space Amoeba* (1970), and *Zigra* (1971). Every year Tokyo, Yokohama, Osaka and points east are razed to the ground; every year the monsters are destroyed; and every year Tokyo and Co rise again, as do the monsters. It is a circle of cinematic spectacle that shows no sign of disappearing up its own sprocket-hole. As long as it continues, vicariously satisfying a human urge to destroy, it may keep real-life destruction at bay.

Radioactive contamination mutated the traditional horror film, too. Poor old Bela Lugosi was the first to suffer. In *Bride of the Atom* (1955) he tried to make an atomic superman but what he got was Tor Johnson, a bald and bulgy wrestler. Zombies got the nuclear treatment in *Creature With the Atom Brain* (1955), a Curt Siodmak script. Steven Ritch turned into *The Werewolf* (1956), victim of a misguided plan for H-Bomb survival, and John Beal was the atomic scientist who drew blood as *The Vampire* (1957). Boris Karloff, too, suffered from fall-out. He played Baron Victor, last of the Frankensteins (and Karloff's first as a genuine member of the family) in *Frankenstein 1970*, which was made in 1958. He used an atomic reactor to revive his ancestor's experiment; they both perished in a gush of 'atomic steam'.

'Children of all ages should be allowed to see horror films. I am sure that Frankenstein and Dracula would not have any serious effect on children's minds. After all, I saw them myself when I was a kid, and they didn't affect me!'

Herman Cohen, producer, protesting against the British censor's decision to award his film an 'X' for Adults Only certificate, and failing to give credit where it was due. For without his own early exposure to Karloff and Lugosi, would he have created one of the greatest titles in the history of movies, *I Was A Teenage Werewolf* (1957)? It deserved its stupendous success at the box office: Cohen's investment of 150,000 dollars profited him nearly two-and-a-half million. He almost did it again with *I Was a Teenage Frankenstein* (1957),

but none of his instant imitators came anywhere near, even with *Teenage Monster* (1957), *Teenage Zombies* (1958), *Teenage Cavemen* (1958), or *Teenagers From Outer Space* (1959). Cohen came to England to make *I Was a Teenage Gorilla*, but by the time it was ready there had been too many teenagers on the scene for even as keen a teen-lover as Cohen. The film went out as *Konga* (1961).

In the changing pattern of picture-making, the independent producer has emerged to replace the old 'B' picture units run by the major studios. William Castle, like Charles Schneer and Herman Cohen, has a fondness for the fantastic, and also like the others shuttles between America and England. Unlike them, however, Castle also directs his own films. He learned his quick trade turning out *Boston Blackie*, *Whistler*, and *Crime Doctor* series in Columbia's 'B' unit, but is economically unable to give his independent productions that built-in big studio gloss. He makes up for this by wildly imaginative devices to pull in his public.

Macabre (1955) began it all: the audience was issued with thousand-dollar insurance policies against being scared to death. Castle played it safe: the movie was little more than a murder mystery. 'Emergo' was the gimmick with *The House on Haunted Hill* (1958): as Vincent Price turns a handle on screen, a dangling skeleton cranks across the auditorium (provided the projectionist is on cue!). Price was back in *The Tingler* (1959), warning the audience that materialized fright in the shape of a clutching crab was loose among them. Lucky patrons felt its touch when their electrically-wired seats gave them a shock! 'Ghost Viewers' were handed out with the tickets for *13 Ghosts* (1960), red/green glasses that added an extra dimension to the materializations. Cohen followed Castle by inserting 'Hypnovista' sequences into the American release print of his British *Horrors of the Black Museum* (1959), but the craze for Psychoramas, Fright Breaks, and stereo 'Masks' seems to have gone the way of 3-D. Castle's most frightening film to date has been the only one he did not direct: Roman Polanski's *Rosemary's Baby* (1968).

The macabre melancholy of Edgar Allan Poe had attracted American movie-makers for fifty years. The lure of Poe's poetics may have been the desire to create a genuinely native horror film, the challenge to translate his imaginative imagery into movie visuals, or the fact that he was out of copyright. To 1960 the most successful movies, as

185

The Corman Cometh: Roger Corman, whizz-kid of the quickies, came to England to make *Masque of the Red Death* (American International 1964). He might as well have stayed at home, for the end-product was just like his other pieces of Poe, right down to his star, Vincent Price. British budgeting did allow for a few more extras to be available for the orgy scene, however (*right*). Hazel Court's sacrificial slashing (*below*) was cut by the British Censor. *Opposite:* John Beal as *The Vampire* (Gramercy 1957) keeps the home fires burning.

Price of Fame: Vincent Price is today's king of the horror movie, the inheritor of Karloff's crown. Seldom a man for monstrous makeup, Price permutates his familiar features with a trimming of whiskers, a brush of pomade, a pair of dark glasses. *Opposite* he is seen in *The Tomb of Ligeia* (American International 1964; *above*), yet another pot of Poe by Corman, and *below*, surrounded by the mutants of *The Haunted Palace* (American International 1963). This was pretended Poe by Corman. *Above left*, Price is in Poe-Corman's *House of Usher* (American International 1960), and, *left*, in Corman-Poe's *The Raven* (American International 1963). Peeping round is Peter Lorre. *Above* is the Price poster for *House on Haunted Hill* (Allied Artists 1958), by William Castle for a change.

horror movies, had been the Universal series, which had simply taken a Poe title and theme and let Karloff and Lugosi take it from there. Suddenly Poe found a new interpreter in, of all people, Roger Corman. The king of the quickies was tired of making back-to-back movies. Now, he asked American International, instead of making two pictures for the price of one, could he make one for the price of two? Nicholson and Arkoff, aghast, were aghast again when Corman told them the tale he had in mind was 'The Fall of the House of Usher'. Acutely aware of their teenage audience, one half of AIP pointed out that as high school students had to study Poe they would naturally hate him! The other half pointed out that there was no monster in the story, and horror pictures had to have a monster. 'The house is the monster,' retorted glib Mr Corman.

House of Usher (1960) had everything that Corman's quickies lacked. Colour (Pathecolor applied with unusual selectivity), CinemaScope (photographed with unusual mobility by Floyd Crosby), music (written with unusual sensitivity by Les Baxter), mood (designed with unusual period sense by Daniel Haller), literacy (scripted with unusual care by novelist Richard Matheson), acting (played with unusual restraint by Vincent Price). Unfortunately it also had length, eighty minutes compared with the usual sixty, and the extra twenty minutes made their presence felt early on as it became clear that Corman had not been able to avoid one hangover from his old days: a low budget. Having paid for his big star he had room for only three more actors. As two of these were in the teenage mould, insurance for AIP's

regular customers, the longueurs were longer than ever. In a desperate bid for variety Corman threw in a shot in which the entire Usher family tree materialized in the form of ten bit-part players. Yet riding as it did upon the Hammer wave of horror, the fall of Usher marked the rise of Corman.

Suddenly, it's Poe! Having run his monsters, teenagers, rock'n'rollers, and dragstrippers into the ground, Corman embarked upon a cinematic campaign to do the same for poor Poe. *The Pit and the Pendulum* (1961); *The Premature Burial* (1962); *Tales of Terror* (1962) which were 'The Case of M. Valdemar', 'The Black Cat', and 'Morella'; *The Raven* (1963); *The Haunted Palace* (1963), which was really H.P.Lovecraft's 'The Case of Charles Dexter Ward'; *The Masque of the Red Death* (1964); *The Tomb of Ligeia* (1964). The last two Corman made in England, yet hardly needed to have made the trip. They were as much formula as the others; the dominant Price, the arty credits, the tracking shots, the familiar corridors, the old house.

Even with his luxurious new schedules, four weeks instead of two, Corman felt the urge to rush things. *The Raven* was polished off with three days to spare. Instead of giving his star, the venerable Boris Karloff, a breather, Corman had a script whipped up overnight, and while two assistants shot backgrounds in the Big Sur, he propped his aged trouper against those *Raven* sets still standing and called the hastily-pasted end-product *The Terror* (1963).

The difference between the formula-bound Corman and a film-maker can be seen in the work of one of his protégés, Peter Bogdanovich. Using Corman techniques – clips from *The Terror* spliced into improvised location shooting, plus two days of Boris Karloff's services left over from a Corman contract – Bagdanovich made *Targets* (1968). It was a brilliant debut by any standards, and remains one of Karloff's finest films ever. The grand old monster plays himself, thinly disguised as Byron Orlok, musing over the golden age of horror films, disliking modern trends in the genre, then accidentally caught up in real-life horror involving a teenage sniper. Karloff made more films before he died in England, on 2 February 1969, at the age of eighty-two. But it is *Targets* that remains, the perfect obituary, and the only horror film completely to bridge the gap between the horror that was golden and the horror that is today.

Unwelcome Visitors: *Invisible Invaders* (UA 1959; *above*); *Willard* (Crosby 1970; *opposite*).

THE BEST OF BRITISH BLOOD

In which there is a Murder at the Red Barn, a Face at the Window, a Demon Barber in Fleet Street, and blood on the Hammer.

The Frankenstein Monster, Dr Jekyll and Mr Hyde, Count Dracula, The Invisible Man: in order of their appearance, the great monsters of literature. And all British. Karloff, Clive, Laughton, Thesiger, Rains, Rathbone, Atwill, Banks, Hardwicke, Zucco: the great players of horror, as British as R.C.Sherriff who wrote and James Whale who directed. A heritage of horror, hallowed by Hollywood, ignored by England.

The horror film was the perfect native product: yet it was untouched by an industry that sneered at America's England, that fogbound London of hansom cabbies and bribable bobbies, equalled only by fogbound Cornwall or fogbound Wales, where the autumn moon beamed, the wolfbane bloomed, the garlic wreathed, and there was breathing in the barn. Universal Europe: where the moors of Llanwelly subbed for the plains of Vasaria, where villagers crossed themselves in cockney or 'country' before lighting their flaming torches and proceeding up the Borgo Pass. The settings were interchangeable, the ambiance unchangeable. This was the secret of the Universal universe. It gave the great films a continuity that was comforting to come back to, whatever the horror that walked abroad. Familiar faces, familiar places: a sort of security in a world of fear. It was easier to suspend belief when the impossible took place in a tight, false world of studio-built landscape, where every tree was carefully gnarled in expressionistic fright, every house cunningly gabled in Gothic mystery, every shadow beautifully lit into lurking terror; and where every actor was caught in the closing ring of horrors, untouched by the possibility of a normal world beyond. Perhaps, then, it was for the best that British cinema left the horrors to Hollywood.

One other great British tradition almost made it as a native school of horror movie: the theatre of blood and thunder. The Victorian taste for vicarious violence was satisfied by the once-weekly, twice-nightly welter of gore called melodrama.

William Corder had murdered Maria Marten, mistress and mole-catcher's daughter, in 1827. Her old mother dreamed the body was in the barn. The floor was dug up, the corpse uncovered, and Corder was hanged. The case and its supernatural solution caught the public's fancy. It was re-enacted by puppets and peep-shows, penny dreadfuls and penny-gaffs, and remained in repertory for more than a century. Dicky Winslow, a theatrical gent who stage-managed the movies sold by George Harrison & Co of Berners Street (today we would call him the director), cranked his camera on a sketch company version then touring the Music Halls. *Maria Martin; or, The Murder in the Red Barn* (1902) packed six scenes into five minutes: Maria's Disguise . . . The Murder in the Red Barn . . . The Dream . . . The Arrest of Corder . . . The Condemned Cell . . . The Apparition of Maria. Mr and Mrs A.W.Fitzgerald played Corder and Maria, then immediately played the leads in an unlikely item called *A Fight With Sledgehammers* (1902).

Melodrama went West: to Wales where William Haggar toured the village fairgrounds as 'The Old'un of Aberdare'. One of his sideshows was the Great American Bioscope and he used it to turn out his own flickering epics. With his enormous family playing all the parts, Haggar's Sensationals were snapped up by the London offices of Frenchman Gaumont and American Urban. Their main English trade was with the fairground exhibitors and Haggar knew exactly what those wanderers, and their audiences, wanted. Where Harrison produced complete, if condensed, stories, Haggar showed simply the meat. And red meat it was.

The Two Orphans (1902), Adolphe Dennery's mighty melodrama, came out as 'A knife duel between a Cripple and a Marquis'. *True as Steel* (1902), 'scenes from the drama of the same name', was little more than a 'Sensational fight between

Bars Sinister: Boris Karloff as *The Ghoul* (Gaumont British 1933).

a Knight and a Forest Hermit'. Of Haggar's remaining releases for 1902 apparently titles alone were enough to guarantee sales: *The Wild Man of Borneo* and *The Maniac's Guillotine*. Haggar caught wind of *The Life of Charles Peace* (1905) being filmed in Sheffield, and rushed through his own version, casting son Walter as 'The Modern Ishmael'. Haggar's grisly climax, a realistic representation of the murderous burglar's execution, must have stirred memories for the older generation: Haggar's movie was the first public hanging since 1868! The Sheffield Photo Company was more squeamish: 'It has been decided *not* to reproduce the Execution Scene, as we believe it is too ghastly and repulsive.' Haggar got round to Corder's crime, too, but evidently the confusion of the two Charley Peace films left their mark. Haggar reversed his title to *The Red Barn Crime; or, Maria Martin* (1908). Son Walter, as Corder, was hanged again. Maurice Elvey, who would finally emerge as Britain's most prolific popular director, was the first to get the girl's name right. His *Maria Marten; or, The Murder in the Red Barn* (1913) was even more historic. Elvey actually filmed it in the original Red Barn in Polstead, Suffolk. Fred Groves was the squire and Elizabeth Risdon the farmer's daughter.

That last year of peace saw a small revival in British films and British horror. *Dr Trimball's Verdict* (1913), a Cecil Hepworth Production, had Alec Worcester as the doctor who murders his rival. Later he buys a skeleton for his study. It turns out to be his victim's: his ghost materializes upon his own bones. Dr Trimball dies of shock. *The Vampire* (1913) was set in India and showed a native lady turning into a snake to bite the explorer who shot her. *The Grip of Iron* (1913), Arthur Shirley's melodrama founded upon 'Les Etrangleurs de Paris', was filmed in Brighton. Fred Powell played the insurance clerk who secretly strangled for the sake of his extravagant daughter. *The Fakir's Spell* (1914) changed an Indian girl's English lover into a gorilla. He is captured by a circus, but reverts to his old self when his cage catches fire. *Heba the Snake Woman* (1915) was a transformation too: identical with *The Vampire* except Heba was an Aztec. *A Cry in the Night* (1915) was heard when the heroine's father was killed by a mad doctor's winged gorilla. Under the fur and feathers was James Russell, an ex-Karno comic.

British Blood: 1902 (*above*), and 1939 (*below*) – Bela Lugosi in Edgar Wallace's *Dark Eyes of London* (Argyle).

The first feature-length British horror was *The Avenging Hand* (1915): the ghost of an Egyptian Princess came to London looking for her severed member. There was a hypnotized chimp that strangled to order in *Crime and the Penalty* (1916), and *The Man Without a Soul* (1916) was Milton Rosmer back from the dead. George Loane Tucker directed this rather religious piece, then went home to America to make *The Miracle Man*. Leal Douglas was another spectral emigrant from Ancient Egypt. She brought vengeance upon an MP in – and as – *The Beetle* (1919). The strangler of Paris struck again in *The Grip of Iron* (1920); this time the doubled-up Jagon and Simmonnet was played by George Foley. Paris was again the setting for a film of an 1897 melodrama by F. Brooke Warren, whose title gave the world a phrase of fright.

The Face at the Window (1920), with its science-fictional set-piece of a corpse revived by electricity, also had the double-life ploy. Banker Lucio Degradoff is even less innocent than he sounds. By night he is Le Loup (The Wolf), a murdering burglar. His latest victim was killed in the act of writing: 'I am murdered by Luc. . . .' Naturally, handsome bank-clerk Lucien Cartwright is arrested, but an application of galvanism by Dr LeBlanc enables the corpse to complete his final act. He writes '. . . io' and the right man is copped by detective C. Aubrey Smith.

Grand Guignol arrived in England in 1921 in a series of short films of that generic title. Tales filmed included George Saxon's *A Bit of Black Stuff* and G.B.Stern's *The Curse of Westacott*. It was a time for shorts, and Lyn Harding played Svengali in a potted *Trilby* (1922) while Booth Conway was Quasimodo to Sybil Thorndike's *Esmeralda* (1922). A short story blown to feature length was W.W.Jacobs' classic *The Monkey's Paw* (1923): Moore Marriott and Marie Ault wished their dead son alive again and quickly wished they hadn't.

Adrian Brunel, who had played the lively corpse in *The Face at the Window*, promoted himself to director for *The Man Without Desire* (1923). There was a sensation at the première when a woman screamed and fainted as Ivor Novello clambered out of his coffin. A foretaste of different screams to come for England's greatest matinée idol. In the film he was Count Vittorio Dondolo who, distraught when his sweetheart is poisoned, submits to a scientist's experiment in suspended animation. Revived 300 years later he encounters his old love's descendant but alas, the old spark has gone.

Dead Heads: Decapitation has increased in popularity since Claude Rains was *The Man Who Reclaimed His Head* in 1934. Peter Lorre lost his head in *Tales of Terror* (1962), a typical Price-Poe-Corman-American International picture (*below*). *Right:* one of *The Four Skulls of Jonathan Drake* (Vogue 1959) as shrunk by Paul Wexler. *Bottom left: The Man Without a Body* (Eros 1957) was Nostradamus. *Bottom right: The Curse of the Living Corpse* (Twentieth Century-Fox 1964).

Faces at the Window: *opposite, Vampyr* (Dreyer 1932; *above left*) and *The Ghost Breakers* (Paramount 1940; *above right*); *below, Curse of the Dead* (F.U.L. 1966).

Familiar Faces: If the face isn't familiar, the makeup is. British horror films tend to go for American stars like Akim Tamiroff (*opposite above left*), who got atomically mixed with *The Vulture* (Paramount 1966), Bryant Haliday who was anatomically mixed as *The Projected Man* (Compton 1966; *opposite above right*) and Joan Crawford who got mixed up with *Trog* (Cohen 1970; *opposite below*). Boris Karloff, American star born in Britain, came home for *Grip of the Strangler* (MGM 1958; *loft*) and Herman Cohen, American producer, came over for *Horrors of the Black Museum* (1959; *below*). Hammer, usually derivative, tried a new tack by turning Jacqueline Pearce into *The Reptile* (1966; *below left*).

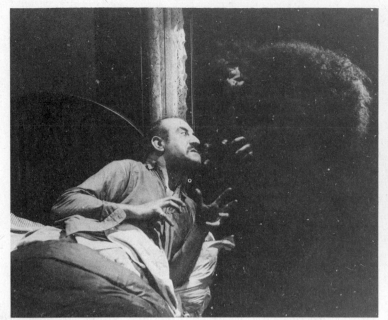

Dr Fu Manchu looked anything but a Yellow Peril in the person of Harry Agar Lyons, but Harry Rignold was ideally cast as *The Coughing Horror* (1924). This hirsute henchman, flogged into fury, climbed through Nayland Smith's window and got his arm chopped off for his pains.

British films experienced a revival in the late silent period, thanks to the Government's new Quota Act. *Maria Marten* (1928) was revived, too, with Warwick Ward and Trilby Clark. Walter West directed, as he did a companion piece, *Sweeney Todd* (1928). Moore Marriott played the Demon Barber of Fleet Street, first seen in 1847 in the melodrama, 'The String of Pearls', by George Dibdin Pitt. This legend of bloody butchery – the barber uses his cut-throat razor to slash his customers and tip them into his cellar, whence the corpses are cooked into penny pies by the lady next door – turned out, in this version, to be a dream. The last silent movie in the genre was *Chamber of Horrors* (1929): Frank Stanmore going mad whilst spending the night in Madame Tussaud's waxworks. Again, it was all a dream.

The first true horror films arrived in Britain in 1931, and nobody was more horrified than the British censor. He cut them, fussed in the press, and initiated a system of 'Notification to the Home Office' for films 'of an horrific nature'. If any British studio had wanted to make horror films, this was more than enough to put them off. British films were carefully budgeted to bring returns on full circuit distribution: a limitation of patrons to the over-sixteens would completely eliminate profits. Only the smallest, cheapest studio dared to flirt with the form. *Castle Sinister* (1932) was made by Delta at Bushey. Eric Adeney failed to insert the

British Tradition: The traditional British melodrama could have found its film form with Tod Slaughter, who near-burlesqued himself in *Crimes At the Dark House* (King 1940; *above*). Earlier, Harry Rignold played a silent *Coughing Horror* (Stoll 1924; *above left*); later Karloff played *The Man Who Changed His Mind* (Gaumont 1936; *opposite*).

heroine's brain into an apeman's head, just as Widgey Newman failed to direct a good film. He failed again with *The Unholy Quest* (1934), despite letting R.W.Lotinga direct. Claude Bailey failed to revive an embalmed crusader. More successful was Leslie Hiscott's remake of *The Face at the Window* (1932). This time Raymond Massey sorted out Lucio Fournal from Lucien Courtier via Dr Renard's machinery.

Boris Karloff came home in 1933. It was a working holiday. He called on his delighted brothers, then made *The Ghoul* (1933) at Shepherd's Bush. It was old home week on all counts, for as Professor Morlant, Egyptologist, he rose glowing from his grave to seek a sacred jewel. Cedric Hardwicke lent stolid support and Ernest Thesiger lent his nostrils. T. Hayes Hunter's piece of fogbound Gothic, photographed by Gunther Krampf, was the only British horror film in the true Hollywood tradition, and the first to be 'notified as horrific'. This honour was also awarded to two more minor works, Brian Desmond Hurst's *The Tell-Tale Heart* (1934) from Poe, and Vernon Sewell's *The Medium* (1934). Sewell used his ghostly inspiration, a *Grand Guignol* play called 'L'Angoisse', four or more times during his directorial career.

Karloff came back for *The Man Who Changed His Mind* (1936), a clever title suiting John Balderston's story of personality exchange, dropped by the Americans for the more box-office *The Man Who Lived Again*. Karloff was Dr Laurience, swapping magnate Frank Cellier's

Monsters International: The British revival initiated by Hammer stimulated first the smaller British producers, then the Continentals. One of the better Hammers was *Plague of the Zombies* (1966; *right*), a tale of the Cornish tin mines. *Blood on Satan's Claw* (Tigon 1970; *below left*) was another rural episode, originally shown as *Satan's Skin*. The urban adventure (*below right*) *The Phantom of Soho* (CCC 1963) was made in Germany. *Opposite: The Murder Clinic* (Leone-Orphée 1966; *above right*) was made by France and Italy together, *Revenge of the Blood Beast* (Leith 1965; *below*) by Italy alone – although the director was British (Michael Reeves). *Castle Sinister* (*above left*) was made by Equity British in 1948.

GOLDEN ERA
present
"THE PHANTOM OF SOHO"
'SCOPE 'X'Cert.
Released by Golden Era Film Distributors

soul with crippled Donald Calthrop's, then his own with John Loder's for love of Anna Lee. Whither Karloff, thither Lugosi, although, as ever, to the lesser studios. *Phantom Ship* was the title Americans gave to *The Mystery of the Mary Celeste* (1935), in which Denison Clift sought to solve that classic mystery of the sea by claiming Lugosi went mad and threw everybody overboard. It was one of the first films produced by a company of whom more would be heard, Hammer Films.

Lugosi returned to England for *Dark Eyes of London* (1939), an Edgar Wallace thriller directed by Walter Summers. America saw it as *The Human Monster*. Lugosi, in wig, whiskers, and dubbed British accent, was the kindly old gent who ran the Dearborn Institute for the Blind. Removing wig, whiskers, and dubbed British accent, he became Dr Orloff, insurance swindler. He uses big, blind Jake (Wilfrid Walter) to drown his victims in a tank and dump them in the Thames. Jake turns on him when Lugosi kills his only friend, Dumb Lew, having first made the poor little man deaf. It was the first British film to win the censor's new 'H' certificate. Horrific it was, especially in taste.

Taste is delicate and instinctive. The blood of melodrama ran red, yet such was the gusto of Tod Slaughter, last in the line of Victorian villains, that his films never offended. Slashing throats or snapping spines, he weltered in his glorious gore, leering and chuckling, winking and nudging his audience to laugh along with him on the road to hell. He was Corder, of course, in *Maria Marten* (1935), and the Demon Barber, of course, in *Sweeney Todd* (1936). He was also Squire Meadows in the old Charles Reade melodrama *It's Never too Late to Mend* (1937), condemning his love rival to a living hell, and the Tiger, king of the underworld, in Tom Taylor's venerable *The Ticket-of-Leave Man* (1937). He played half the title roles in *Sexton Blake and the Hooded Terror* (1938), and Chevalier del Gardo in the best version yet of *The Face at the Window* (1939). Wilkie Collins' 'The Woman in White' was made over for him as *Crimes at the Dark House* (1940), with Slaughter as wicked Sir Percival Glyde, and another old piece, 'Spring-heeled Jack, the Terror of London', was dressed up as *The Curse of the Wraydons* (1946). Barrel-chested, beer-bellied, 61-year-old Slaughter made an unlikely leaper.

Slaughter, happy in his work ('You have a beautiful throat for a razor, sir. O, how I should love to polish you off!'), ran afoul of the censor only once. Henry Oscar and he played Burke and Hare for Bushey Studios, and the censor refused to pass the film. Not because of their ghoulish grave-robbing, but because of their names! Redubbed throughout as Moore and Hart, the film was cheerfully passed under its new title, *The Greed of William Hart* (1948). The writer, John Gilling, in a more permissive age, directed his old Slaughter screenplay as *The Flesh and the Fiends* (1960); there was no trouble, nor was there when Vernon Sewell made his even more permissive version, *Burke and Hare* (1972). Given bigger budgets and better studios, Tod Slaughter could have been the great British monster. He died in 1956, up to his elbows in bright red blood, stalking the boards as Sweeney Todd: bloodied, bankrupt, but unbowed. By now he should be ripe for rediscovery.

There were no horror films made in England during the war, evidently in keeping with some official policy implemented by the censor. There were several supernatural pictures, notably the near-horrific *Dead of Night* (1945), an Ealing omnibus of classic ghost stories. First in the field after the war was George Barnett of Brighton, that outpost of early pioneers. He got an 'H' for his pot of Poe, *The Fall of the House of Usher* (1948). Unshown for two years it finally played one week in Tottenham Court Road. Then, in 1953, came the first signs of something nasty stirring in the woodshed. Not so much a woodshed, more a country house. Down Place, Maidenhead Road, Bray: an ideal studio for a small company with enterprising but inexpensive ideas. The old firm of Hammer Films was ready to strike again.

'See! A strange and beautiful woman created before your eyes! See! The mad scientist of Howdean defy the laws of life!' *Four Sided Triangle* (1953) was cheap but flashy: Stephen Murray electrically producing two Barbara Paytons for the price of one contract, in a hooped duplicator modelled on, if not salvaged from, *Metropolis*. But it was a start, and it helped director Terence Fisher, who had fallen from Gainsborough gloss to 'B' movie dross, pay the rent. Four years later he was back with a film that shocked the world and rocked the box offices. It was the first British film to hit the sensation-exploitation market. It made little old Hammer Films a force to be reckoned with, staid old Terence Fisher a director to be noticed, familiar-faced old Peter Cushing and Christopher Lee into international stars, and proved Mary's old Monster truly immortal.

The Curse of Frankenstein (1957) re-established the traditional horror film after more than a decade spent out of this world in science-fiction.

Out for the Count: The lives of Christopher Lee and Count Dracula are today as entwined as those of Lugosi and Dracula, years ago. Lee owns Lugosi's Dracula ring, but it is unlikely that, like his late mentor, he will insist on being buried in his Dracula cape. Lee's Dracula has the gift of eternal life beyond the wildest dreams of his creator, Bram Stoker. He lives beyond legend, having survived reduction to dust, evaporation, drowning in *Dracula Prince of Darkness* (Hammer 1965; *left*) and impalement: *Dracula Has Risen From the Grave* (Hammer 1968; *below*). The laws of the box office reach beyond the lores of logic and legend.

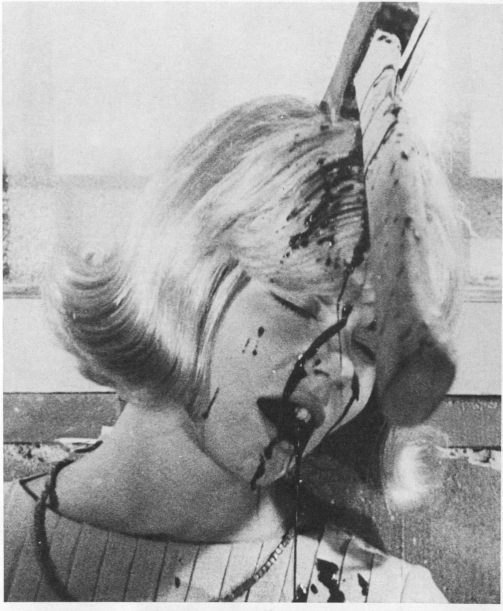

New Blood: Hammer tapped a new vein of horror when they turned on the Technicolor: blood ran red and is still running. Poe's *The Black Cat* (*right*) was given the new look by Hemisphere Pictures in 1966, while, *below left*, Edith Scob wears a mask to conceal her flayed flesh in *Eyes Without a Face* (Champs-Elysées 1960). Georges Franju's clinical experiment was shown in America as *Horror Chamber of Dr Faustus*. Tissue transplants also upset Alberto Lupo in *Seddok* (Lion 1960; *below right*). Another Italian monster was Doctor Hichcock, who first had an *Orribile Segreto*, then struck back as *The Spectre* (Panda 1963; *opposite above left*). *The Blood Beast Terror* (Tigon 1967; *opposite above right*) was an outsize death's-head moth. *Opposite below:* the chlorophyll man, a Philippino favourite, was all washed up in *Mad Doctor of Blood Island* (Hemisphere 1970) – but struck again in *Blood Devils*.

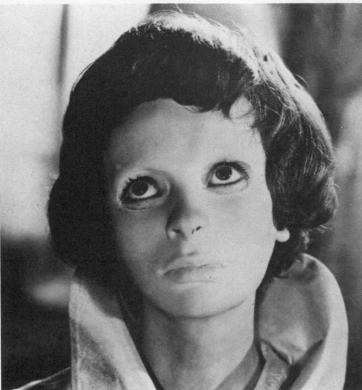

It sparked off cycles, spun off sequels, inspired revivals. 'This is where we came in'; but this time there was a difference. The new age of horror was geared to a new taste. Where the old films had quickly cut away from the sight of blood, Hammer cut in for a closeup. The old age had been a golden one in spite of its monochrome. The new age would be red, red as blood, and all in Glorious but inexpensive Eastmancolor.

Christopher Lee's Monster had little of Karloff's pathos, none of Karloff's appearance. The novel was out of copyright; not so Universal's movie. Phil Leakey plastered up the new 'Creature' (even its name was changed, just to be safe) and mid-way through the movie shot half its face away. Hammer made one fatal error: they killed the Creature in an acid bath. So when the time came for a sequel, they made Frankenstein the continuing thread instead. Peter Cushing played the Baron four more times, each time making a different Monster. Finally, running out of ideas, Hammer went back to the beginning again and remade their first film. *Horror of Frankenstein* (1970) introduced Ralph Bates as the more modern Prometheus.

Lee was promoted to *Dracula* (1958), a film which, like that vampire, had difficulty in crossing running water. Universal's copyright meant it had to be shown in America as *Horror of Dracula*. Reduced to dust by Cushing's crucifix, Lee was understandably absent from *Brides of Dracula* (1960). Equally understandably, he was back in red-lined cloak with eyeballs to match in *Dracula, Prince of Darkness* (1965). Once again the powers of darkness had been vanquished by the good god gold. Five revivals have happened since, including one in whiskers shot in Spain, but excluding the catch-penny *Countess Dracula* (1970). Extending this policy beyond Shelley and Stoker, Hammer exhumed a short story by J. Sheridan LeFanu, and so far have spun three features from 'Carmilla'. The first, *The Vampire Lovers* (1970), shifted the centre of fanging from neck to nipple, and as both vampire and victim are female, the future seems sexy if uncertain.

Hammer horrors have run the traditional gamut: *The Mummy* remade with Lee in 1959, *The Phantom of the Opera* remade with Herbert Lom in 1962, *One Million Years BC* remade with Raquel Welch in 1966, *Dr Jekyll and Mr Hyde* remade twice, lately with a sex-change twist as *Dr Jekyll and Sister Hyde* (1971). There has been *The Curse of the Werewolf* (1961), a *Plague of the Zombies* (1965), and three science-fiction pieces based on television's *Quatermass* serials. In quantity Hammer films are fast approaching Universal, but in quality they have yet to reach Monogram. Meanwhile they can admire their Queen's Award for Industry and scream all the way to the bank.

Of the Old Monsters, only Chaney remains.

'I used to enjoy horror films when there was thought and sympathy involved. Then they became comedies. Abbott and Costello ruined the horror field: they made buffoons out of the monsters. Then the cheap producers came along and made worse buffoons of them, because they killed for the sake of killing, there was blood for the sake of blood. There was no thought, no true expression of acting, no true expression of feeling. We used to make up our minds before we started that this is a little fantastic, but let's take it seriously. And they were sold seriously. But all this foolishness today, it isn't sold seriously. It's made as a joke, a laugh, for the kids to go in and have a ball.'

The elder Chaney, Karloff, Lugosi . . . Laughton and Lorre and Veidt . . . Rathbone and Rains . . . Whale and Laemmle and Browning. . . . The Scroll of Thoth runs from Atwill to Zucco. Yet they will be back, at the flicker of a projector, the touch of a TV switch, through their own medium – the only medium truly to revive the dead. The cinema.

So charge your glasses – with gin, of course – and join Dr Pretorius in his toast:

'To a new world of Gods and Monsters!'

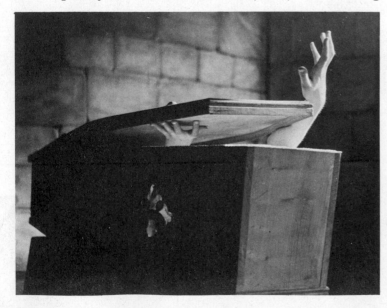

Last Laugh: *Fall of the House of Usher* (GIB 1948; *left*); *Carry On Screaming* (Anglo-Amalgamated 1966; *opposite*).

APPENDIX

The 'H' Certificate

The horror film was officially born on 1 January 1937. On that date the British Board of Film Censors introduced their 'H' for Horrific certificate, which prevented persons under the age of sixteen from seeing any film so certified. Previous to this, horror films were awarded the 'A' for Adult certificate (persons under sixteen admitted in the company of adults), but were 'notified to the Home Office as being, in the Board's opinion, horrific in character'. The 'H' certificate was replaced from 1 January 1951 by the 'X' certificate, an all-embracing category for films of an adult nature. This is the complete list of the 18 'A' films and 37 'H' films certified by the Board, together with five films banned outright.

1933
Jan *Vampire (Vampyr)* — Carl Dreyer
Mar *Vampire Bat* — Majestic
Jul *The Ghoul* — Gaumont-British
Oct *King Klunk* — Universal
Nov *The Invisible Man* — Universal
1934
Jan *The Tell-Tale Heart* — Clifton-Hurst
Jan *Son of Kong* — Radio
Feb *The Medium* — Film Tests
Apr *The Ninth Guest* — Columbia
Aug *The House of Doom (The Black Cat)* — Universal
1935
Jan *The Night on the Lonely Mountain* — Alexeyev
May *Mark of the Vampire* — MGM
May *Werewolf of London* — Universal
May *The Bride of Frankenstein* — Universal
Jun *The Raven* — Universal
Jul *The Hands of Orlac (Mad Love)* — MGM
1936
Aug *The Devil Doll* — MGM
Aug *The Man Who Changed His Mind* — Gaumont-British
1937
('H' Certificate introduced)
May *The Thirteenth Chair* — MGM
1938
Apr *J'Accuse* — Abel Gance
1939
Jan *Son of Frankenstein* — Universal
Mar *The Monster Walks* — Mayfair
Apr *Boy Slaves* — RKO-Radio
Jun *The Gorilla* — Twentieth Century-Fox
Jun *The Dark Eyes of London* — Argyle
Jul *Hell's Kitchen* — Warner Bros
Aug *On Borrowed Time* — MGM
Sept *A Child Is Born* — Warner Bros
Sept *The Man They Could Not Hang* — Columbia
Nov *The Return of Dr X* — Warner Bros
Nov *The Cat and the Canary* — Paramount
1941
Sept *The Monster and the Girl* — Paramount
1942
May *The Ghost of Frankenstein* — Universal
1945
Nov *United Nations War Crimes Film* — United Nations
Dec *The Invisible Man's Revenge* — Universal

Dec *The Return of the Vampire* — Columbia
1946
Jan *The Mad Ghoul* — Universal
Feb *The Lady and the Monster* — Republic
Mar *Frankenstein Meets the Wolf Man* — Universal
Apr *The Ape Man* — Monogram
Jun *Voodoo Man* — Monogram
Jun *The Corpse Vanishes* — Monogram
Jul *The Mummy's Curse* — Universal
Jul *House of Frankenstein* — Universal
Aug *The Mysterious Doctor* — Warner Bros
Sept *The Vampire's Ghost* — Republic
Dec *Jungle Captive* — Universal
1947
Jan *The Mummy's Ghost* — Universal
Jan *The Mummy's Tomb* — Universal
1948
Jan *House of Dracula* — Universal
May *The Fall of the House of Usher* — G.I.B.
Jun *Dead Men Walk* — P.R.C.
Jun *The Monster Maker* — P.R.C.
Jun *Tall, Dark and Gruesome* — Columbia
1950
Jul *Captive Wild Woman* — Universal
Banned by the Censor
1914 *Dr Zanikoff's Experiences in Grafting*
1932 *Freaks* — MGM
1932 *The Island of Dr Moreau* — Paramount
1934 *Life Returns* — Universal
1946 *Bedlam* — RKO

Filmography: A Collector's Guide

In recent years the introduction of the 8mm gauge (in both standard and super-8 format) has made it possible for every enthusiast to rent, and even purchase, prints of his favourite films. As a handy reference guide for the growing band of film collectors, here is an alphabetical title list of the 165 horror films released on 8mm to date, together with a note as to sound [*] or silent availability, length in reels and name of main distributor. (See 'Moviemaker Magazine' [UK] and 'Classic Film Collector' [US] for distributors' addresses. Editor)

Abbott and Costello Meet Dr Jekyll & Mr Hyde (1) [*] Castle
Abbott and Costello Meet Frankenstein (1) [*] Castle
Abbott and Costello Meet the Mummy (1) [*] Castle
The Ape (7) [*] Derann
The Avenging Conscience (6) Cine Service
Baron Munchausen's Dream (Méliès) (1) Blackhawk
Battle in Outer Space (colour) (1) [*] Columbia
Battle of the Giants (One Million BC) (1) [*] Castle
The Beast from Haunted Cave (7) [*] Heritage
The Beast with Five Fingers (1) UA
The Bells (7) Entertainment
The Birth of Frankenstein (Curse of Frankenstein) (1) Americom
The Black Zoo (colour/cinemascope) (9) [*] Derann

The Blob (1) Republic
Blood of Dracula's Castle (colour) (9) [*] Derann
Blood on his Lips (Hideous Sun Demon) (9) [*] Mountain
Bloodlust (8) [*] Derann
Bride of Frankenstein (1) [*] Castle
The Cabinet of Dr Caligari (5) Entertainment
The Cat and the Canary (6) Perry
Chamber of Horrors (Door with Seven Locks) (1) Entertainment
City of the Dead (8) [*] Derann
Comédie et Magie de Méliès (compilation) (1) Blackhawk
Conquest of the Pole (Méliès) (1) Blackhawk
Cosmic Monsters (Strange World of Planet X) (1) Republic
The Coughing Horror (2) Watsofilms
The Creature from the Black Lagoon (1) [*] Castle
The Creature Walks Among Us (1) [*] Castle
Curse of Dracula (Return of Dracula) (1) UA
Curse of Frankenstein (1) Americom
Curse of Simba (colour) (8) Derann
Curse of the Demon (1) Columbia
Curse of the Mummy's Tomb (1) [*] Columbia
Dante in the Inferno (Dante's Inferno) (1) Watsofilms
The Deadly Mantis (1) [*] Castle
The Demon Doctor (9) [*] Mountain
Destination Inner Space (colour) (9) [*] Derann
Devil Doll (9) [*] Derann
Dinosaurus (1) Republic
Dr Cyclops (1) [*] Castle
Dr Jekyll and Mr Hyde (James Cruze) (1) Blackhawk
Dr Jekyll and Mr Hyde (John Barrymore) (6) Blackhawk
Dr Jekyll and Mr Hyde (Sheldon Lewis) (5) Essex
Dr X (1) UA
Doom of Dracula (House of Dracula) (1) [*] Castle
Dracula (1) [*] Castle
Dracula's Desire (Mother Riley Meets the Vampire) (1) [*] Walton
Earth versus Flying Saucers (1) [*] Columbia
East Side Kids Meet Bela Lugosi (Spooks Run Wild) (1) [*] Entertainment
Exploits of Elaine (Death Ray; Life Current) (4) Blackhawk
Evil of Frankenstein (colour) (10) [*] Derann
Face of Fu Manchu (1) Americom
The Fall of the House of Usher (1928) (1) Perry
The Fall of the House of Usher (8) [*] Derann
Fantasie de Méliès (compilation) (1) Blackhawk
The Fatal Passion of Doctor Mabuse (9) Cine Service
First Men on the Moon (cinemascope) (1) [*] Columbia
The Flesh Eaters (10) [*] Derann

210

Frankenstein (1) [*] Castle
Frankenstein Meets the Space Monster (1) Ken
Frankenstein Meets the Wolf Man (1) [*] Castle
Frankenstein Must Be Destroyed (1) Ken
Frankenstein's Cat (cartoon) (1) Ken
Frankenstein's Daughter (4) [*] Entertainment
Frozen Alive (7) [*] Derann
The German Giants (compilation) (2) Perry
Ghidrah the Three Headed Monster (Japan) (1) Ken
Ghost of Frankenstein (8) [*] Derann
Ghost of Slumber Mountain (1) Entertainment
The Giant Behemoth (*Behemoth the Sea Monster*) (1) Ken
Godzilla versus The Thing (Japan) (1) Ken
The Golem (6) Perry
The Haunted House (*Our Gang*) (1) Ken
Highlights of Horror (compilation) (1) Perry
Horror of Dracula (1) Americom
Horror of Fu Manchu (1) Americom
House of Dracula (1) [*] Castle
House of Frankenstein (1) [*] Castle
The Human Monster (*Dark Eyes of London*) (2) Entertainment
The Hunchback of Notre Dame (Chaney) (10) Blackhawk
The Hunchback of Notre Dame (Laughton) (1) Ken
I Was a Teenage Frankenstein (1) Ken
I Was a Teenage Werewolf (1) Ken
The Imaginative Georges Méliès (compilation) (1) Blackhawk
The Incredible Shrinking Man (1) [*] Castle
The Invisible Ghost (1) Entertainment
The Invisible Man (8) [*] Derann
It Came from Outer Space (1) [*] Castle
Jack the Ripper (colour) (1) [*] Heritage
Jason and the Argonauts (colour) (4) [*] Columbia
King Kong (2) Watsofilms
The Long Hair of Death (10) [*] Derann
The Lost World (5) Perry
Lust of a Vampire (1) Watsofilms
The Mad Magician (stereo) (1) [*] Columbia
The Magic of Méliès (compilation) (1) Blackhawk
Man Made Monster (1) [*] Castle
Master of Terror (*The 4D Man*) (1) Republic
Metropolis (8) Niles
Mighty Joe Young (1) Ken
Missile to the Moon (1) Entertainment
Monster from Piedras Blancas (7) [*] Heritage
Monster of All Monsters (*Ghidrah*) (1) Ken
Monster of Death (*Hideous Sun Demon*) (2) [*] Mountain
Monster that Challenged the World (1) UA
Mother Riley Meets the Vampire (6) [*] Walton
Movie Milestones No. 1 (*The Miracle Man*) (1) [*] Walton
The Mummy (1) [*] Castle
The Mummy's Ghost (1) [*] Castle
The Mummy's Tomb (1) [*] Castle
Munster Go Home (10) [*] Powell
My Son the Vampire (*Mother Riley Meets the Vampire*) (1) Republic
The Night Caller (9) [*] Macro
Nightmare in Wax (colour) (9) [*] Derann
Nosferatu (3) Blackhawk
One Million BC (1) Castle
The Phantom of the Opera (Chaney) (8) Blackhawk
The Phantom of the Opera (Lom) (8) [*] Powell
Plan 9 from Outer Space (7) [*] Heritage
Playgirls and the Vampire (1) Watsofilms

Psycho (10) [*] Derann
The Quatermass Experiment (8) [*] Derann
Revenge of Frankenstein (colour) (1) [*] Columbia
The Revenge of the Creature (1) [*] Castle
Rodan the Flying Monster (Japan) (1) Ken
Seddok (1) Mountain
The Seventh Voyage of Sinbad (colour) (4) [*] Columbia
She (Marguerite Snow) (2) Perry
She (Betty Blythe) (5) Blackhawk
The Shock (6) Blackhawk
Slaughter of the Vampires (9) [*] Mountain
Son of Frankenstein (1) [*] Castle
Son of Kong (1) Ken
Son of Satan (*Seddok*) (1) Mountain
The Spider (1) Ken
Spooks (stereo) (1) Columbia
The Supernatural of Méliès (compilation) (1) Blackhawk
The Surrealism of Méliès (compilation) (1) Blackhawk
Svengali (9) [*] Derann
Tails of Horror (stereo) (1) Columbia
Tales of Terror (Méliès compilation) (1) Blackhawk
Tarantula (1) [*] Castle
The Tell-Tale Heart (cartoon) (1) [*] Columbia
Terror of Dracula (*Nosferatu*) (2) Entertainment
Theatre of Death (colour) (10) [*] Derann
The Thing (1) Ken
A Trip to the Moon (Mehes) (1) Entertainment
Twenty Million Miles to Earth (1) [*] Columbia
Twenty Thousand Leagues Under the Sea (8) Blackhawk
Twenty Thousand Leagues Under the Sea (Disney) (1) Disney
Ulysses (1) Americom
The Undead (1) Ken
The Vampire and the Ballerina (1) UA
The Vampire Bat (1) Entertainment
The Vampire's Curse (2) [*] Mountain
The Vampire's Last Fling (1) Watsofilms
Varan the Unbelievable (Japan) (1) Ken
Voyage to the Bottom of the Sea (4) Americom
War of the Colossal Beast (1) Ken
War of the Planets (1) Castle
The Wasp Woman (7) [*] Heritage
Waxworks (6) Perry
We Want Our Mummy (1) [*] Columbia
The Werewolf (1) [*] Columbia
The Wolf Man (1) [*] Castle

Bibliography: Books

Ackerman, Forrest J. – *The Best from Famous Monsters of Filmland* – New York 1964 – *Son of Famous Monsters of Filmland* – New York 1964 – *Famous Monsters of Filmland Strike Back* – New York 1965 – *The Frankenscience Monster* – New York 1969 – *Science Fiction Worlds of Forrest J. Ackerman and Friends* – California 1969
Anderson, J. and Ritchie, D. – *The Japanese Film* – Tokyo/Vermont 1959
Anderson, Robert G. – *Faces, Forms, Films* – New Jersey 1971
Barbour, Alan G. – *A Thousand and One Delights* – New York 1971 – *Days of Thrills and Adventure* – New York 1970
Baxter, John – *Hollywood in the Thirties* – London/New York 1968 *Science Fiction in the Cinema* – London/New York 1970
Bessy, M. and Lo Duca – *Georges Méliès Mage* – Paris 1945
Bogdanovich, Peter – *Fritz Lang in America* – London 1967
Bouyxou, Jean-Pierre – *Frankenstein* – Paris
Boullet, Jean – *La Belle et La Bête* – Paris 1958
Butler, Ivan – *Horror in the Cinema* – London 1970
Clarens, Carlos – *An Illustrated History of the Horror Film* – New York 1967 – *Horror Movies* – London 1968

Douglas, Drake – *Horror* – New York 1966
Eisner, Lotte H. – *L'Ecran Démoniaque* – Paris 1952 – *The Haunted Screen* – London 1969
Everson, William K. – *The Bad Guys* – New York 1964
Eyles, Allen – *Horror Album* – London 1971
Franklin, Joe – *Classics of the Silent Screen* – New York 1959
Gifford, Denis – *Movie Monsters* – London/New York 1969 – *Science Fiction Film* – London/New York 1971
Goodman, Ezra – *The Fifty Year Decline and Fall of Hollywood* – New York 1961
Gow, Gordon – *Suspense in the Cinema* – London 1968
Harryhausen, Ray – *Film Fantasy Scrapbook* – New York 1972
Higham, C. and Greenberg, J. – *Hollywood in the Forties* – London/New York 1968 – *The Celluloid Muse* – London 1969
Jensen, Paul M. – *The Cinema of Fritz Lang* – London/New York 1969
Kracauer, Siegfried – *From Caligari to Hitler* – Princeton 1947
Kyrou, Ado – *Le Surréalisme au Cinéma* – Paris 1964
Laclos, Michel – *Le Fantastique au Cinéma* – Paris 1958
Lahue, Kalton C. – *Continued Next Week* – Oklahoma 1964
Milne, Tom – *The Cinema of Carl Dreyer* – London 1971
Robinson, David – *Hollywood in the Twenties* – London/New York 1968
Robinson, W. R. – *Man and the Movies* – Louisiana 1967
Sadoul, Georges – *Georges Méliès* – Paris 1961
Steiger, Brad – *Master Movie Monsters* – Chicago 1965 – *Monsters, Maidens and Mayhem* – Chicago 1965
Underwood, Peter – *Horror Man* – London 1972
Weiss, K. and Goodgold, E. – *To be Continued* – New York 1972
Wiene, Robert – *The Cabinet of Dr Caligari* – London 1972
Willemen, Pirie, Will, Myles – *Roger Corman* – Cambridge 1970

Bibliography: Magazines

Bizarre – Paris 1960
Castle of Frankenstein – New Jersey 1962
Certificate X – Manchester 1965
Chilling Monster Tales – New York 1966
Famous Monsters of Filmland – Philadelphia 1958
Fantastic Monsters of the Films – California 1962
For Monsters Only – New York 1965
Gothique – Brentford 1965
Horror Monsters – Connecticut 1961
L'Incroyable Cinéma – Salford 1969
Insight – London 1965
Journal of Frankenstein – New Jersey 1961
Mad Monsters – Connecticut 1961
Masque – London 1970
La Méthode – Paris 1961
Midi-Minuit Fantastique – Paris 1962
Miroir du Fantastique – Paris 1968
Modern Monsters – California 1966
Monster Howls – New York 1966
Monster Mania – New York 1966
Monster Parade – New York 1958
The Monster Times – New York 1972
Monster World – Philadelphia 1964
Monsters and Things – New York 1959
Monsters to Laugh With – New York 1964
Monsters Unlimited – New York 1965
Movies International – California 1969
Photon – New York 1966
Screen Chills – London 1957
Screen Facts – New York 1963
Screen Thrills Illustrated – Philadelphia 1962
Shock Tales – New York 1959
Shriek – New York 1965
Spacemen – Philadelphia 1961
Supernatural – Bournemouth 1964
3-D Monsters – New York 1964
Trumpet – Texas 1965
Twylight – Kent 1965
World Famous Creatures – New York 1958

INDEX

Comedy of Terrors (American International 1963)

The Golem (Union 1920)

Grip of the Strangler (MGM 1958)

House of Dark Shadows (MGM 1970)

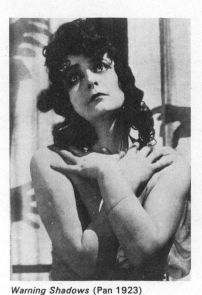
Acknowledgments

The stills in this book come from the author's collection, with additional help from Garry Parfitt and Michael Pointer. Stills are copyright of the companies as credited in the captions.